The Complete Idiot's Reference Card

Taking A Quick Look at Excel

COLUMN HEADINGS · CELL CURSOR · TITLE BAR · MENU BAR · STAN... TO... · FO... T...

ACTIVE CELL · ROW HEADINGS · WORKBOOK SCROLL ARROWS · SCROLL BARS

STATUS BAR · WORKSHEET TABS · GRIDLINES

Microsoft Excel - Book1

File Edit View Insert Format Tools Data Window Help

Arial · 10 · B I U · $ % ,

A1

Sheet1 / Sheet2 / Sheet3 / Sheet4 / Sheet5 / Sheet6

Ready · NUM

Taking Shortcuts

Press	To
F1	Get help
Ctrl+N	Open a new file
Ctrl+O	Open an existing file
Ctrl+S	Save a file
Ctrl+P	Print a file
Ctrl+Z	Undo a mistake
F4	Repeat an option
Ctrl+X	Cut
Ctrl+C	Copy
Ctrl+V	Paste
Ctrl+D	Fill down
Ctrl+R	Fill right
Ctrl+1	Format cells
F7	Check your spelling

Moving Around Quickly

Press	To Move
Arrow	One cell in the arrow direction
Tab	To the next unlocked cell in a protected worksheet
Home	To leftmost cell in row
Ctrl+Home	To top left cell in worksheet
Ctrl+End	To bottom right cell in worksheet
Page Down	Down one screenful
Page Up	Up one screenful
Alt+Page Down	Right one screenful
Alt+Page Up	Left one screenful
Ctrl+Page Down	To next sheet in workbook
Ctrl+Page Up	To previous sheet in workbook

alpha books

Tools on Bars

Excel opens up with two toolbars visible: Standard and Formatting. Here's a rundown on the tools on each one and their purpose:

Standard Toolbar

Icon	Tool
	New Workbook
	Open
	Save
	Print
	Print Preview
	Spelling
	Cut
	Copy
	Paste
	Format Painter
	Undo
	Repeat
	Sort Ascending
	Sort Descending
	AutoSum
	Function Wizard
	ChartWizard
	Text Box
	Drawing
	Zoom Control
	Tip Wizard
	Help

Formatting Toolbar

Icon	Tool
Arial	Font
10	Font Size
B	Bold
I	Italic
U	Underline
	Align Left
	Center
	Align Right
	Center Across Columns
$	Currency Style
%	Format Style
,	Comma Style
	Increase Decimal
	Decrease Decimal
	Border
	Cell Color
	Font Color

Just Mousin' Around

Point	To move the mouse until the on-screen pointer points to the desired object.
Click	To press and release the left mouse button once.
Double-click	To press and release the left mouse button twice in a row quickly.
Drag	To press and hold the left mouse button, and then move the mouse.
Right-click	To press and release the *right* mouse button once.

The Complete IDIOT'S Guide to EXCEL

by Ricardo Birmele

alpha books

A Division of Prentice Hall Computer Publishing
201 W. 103rd Street, Indianapolis, Indiana 46220 USA

I'd like to dedicate this book to The Good Lord, Who made it possible; to my wife, Bevy, for making it so pleasant; and to my sons, Chris and Misha, for making it necessary.

©1993 Alpha Books

International Standard Book Number: 1-56761-318-7
Library of Congress Catalog Card Number: 93-72163

95 94   9 8 7 6 5 4

Interpretation of the printing code: the rightmost number of the first series of numbers is the year of the book's printing; the rightmost number of the second series of numbers is the number of the book's printing. For example, a printing code of 93-1 shows that the first printing of the book occurred in 1993.

Screen reproductions in this book were created by means of the program Collage Plus from Inner Media, Inc., Hollis, NH.

Printed in the United States of America

Publisher
Marie Butler-Knight

Associate Publisher
Lisa A. Bucki

Managing Editor
Elizabeth Keaffaber

Development Editor
Faithe Wempen

Acquisitions Manager
Stephen R. Poland

Production Editor
Michelle Shaw

Copy Editor
San Dee Phillips

Cover Designer
Scott Cook

Designer
Amy Peppler-Adams, Roger Morgan

Illustrations
Steve Vanderbosch

Indexer
Craig Small

Production Team
*Gary Adair, Diana Bigham-Griffin, Kate Bodenmiller, Brad Chinn,
Kim Cofer, Meshell Dinn, Stephanie Gregory,
Jennifer Kucera, Beth Rago, Marc Shecter, Greg Simsic*

*Special thanks to C. Herbert Feltner for ensuring
the technical accuracy of this book.*

Contents at a Glance

Part I: Let's Start at the Beginning — **1**

1 The Least You Need to Know — 3
2 No More Broken Pencils: An Excel Overview — 7
3 But I've Never Done Windows — 17
4 Taking a Quick Plunge — 33
5 Taking Control of Your Workbook — 51
6 Rats! I Need Help, Now! — 61
7 I'll Be Back — 71

Part II: Doing Something Useful — **79**

8 A Range By Any Other Name — 81
9 Calculations for Non-Rocket-Scientist Types — 91
10 Tidying Up the Place — 103
11 A Thing of Beauty — 115
12 I Output, Therefore I Print — 129

Part III: Data Lists Unlimited — **141**

13 Making A List — 143
14 Shape It, Sort It — 151
15 Summing Up A List — 159
16 Pivot Tables: Some Assembly Required — 167
17 Fetching and Merging Data — 181

Part IV: Other Stuff You Wanted to Know — **191**

18 A Chart Is Worth A Thousand Words — 193
19 Let The Macro Do It — 205
20 Beyond the Defaults — 215

Appendixes — **221**

A Installing Excel — 221
B Twenty Great Ideas — 223
C A Function Bestiary — 243
D Help for Excel 4 Fans — 263
E Speak Like a Geek: The Complete Archive — 267

Index — 275

Contents

Part I: Let's Start at the Beginning   **1**

1 The Least You Need to Know   **3**

It's a Windows Program 3
Files are Called Workbooks 3
Row + Column = Cell 4
Press F1 for Help 4
Label Everything! 4
Appearance is Everything 4
Print It Out 5
Excel Makes a Slick Address Book 5
Charts Help Readers Understand Quickly....................5
It's Easier to Automate 5

2 No More Broken Pencils: An Excel Overview   **7**

Pleased to Meet You 8
What Does a Worksheet Look Like? 8
A Tale of One Worksheet 12
More Than Just a Pretty Worksheet 14

3 But I've Never Done Windows   **17**

First Things First 18
Yeek! A Mouse! 20
Groups and Individuals..21
Time to Experiment 22
    Borders, Borders 23
    Move It, Buddy 24
    Menus, Menus 24
Keyboarding: Doing It the Old-Fashioned Way 25
    The Keys to Windows...25
A Bit of Dialog 28
I'm Outta Here! 30

4 Taking a Quick Plunge   33

The Splash (Launching Excel) 34
The Big Screen: A Tour 34
  Worksheet Workout 35
  A Cellular Affair 36
  A Fashionable Address 37
  Menu Mania 38
  The Right Toolbar for the Job 39
Doing Something Real 43
  Identification, Please! 44
  And the Number Is 45
  Tis What's Worth 46
  Adding Sideways...47
The Dash 48

5 Taking Control of Your Workbook   51

Going Mobile 52
  Moving Around with the Keyboard 52
  Scrolling Around with the Mouse 52
  Shuffling Through the Sheets 53
Zooming Around 54
A New Arrangement 54
The Big Split 56
Moving and Copying Entire Worksheets 58
Renaming Worksheets 59
Keeping Out the Snoops 59

6 Rats! I Need Help, Now!   61

A Menu of Help 62
  Contents: Your First Stop 63
  Searching for Help 64
  Using the Help Index 65
  Just Follow the Example 65
  Help for Lotus 1-2-3 Users 66
  Help for Multiplan Users 66
  A Technical Question 67
  Read All About It 67
For Instant Help, Press F1 Now 68

Using the Toolbar's Help Button 68
Have I Got a Tip for You! 69
Putting It to Bed 69

7 I'll Be Back!   **71**

Picking Valid File Names...72
What's Wrong with This Picture 72
How to Save a Workbook 73
Saving (the First Time) 74
What Are My Options? 75
A Bit of Protection 76
Summary Information 76
Saving Again 77
When Should I Save? 77
Saving on Time 77
Au Revoir 78

Part II: Doing Something Useful   **79**

8 A Range by Any Other Name   **81**

Home on the Range 82
Naming Cells and Ranges 83
Why Should I Name Things? 83
Deciding on a Name..84
Assigning the Name 85
Making Excel Assign the Names 87
Naming Scattered Cells 88
An Expanded Name..88
I've Changed My Mind! 88
What Can I Do with a Name?......................................89
Okay, Move It, Buster! 89
Let's Go There 90

9 Calculations for Non-Rocket-Scientist Types   **91**

The Formula for Success..92
Easing into Functions 93
Functions: Excel's Power Tools 94
What a Function Looks Like 94

It Takes All Kinds 95
Ask for It by Name 96
What's Wrong with This Picture? 98
I Can Figure It Out by Myself 98
Giving Function Wizard a Try 99
A Function Within a Function 100

10   Tidying Up the Place   **103**

Moving (and Copying) Made Easy 104
The Easy Way to Move or Copy 104
Multi-Sheet Moves and Copies 105
Autofill 'Er Up! 105
Painting a Format 107
Shooting Blanks into a Sheet 107
A Squeeze Play 108
Away with You 108
A Built-In Spelling Bee 109
Your Own Little Dictionary 110
Find It! Fix It! 110
I Hate It When a Dentist Says "Oops!" 111
A Matter of Style 112
It's One of Your Own 112
Deleting Styles 113
Copying Styles Between Workbooks 113

11   A Thing of Beauty   **115**

The Wonders of Number AutoFormatting 116
A Cellular Format 118
AutoFormatting a Whole Sheet 120
I Want to Do It Myself! 122
On the Border 122
A Bit of Shade 123
Trying on a New Font 124
Color Me Dotted 124
Using the Formatting Toolbar 125
Some Basic Design Rules 126

12 I Output, Therefore I Print   129

Pushbutton Printing 130
Talk About Printing! 130
How the Page Should Look 132
   The Lowdown on Headers and Footers 133
Taking a Peek 134
   A Marginal Experience 135
   A Zoomin' View 135
Breakin' Pages 136
Your Friend, the Printer 137

Part III: Data Lists Unlimited   141

13 Making a List   143

List Rules and Regulations 144
But Is It a Database? 145
Form(al) Editing 145
   What's a Data Form? 146
   Using a Form to Find Data 146
   Adding and Editing Records with a Form 148
   Deleting a Record 148

14 Shape It, Sort It   151

Sorting Data from A to Z . . . or Z to A 151
   Sorting, Oh-So-Simply 152
   A More Complicated Sort 154
Getting Less List 155
   Filtering a List with AutoFilter 155
   Filtering for Those with Special Needs 156
   Copying a Filtered List 157

15 Summing Up a List   159

Subtotaling Your List 160
   Preparing Your List 160
   Doing It 161
Showing More or Less Detail 162
Using Your Subtotaled List as a Report 163

16 Pivot Tables: Some Assembly Required   **167**

The Not-So-Big Picture 168
Doing Your Own Pivot Table 169
  Making a Table Out of Neighboring Cells 170
  Using Multiple Ranges or Worksheets 171
Customizing Your Pivot Table 172
  Pivoting Your Table 172
  Adding and Removing Data 173
  Editing and Updating a Pivot Table 174
  Changing the Calculations for the Data Area 174
  Grouping and Ungrouping Data 176
  Hiding and Showing Detail 177
  Formatting a Pivot Table 178

17 Fetching and Merging Data   **181**

What Is Microsoft Query? 182
Pre-Flight Check List 183
A Painless Extraction 184
Changing a Query 186
Recycling Your Queries 186
Getting More Focused 187

Part IV: Other Stuff You Wanted To Know   **191**

18 A Chart Is Worth a Thousand Words   **193**

Why A Chart? 194
What Is a Chart? 194
  Creating a Chart 194
This Is This, That Is That 195
Which Chart Do I Use When? 196
Seven Steps to the Perfect Chart 197
  Step 1: Highlight the Data 198
  Step 2: Start the Process 198
  Step 3: Choose a Chart Type 199
  Step 4: Select a Chart Format 199
  Step 5: Make Some Decisions 199
  Step 6: Add the Finishing Touches 200
  Step 7: Sit Back and Admire Your Work 200

The Chart Toolbar 201
A Few Finishing Touches 202
   Chart Cheating 202

19 Let the Macro Do It   205

What, Pray Tell, Is a Macro? 206
Let's Play Follow the Leader................................206
   Writing the Macro 208
   Let's Give It a Try! 209
An Anatomy of a Macro 210
   The Heading 211
   The Macro Itself...211
Running Macros 212
Anti-Macro 213
Macros for 1-2-3 Refugees 213

20 Beyond the Defaults   215

Your Workspace the Way You Want It..................215
Your Way at the Start...218
Templates 218
Add-Ins 219

A Installing Excel   221

B Twenty Great Ideas   223

Address Book 223
Emergency Phone Numbers 224
Car Maintenance 225
Student Grades 226
Sports Scores 227
Exercise Log 228
Wedding Planner 229
Project Manager 230
Day Planner Pages 231
Calendar 232
Presentation Graphics 233
Household Budget 234
Checkbook 235

Chores List...236
Sales Contacts..237
Class Schedule 237
Mortgage Amortization 238
Home Inventory 240
CD/Video Collection 241
Invoice 242

C A Function Beastiary   **243**

Why Use Functions? 243
Yet Another Look at an Excel Function 243
Financial Functions 244
Math & Trigonometry Functions 247
Database Functions 250
Date & Time Functions 251
Statistical Functions 253
Information Functions 257
Lookup & Reference Functions 258
Logical Functions 259
Text Functions 260

D Help for Excel 4 Fans   **263**

No! I Refuse to Upgrade to Version 5! 263
Worksheets, Workbooks, Etc. 263
Minus a Few Extras..263
Different Toolbar Buttons 264
Help! I've Upgraded to Version 5 and I'm Lost! 265
Can I Use My Old Files? 266

E Speak Like a Geek: The Complete Archive   **267**

Index   **275**

Introduction

For Whom I Wrote This Book

Well, for you, of course. And now that I've gone through all the effort of writing it, I'm glad that you're willing to take the time to read it. As you do, you'll learn all the really important stuff that will allow you to run your computer so well that it'll become a useful tool. No longer will you fear it, or want to beat it to death.

I know that some software can be kind of confusing at first. And when you're trying to get numbers crunched and work done under time pressure, you don't need obstacles; you need solutions. That's just what you'll get as you learn and use Excel.

What We've Got Here Is an Ability to Communicate

As you read this book, I'll lead you to the point where Excel will become easy to use. Best of all, you'll learn enough so that you'll be able to solve those pesky problems that seem to spring up no matter what you do—and you'll do it on your own. Pretty soon, people will even be coming to *you* for advice!

A Short History

In the Beginning . . . spreadsheet software meant VisiCalc, a humble but useful program by Dan Bricklin. Thousands of people bought their first microcomputer just so they would be able to use this new electronic spreadsheet. VisiCalc begat Lotus Development's 1-2-3, which catalyzed the microcomputer revolution and became a standard in the MS-DOS world. And thus was the state of the world for a couple of years.

Meanwhile, off in a quiet Hungarian meadow, a brilliant and young—they are *always* young—software engineer considered this. He was uncomfortable with the situation. For one thing, the young programmer disliked the single-mindedness that is MS-DOS' biggest limitation. For another, it was winter, and he had forgotten his overcoat.

> ## By the Way . . .
>
> While most of this book is true, any resemblance between characters depicted herein and people living, dead, or merely hung-over is simply amazing to the author.

MS-DOS   Short for Microsoft Disk Operating System. MS-DOS is the software that actually "runs" your computer's hardware, while Excel (and Windows) work together with you to help you do your job.

Thinking grand thoughts, the young man decided that if he ever found himself in a comfortably warm place—say Redmond, Washington, USA—he would get together with other brilliant, young programmers to create a new kind of software. It would be something to replace *MS-DOS*. And the more he thought about it, the more excited that young fellow became.

His new kind of operating system would use pictures called *icons* to represent programs. And he'd include a yet-to-be-named soap-shaped roller ball with buttons to select those icons. He'd call his new software, Ablaka! Better still—because then he'd be in America, where everyone speaks English—he would call it Windows!

So it came to pass that the Windows graphical environment came into being. And none too soon! Because one of the very first important pieces of software to be written to run under Windows was—you guessed it—Excel.

> ## By the Way . . .
>
> I'll bet you didn't know that Excel was originally to be an MS-DOS based product. Excel was a replacement for the already-clunky Multiplan. Fortunately, someone saw the light just in time.

What You Need to Do This Stuff

Now's a good time for you to step back a moment and make sure you're ready for the good stuff that's coming. I'm going to assume that you have a computer with Microsoft Windows and Excel already loaded on it. I'll also figure that you're basically able to turn on the computer and start Windows running. If you haven't installed Excel yet, turn to Appendix A in the back of this book for help.

If you've never actually done a lot of work with either program, that's not a problem. I'll tell you everything you need to know as we go along.

How Should You Use This Book?

I figure that you—like most of us—are in a hurry. Your best bet is to look in the Table of Contents or Index to see where the information you need might be located. Each chapter stands pretty much on its own, and contains just what you need to know.

While you're doing the examples, if I want you to press a key, you'll see the name of the key in bold, like:

Press **Enter** to continue.

Sometimes, you'll need to type the dreaded *key combination*: jargon for "press two keys at the same time." I'll show you key combinations by putting a plus sign between the two keys you should press together. For instance,

Press **Alt+M** to open the Macro menu.

When you see something like that, you'll know to press and hold the **Alt** key while you type **M**. Then Excel will do something; in this case, it will open the Macro menu. You may want to make friends with the **Alt** key. It's used with other keys an awful lot as a shortcut to getting things done (about which, more later). By the way, the bold **M** here is our way of telling you to press **M** with the **Alt** key (this time). (The **M** is called the *selection letter*.)

There are some boxed notes in this book used to bring out special information:

By the Way . . .
These are special hints from your most humble, but illustrious, author.

Put It to Work
A bit of practice for you to perfect your new skills.

Simple little definitions to keep you up with the jargon.

Really deep, techy stuff that you can skip—unless you're really motivated.

A quick tip on an easier way (hopefully) to do something.

A bit of assistance when things hit the fan.

Acknowledgments

My heartfelt thanks to everyone at Alpha who helped with this book. Especially for the enthusiasm and pointers from Faithe, the patience and foresight of Steve, and the stick-to-itiveness of Marie.

Trademarks

All terms mentioned in this book that are known to be trademarks or service marks are listed below. Additionally, terms suspected of being either have been appropriately capitalized. Alpha Books cannot attest to the accuracy of this information. Use of a term in this book should not be regarded as affecting the validity of any trademark or service mark.

Microsoft Excel, Microsoft Multiplan, and Microsoft Windows are registered trademarks of Microsoft Corporation.

Lotus 1-2-3 is a registered trademark of Lotus Development.

Part I
Let's Start at the Beginning

You say you're a total novice, without a clue? You've never used a spreadsheet before, let alone Excel? You wonder what those little pictures on the screen represent? You've come to the right place. In this part of the book, you'll ease into Excel by learning some basic facts about spreadsheets in general, about Windows, and about using Excel's features to get the job done. Nothing too technical here. You can handle it.

Chapter 1
The Least You Need to Know

Okay, you're a beginner. Not a problem. Even I, your illustrious author and guide, was a beginner once. As you start learning Excel, I'd like you to remember some of the best computer advice I was ever given: "You'll never break anything by pressing buttons." Feel free to experiment, to press buttons, to play with the software—to have fun while you learn. What you do by mistake, you can usually undo. And if not, fixing the result is always easy.

As you're getting acquainted with Excel, here are a few things to keep in mind:

1. It's a Windows Program

Excel is a Windows program, so you need to know something about Windows to use it. If you need help with Windows, check out Chapter 3.

2. Files are Called Workbooks

The basic Excel document is called a *workbook*. A workbook consists of up to 256 pages, or worksheets. For simple projects, you may only use a single worksheet in a workbook—don't worry, you're not being wasteful. For other projects, you may use many worksheets. Chapter 2 will explore the wonders of workbooks and their worksheets.

3. Row + Column = Cell

On a worksheet, there are numbered rows and lettered columns that intersect to form *cells*. A cell's name consists of its column letter and row number: for example, B3, F14, A1. You enter data into a cell by positioning the *cell pointer* (a dark rectangle) on that cell and then typing. You'll learn more about cells in Chapter 2, and you'll actually enter something into a cell in Chapter 4.

4. Press F1 for Help

I remember reading about Albert Einstein, and how he didn't even know his own telephone number. He felt that he shouldn't have to be bothered keeping track of information he could easily look up. It's the same way with Excel—especially when you're starting out. You don't have to memorize everything because you're never far away from help. Make friends with the **F1** key. Press it early and often. When you do, Excel will probably have something helpful to show you about where in the program you are. You can learn about this lifeline in Chapter 6.

5. Label Everything!

If your mind is as much a sieve as mine, you can type a number into a worksheet cell and forget in a trice what that number is supposed to represent. (Don't you just hate trices? And why do we get forgetful just because we've gotten into one?) That's why, if you type a number into a cell, the cell to the left of it should always contain a *label* (text that in some way describes the number or its purpose). You'll get the full scoop in Chapter 4.

6. Appearance is Everything

Accurate data is not much good if it looks boring and puts the reader to sleep. In Chapter 11, you'll learn how to jazz up your worksheets with color, borders, shading, and fancy fonts, and make sure that your dollar signs and decimal points are in the right places.

7. Print It Out

Print your worksheets using the **Print** command, which is found on the File menu. While it might be pleasant, in a narcissistic sense, merely admiring the figures in a worksheet is pretty useless. Besides which, there's nothing like a neatly printed worksheet to show your boss that you've accomplished something. (Now if you could just get him off of his fat— um, I mean—get him to sit up and take notice.) Chapter 12 describes the ins and outs of printing.

8. Excel Makes a Slick Address Book

I'll bet you'd be surprised to know that most people who use Excel don't use it to keep track of financial minutiae. You know what they use it for instead? *To manage lists of data!* Like mailing lists, for instance, with names, addresses, and telephone numbers. Or they use Excel to manage tasks they have to accomplish or items of inventory they'll need to find later. Part III of this book is dedicated to Excel's database capabilities.

9. Charts Help Readers Understand Quickly

I don't know about you, but I get bleary-eyed quickly looking at columns of figures. And when I do, whatever I'm supposed to learn from those numbers simply doesn't penetrate. Adding to my frustration, most often the numbers themselves aren't all that important. It's their *relationship* to one another that matters. Excel helps out with a sophisticated and easy-to-use charting facility. In no time flat, you can create an attractive chart—with notes and highlights, even—and incorporate it right into your worksheet. Chapter 18 tells you enough about charting that you'll feel comfortable with it right away.

10. It's Easier to Automate

When you first start working with a piece of software, every keystroke can be an adventure. In a while, however, you will learn the software. Those same keystrokes can quickly become drudgery. Excel lets you escape such toil if you teach it to remember your repetitive tasks. Chapter 19 is where to go to find out more.

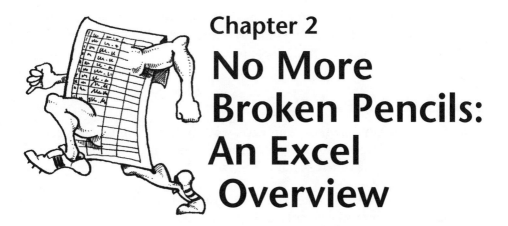

Chapter 2
No More Broken Pencils: An Excel Overview

In This Chapter

- ☛ What is a worksheet?
- ☛ Why an electronic worksheet is better than a paper one
- ☛ The parts of the Excel screen
- ☛ A quick look at the worksheet creation process
- ☛ Nifty tools, besides worksheets

When I think of a worksheet, in my mind's eye, I see the Dickens character, Bob Cratchit, bent over his ledgers. In his hand, he holds a stubby pencil as he adds columns of figures. On his head, Bob wears a green eyeshade against the meager sun coming in the window above his desk.

Pity is, much hasn't changed in the almost a century and half since *A Christmas Carol* was published. Even today, many people do their figuring laboriously, by hand. Or they rely on tables where they look up numbers that approximate the answer they need. It's not that these people are unintelligent. Perhaps they are afraid. I believe that most often—unlike yourself—they simply haven't felt the need to learn how to do things more quickly and easily.

In this chapter, you'll learn what an electronic worksheet has to offer, and some basics about worksheet software in general. You'll also get acquainted with some of Excel's basic parts.

Pleased to Meet You

When you get right down to it, an Excel worksheet is nothing more than an electronic replacement for a paper ledger. It's also a significant improvement because of the difference in the nature of the two.

When you work with paper, you're working by hand. You have to write each and every number you enter into the ledger. If you ever have to change something, it can lead to a real mess—and I don't just mean the ripped paper, the smell of burned eraser rubber, or the frightened co-workers tiptoeing past your desk. For one thing, you've got to erase the "wrong" number and replace it. That's not too inconvenient if the change comes at the end of a column. If you have to insert a number, well, it's almost impossible.

Another all-too-common problem comes when—not *if*—you make an arithmetic error. Every number depending on the erroneous one will have to be erased, refigured, and rewritten. And if the mistake occurs on a reasonably large paper ledger, you may spend hours just finding all the numbers you have to redo! Bah-humbug!

Excel, being an electronic metaphor for the paper ledger, does away with those kinds of problems. Changing a number is ridiculously easy; all you have to do is retype it. Any dependent numbers are refigured and replaced automatically. As a matter of fact, this is one of a software worksheet's greatest characteristics: the capability to do "what if?" analysis. Here you vary this number or that on your worksheet, just to see the effect on dependent numbers. Arithmetic errors, of course, are a thing of the past.

What Does a Worksheet Look Like?

Excel worksheets come already bound into a *workbook*. A workbook is a bound-together collection of worksheets. It's a kind of electronic simile to a three-ring binder holding printed worksheets. Workbooks are handy because they let you break down a huge collection of worksheets (or one huge, complex worksheet) into smaller, similar ones. Each of the smaller worksheets in a workbook can be easily linked so they can share data.

Enough talk. Let's look at an actual Excel worksheet.

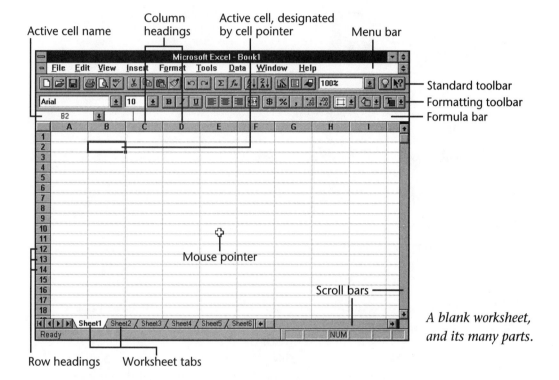

A blank worksheet, and its many parts.

In this worksheet, you'll see several important elements that you'll need to know by heart later, so pay attention now.

Row numbers and column letters   Around the top and left edges of a worksheet are the row and column headings. These help you keep track of the cells' names.

Cell pointer   This dark outline shows you which cell is the active cell at the moment. Whenever you type something, it gets entered into the active cell, so you must be aware of where this cell pointer lies at all times.

Mouse pointer   You use the mouse pointer within the worksheet to choose which cell is active, to select ranges, and to move and copy. Outside of the worksheet, you use the mouse pointer to select menu options and buttons, scroll the view with the scroll bars, and switch among worksheets.

By the Way . . .

The mouse pointer changes shape depending on what Excel thinks you want to do. Normally, the Excel mouse pointer is a *cross* in the worksheet area. This tells you that Excel is ready for you to do something. When the pointer gets close to something that can be acted upon—a menu option or toolbar button, for example—the pointer changes to an *arrow*. When the mouse pointer is pointing to a place where text can be inserted or edited, such as the formula bar, it changes to an *I-beam*.

Menu bar   Pull down menus from the menu bar to issue commands. The Excel menu bar is like any Windows menu bar; see Chapter 3 if you're not familiar with them.

Toolbars   By default, Excel 5 shows the Standard toolbar and the Formatting toolbar. Other toolbars are available too, as you'll learn later in this book. (Right-click on one of the displayed toolbars to see the complete list of toolbars available.) Clicking on a button on a toolbar has the same effect as choosing a command from a pull-down menu.

Cell name   This area tells you the name of the active cell (the one where the cell pointer rests). By default, the cell's name consists of its column letter and row number, such as A1, B12, or C124.

Formula bar   As you type a formula, number, or label into the active cell, it appears both in the cell and in the formula bar. If you enter a formula into a cell, the cell displays the result of the formula, but the formula bar shows the formula itself.

Scroll bars   Each worksheet has many more rows and columns than you can see on-screen at once. The scroll bars let you scroll the off-screen cells into view. They work just like regular Windows scroll bars; see Chapter 3 if you need help with them.

Worksheet tabs   Each workbook has 256 available worksheets. You can choose which worksheet is "on top" by clicking on the worksheet tabs. By default, worksheets have number names, such as Sheet1, Sheet2, and so on.

Gridlines   Gridlines help your eye travel across the worksheet without getting lost. You can turn them off if they get in your way by choosing Tools, Options, View, Gridlines, but leave them up there for awhile if you're a beginner—they help.

Now that you've seen some of the basics, let's take a look at a real worksheet in action. This worksheet is an analysis of a new car purchase. It is an excellent example of how a potentially complicated workbook can be logically organized. In this case, an analysis for each car is contained in its own worksheet.

The active cell, C10, has a name.   A Built-in Excel formula—the PMT function   Lines help divide parts of the worksheet.

Microsoft Excel - Book1							
File Edit View Insert Format Tools Data Window Help							
Arial 10 B I U $ % 100%							
Calculated_p... =PMT(Periodic_rate,Total_payments,-Loan_amount)							

	A	B	C	D	E	F	G
1	**Smith Family Automobile Purchase**						
2	LOAN DATA				TABLE DATA		
3		Loan amount:	**$7,000.00**		Table starts at date:		
4		Annual interest rate:	9.00%		or at payment number:	1	
5		Term in years:	5				
6		Payments per year:	12				
7		First payment due:	12/15/93				
8	PERIODIC PAYMENT						
9		Entered payment:	**$150.00**	*The table uses the calculated periodic payment amount*			
10		Calculated payment:	**$145.31**	*unless you enter a value for "Entered payment".*			
11	CALCULATIONS						
12		Use payment of:	$150.00		Beginning balance at payment 1:		7,000.00
13		1st payment in table:	1		Cumulative interest prior to payment 1:		0.00
14		Payment	Beginning			Ending	Cumulative
15	No.	Date	Balance	Interest	Principal	Balance	Interest
16	1	12/15/93	7,000.00	52.50	97.50	6,902.50	52.50
17	2	01/15/94	6,902.50	51.77	98.23	6,804.27	104.27
18	3	02/15/94	6,804.27	51.03	98.97	6,705.30	155.30

VW / Volvo \ **Toyota** / Plymouth /

Ready

Can we buy the car or not?

Label for cell C3   Worksheet tabs can have meaningful names.

Here are some of the sights to be seen on this worksheet:

Labels and numbers go together like soup and sandwiches. I don't mean to belabor this idea, but without labels, you'll forget what all those numbers represent. You should *always* type a label in the cell immediately above or to the left of every number you enter.

You can assign meaningful labels to worksheets and cells. Notice, for instance, that each worksheet tab has a car name assigned to it, and the active cell isn't just cell C10; it's been named the Calculated Payment cell.

Here's a real-life example of the kind of thing for which people use electronic worksheets.

Fresh water weighs about 62 pounds per cubic foot; salt water is a bit heavier at 64.5 pounds per cubic foot. This means that for two boats of the same type that are loaded equally, the boat in fresh water will ride lower in the water (more deeply) than will the one in salt water.

If you are responsible for keeping a boat afloat in a shallow channel, and your worksheet calculations don't take this kind of "little" disparity into account, it could mean the difference between sailing happily along or calling the Coast Guard Auxiliary to rescue you because you ran your boat aground.

Excel has many built-in formulas called functions. You can identify them easily because they start with an equals sign and several letters, such as **=PMT**, and are followed by a group of variables in parentheses. You'll learn how to use them in Chapter 8.

You can use different fonts and graphic lines to make a worksheet easier to understand. For instance, in this figure, the title (Smith Family Automobile Purchase) is big and bold, and the major sections are separated with vertical and horizontal lines. You'll learn to add your own special fonts and lines in Chapter 10.

A Tale of One Worksheet

Without waxing too rhapsodic, an Excel workbook has a lot in common with a short book of short stories; each one a worksheet. They each have a beginning (the input), a conflict (the number crunching), and the resolution (the resulting figures). Just like a writer creating prose, it's important to make sure that what you've done makes sense.

In this case, the question is: are the numbers correct? You'll know, of course, that there won't be arithmetic errors. But do the calculations result in numbers that make sense?

No matter what you're going to do with your worksheets—calculate trajectory vectors for your starship's translunar orbit insertion, or figure the grade curve for your class of nervous ninth graders—the process is much the same. That's because while each worksheet is different in result, they all have the same kind of start-to-finish flow:

Either you start filling up a new worksheet, or you open an existing one. Well, *that's* a no-brainer; I mean, you've got to start *somewhere*. Before you hop in and press keys, however, I'd take a moment to decide where you want to end up—what result or information this worksheet is to provide. Once you've got a reasonable handle on that, then go ahead and start typing.

Start putting in the numbers. And as you do, arrange them so they make sense. Your best bet is to have input kinds of numbers in one *clearly labeled* place, and outputs in another. Remember: you're probably not the only person who will have to take information from this worksheet at one time or another.

Take off your green eyeshades, and put on an editor's wilted fedora. Here's where you step back and take a quick first look at your work. Ask yourself questions. For instance, do the results of your calculations make sense? Is the worksheet easy to use so when you give it to Hauberk down the hall, he won't be bugging you about it for the next week? (Of course, if you want to get to know Hauberk better, you could just leave the worksheet confusing.) Make your changes (if necessary), and while you're at it, give your spelling a quick check. Excel has the facility built in, and it can save you a bunch of embarrassment.

Save your work; save your work; save your work! Is that clear enough? Or am I being too subtle? Actually, your best bet is to save early and often. You haven't lived until your two-year-old unplugs your computer right in the middle of a high-pressure project—and your last save was just before you found that stupid, convoluted mistake and fixed it.

Give your worksheet one last looking over before you print it. Excel has a very good print preview that shows you a size-reduced version on your computer screen of how your worksheet will look once it's printed. You'll find little margin-moving handles for you to easily adjust how the worksheet will be placed on the pieces of paper.

TECHNO NERD TEACHES

Most electronic worksheets have some kind of macro capability. Usually, the macros are stored in the same worksheet where they are created. Storing macros in separate macro sheets, however, is one of Excel's better ideas. Unlike with the others, you can use the same macros to operate on different Excel worksheets.

More Than Just a Pretty Worksheet

Excel is more than a very clever electronic worksheet. It is a fully integrated package of tools that work together to make your professional life easier. These include the worksheet workbook, of course, but also charts and macros that enhance its usefulness. Here's what I'm talking about.

Workbook   A Workbook is the basic data-holding document of Excel. It is made up of up to 256 worksheets: the big rectangular grid that takes up most of the space on your screen display when you start Excel. The grid you see consists of rows and columns of *cells*—the places where you actually enter your data so that you can work with it.

Charts   A *chart* is a graphical diagram created from the data in your worksheet. Excel includes a number of "canned" chart types, such as line, area, hi-lo-close, bar, pie, and beer (well okay, maybe not beer—but you could take pictures of little beer bottles and use them in a fancy chart like you see on the front page of *USA Today*). With each of these, you can change a number in your worksheet, and Excel will automatically change the chart. Charts are super for showing number trends and results to your audience. You can find out more about charts in Chapter 17.

Macros   An Excel macro is a stored set of keystrokes or menu commands for Excel to perform later—on its own and when you tell it to—written in Microsoft's Visual Basic. You can have Excel run a macro (do those keystrokes or menu commands) when you include the macro's name in an instruction to do so. Macros can save you *a lot* of drudgery time, freeing up your mind for creativity and problem solving. You can find out more about such things in Chapter 18.

The Least You Need to Know

Ah, Excel! The death of number-crunching drudgery. No more arithmetic mistakes; no more dull ledgers. But remember:

- ☞ Excel sure beats a paper worksheet. You can make changes easily, and Excel does all the math calculations.

- ☞ The main component of Excel is the workbook containing up to 256 individual worksheets.

- ☞ Cells are intersections of rows and columns. You type numbers and labels in the cells.

- ☞ The cell with the dark box around it is the active cell. That dark box is called the cell pointer. Whatever you type gets put into the highlighted cell.

- ☞ When entering numbers into a worksheet, label everything. Don't trust your memory, because . . . well, I forget why, just don't.

- ☞ You can tell what Excel is expecting of you by noting the shape of the mouse pointer: crosses for moving, arrows for choosing, I-beams for typing.

- ☞ The general procedure for working with a worksheet is this: enter the numbers and labels, create the formulas that calculate the numbers, check your work, save your work, and then print it.

- ☞ Besides the worksheet, Excel offers some other tools for getting your job done, such as charts and macros. You'll learn more about them later in the book.

**THIS PAGE UNINTENTIONALLY
LEFT BLANK.**

Chapter 3
But I've Never Done Windows

In This Chapter

- Getting Windows up and running
- Using a mouse
- What you'll see in a window
- How to make a window fit
- Shutting a window
- Leaving Windows

In the early days of microcomputers, when there were basically only the IBM-PC and Macintosh, new buyers faced a tough decision. They could go with an IBM-PC and have a fast computer with a boring, blinking command line, or get a slow, friendly, pretty Macintosh. The deciding factor for me, in the end, was price. IBM-PC's were cheap; Macintoshes were expensive. It seemed the better buy, so I went with the PC.

For the next five or six years, I watched PC software evolve. Starting with characters only on the screen, to crude imitations of something similar to the Mac, to less crude imitations, and finally to Windows, version 1.0. Wow! What a big, um, yawn. That clunker software was slower than a West Virginia date on daddy's front porch. And if you didn't hold

TECHNO NERD TEACHES

Ever notice how a light bulb usually blows just as it's turned on? That's because when you first turn on the current, it surges through the wire. If the light bulb filament can take the surge, everything's okay.
If not: something pops.

Inside your computer's monitor there is also a filament, part of a "gun" that sends electrons to make the screen glow in the right places. Just like the light bulb, if your monitor is going to die, it'll probably die when you turn on the power. That's why it's good to leave your monitor on all the time, so it doesn't get strained by the startup surge.

your jaw just right, every now and then it would just stop right in the middle of whatever you were doing. Then came Windows 2.0, Windows 286, Windows 386 . . . well, you get the picture. They kept working at it until they got it right. And, now, you too can own Windows 3.1.

Windows 3.1 is pretty easy to use, after you get used to it. Since Excel is a Windows program, the sooner you get used to Windows, the easier it will be for you to "excel" at Excel. (Sorry, bad pun.) This chapter will help the Windows-impaired among you to get up to speed.

First Things First

Please don't feel offended if I point out the obvious: to use Windows, you have to get it running first. This, in turn, requires that your computer is running. Here's how to accomplish the feat.

Turn on your computer. Look for a switch labeled 1 and 0 (the numbers one and zero). That's an international signage convention where 1 means *on* and 0 means *off*. Sometimes, computer monitors are hooked up to the same computer switch. If not, you'll want to turn it on as well. Ahem.

Now that the computer's on, is Windows running? If so: great! We can be on our way. If not, you'll have to type the following at your DOS prompt (which looks similar to **C:\>**):

WIN

and press **Enter**.

When Windows is running, your computer will look something like this (except you might not have as many icons if you don't have as many programs loaded as I do):

Program Manager window   Program group (open)   Active program group

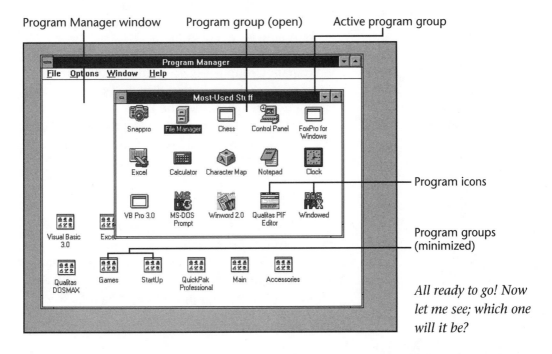

Program icons

Program groups (minimized)

All ready to go! Now let me see; which one will it be?

The Windows interface is very easy to customize, and everyone does it sooner or later. What's important here are the words *Program Manager* at the top of the window. They tell you that you're where you belong when you start Windows: at the beginning.

The **DOS prompt** consists of words or letters that appear on the screen when you're not running a program. They tell you which drive and directory are active. Next to the prompt is a cursor where commands that you type appear.

A **monitor** is the thing that looks like a TV screen that your computer uses to let you know what you're doing as you interact with it.

If you use only three or four of the programs on your hard disk regularly, you may want to put them all together into one *program group* in Windows so you can find them easily. That's what I've done, as you can see in that last figure: I've put my most popular applications into a program group called "Most-Used Stuff." It holds a word processor, Excel (of course), the File Manager, and a couple of diversions. You'll learn how to create a program group later in this chapter.

In the Program Manager window, you can see other windows, like my Most-Used Stuff one. These are called *program group windows*. When a program group is closed, it appears at the bottom of the Program Manager window as an *icon* (a little picture) with its name under it.

Program Group windows hold icons that represent programs on your hard disk. Look again at that last figure; the text under the File Manager icon is in reverse type. This tells you that's the *active* one, the one Windows thinks I'm "looking at." Only one icon can be active at a time. If you press **Enter** when an icon is active, the program it represents will load and run.

Similarly, if you have more than one program group window open, only one of them can be active; the active one's title bar appears in the same color as the title bar of Program Manager itself, and all the other title bars appear in a different color.

Yeek! A Mouse!

Perhaps now, gentle reader, is the time to step back and learn what we are politely to do with our hands—besides engaging them in such mundane activities, such as turning on our computers or typing deft keystrokes. I refer, of course, to the manipulation of our mouses (mice? meeses?). These delicate implements fall easily to hand, and are closely intertwined with the present software.

To continue. . . . Although you can control Windows otherwise, mouses and Windows go together like Rogers and Astaire, like Samson and Delilah, like Prince Charles and Lady Di (oops; perhaps the simile falters a bit). Fortunately, using a mouse is not one of life's more difficult-to-acquire skills.

☞ Place the little darling to one side of your keyboard. It doesn't matter which. Most people find it convenient to use their dominant hand, however. If you have a pad on which to place it, so much the better.

☞ Move the sucker.

Notice how effortlessly your mouse glides across the surface of your desk or pad. Notice also, how the mouse pointer on your screen moves in harmony with it. And that, friend, is pretty much all there is to controlling the mouse pointer on your screen.

Of course, then there's the question of "what are those mouse buttons for?" An excellent question. Once you move the mouse so that the pointer on-screen actually points at something, you'll need to activate the thing by pressing the mouse button(s). Here's a quick rundown:

Click   To press and release the left mouse button once. Clicking on an icon makes it active. Clicking on a menu name opens the menu. In Excel, clicking on a cell makes it active, and clicking on a button on the toolbar issues a command.

Double-click   To press and release the left mouse button twice quickly. Double-clicking an icon runs the program. Double-clicking on a minimized (closed) program group icon opens the group to a window.

Drag   To press and hold down the left mouse button while you move the mouse. The selected object gets "dragged" to the new location of the mouse pointer on-screen. You can drag icons from one program group to another, and, in Excel, you can drag cells to move or copy them.

Groups and Individuals

Icons are Windows' way of keeping you organized. They're what makes Windows special—without pictures, Windows wouldn't be much better than the old DOS prompt. As hinted earlier, Windows has two types of icons: program group icons and program icons.

☞ A program group icon represents a closed program group you can open to reveal program icons.

☞ A program icon represents a program you can run.

TECHNO NERD TEACHES

You can delete an icon from a window by first clicking on it (to select it), and then pressing **Delete**. It won't be gone from your hard disk, or "lost" or anything. Instead, from then on Windows simply doesn't include its icon with the others in your screen display.

But beware! It's much easier to remove an icon than it is to re-create it. Don't delete any icons for programs that you might later need.

The easiest way to tell the difference between program group icons and program icons is to double-click on them. If the thing expands to display a bunch of other icons, you can figure it is a program group. And if a program starts running—well, that's kind of obvious, isn't it?

It's not hard to tell these two types of icons apart. If the icon looks like a miniaturized program group window and sits quietly in the Program Manager window, it's a program group icon. If the icon looks like a unique individual and sits inside a program group window, it's a program icon.

Time to Experiment

One of the neat things about Microsoft Windows is the way the software communicates with you as you manipulate it. Try this:

Click here to open
Control menus.

Click on the Maximize button
to make a window full-screen.

Drag title bars to
move windows.

Click on the Minimize button
to shrink a window to an icon.

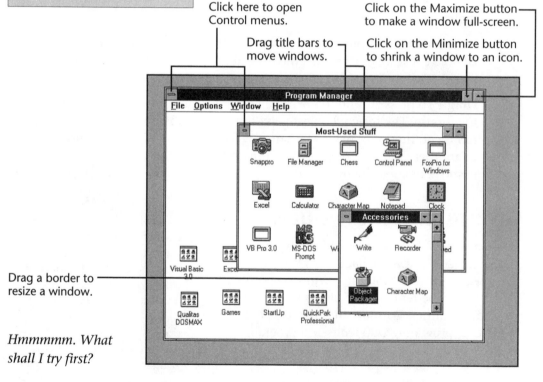

Drag a border to
resize a window.

*Hmmmmm. What
shall I try first?*

Borders, Borders

Move your mouse pointer until it just touches a border on one of your windows. Notice how it turns into a two-headed arrow? This is Windows' way of telling you that it is ready to pull that border in this direction or that to resize the window. The new mouse pointer shapes even let you know in which direction Windows thinks you want to move!

TECHNO NERD TEACHES

Although your mouse probably has two (or three) buttons, Windows recognizes only the left one for its commands. Some Windows applications (such as Excel) recognize the rightmost button, too. Excel uses the right button as a shortcut to pop up a menu.

Holding your mouse pointer there for a moment, press and hold your left mouse button. Now with the mouse button still pressed, move the mouse one way or the other. Notice how the window border gets dragged along? This is that dragging thing I described earlier.

By the Way . . .

This exercise points out a basic difference between a mechanical mouse and its live cousin: Doing this kind of thing with the computer mouse seems natural and easy. If you try it with a live mouse, however, it's real messy and inconvenient and you might get bitten. They just don't seem to be willing to cooperate and get the hang of it. But I digress. . . .

If you've put the mouse pointer on a border corner, notice how it changes into a diagonally-oriented two-headed arrow. That means Windows is ready to resize the window in two axes at the same time.

Now watch how the mouse pointer changes as soon as you move it away from a border. Once again, Windows is telling you that it thinks you will be selecting something like an icon or a menu option, and that it's ready for you to decide.

Try moving to the upper right corner on a window and then clicking once on the **Minimize** button. See how the window shrinks down to being only an icon? Now double-click on the icon to grow the window back again. This is even better than sliced cheese!

Move It, Buddy

Resizing a window to suit yourself is fine, as far as it goes. How about simply moving it to another place on your screen? Once again, it's not a problem.

Move your mouse pointer to the title bar of the window you want to move. (The title bar is the thick line at the top of each window that displays the name of that window.) Press and hold your left mouse button, and drag the window to the new place where you want it to be. Simple, isn't it?

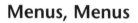

Menus, Menus

Next, move your mouse pointer up to one of the menu names on a menu bar. (The menu bar is the thick line with menu names such as File and Options displayed on it.) Click on it, and watch how the menu drops down so you can get at its commands. If you press and hold your left mouse button as you move the mouse pointer along the menu bar, notice how each menu opens in succession.

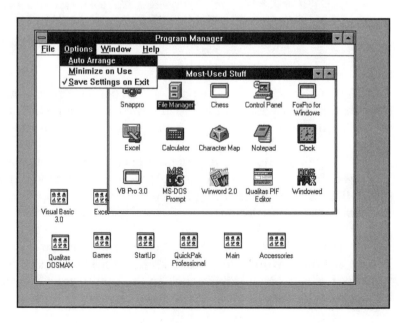

To open a menu, just click on it.

To select a menu command, slide your mouse pointer to the one you want, and click on it. Menu commands that are words by themselves are simple Windows or Excel commands that execute immediately when you select them. Menu commands that end with an ellipsis (...) is Windows' way of letting you know that there is another level to this menu command: a dialog box, which you'll learn about later in this chapter.

If you've opened a menu by mistake, simply move your mouse pointer away from the menu and to another area of your screen. A click with your mouse pointer there will cause the menu to zip itself closed.

Keyboarding: Doing It the Old-Fashioned Way

You know, some people seem to get set in their ways—and not just geezers, either. Back when Windows first came out, one of the big problems Microsoft had in getting people to use it was their distaste for mouses. Seems people were too much in love with their keyboard way of manipulating software. Obligingly, Microsoft made sure that anything you could do with Windows using a mouse, you could also do employing only the keyboard.

The Keys to Windows

If we're going to be able to use our keyboard to run Excel — through Windows, of course—let's take a moment to get acquainted with some computer keys. First, for your excellent perusal, here is an illustration of a representative keyboard.

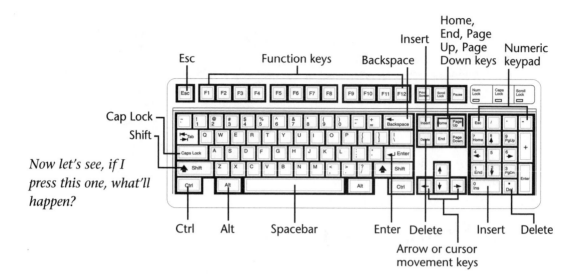

Some of the more useful keys include:

Enter is the "make it so" key, telling Windows that you've finished issuing the order and you want it to be executed. For instance, after you've typed the entire line that you want to put into a cell in Excel, you press **Enter** to place it there. Some keyboards (and computer books) call it the Return key. Same thing.

Esc is a way to say, "Oops, I made a teeny-weeny mistake; now let me gracefully back out of what I'm doing." It let's you *escape* from your current input or action.

F1–F12 are *function* keys. Different programs assign different uses to these keys, but they're generally used as shortcuts for common operations. Since most programs have more than twelve common operations, the function keys are programmed to have different meanings when they're pressed in tandem with other shifting keys, such as **Ctrl**, **Alt**, and **Shift**.

Shift works in much the same way as its traditional counterpart on a typewriter. You press and hold the **Shift** key as you type the alphabetical character you want uppercased. And as I just mentioned, they work in tandem with the function keys to extend the latter's capabilities.

Ctrl keys have been around a long time, even before computer keyboards had function keys. If you wanted some special function that regular typing could not provide, you would press the Control key plus a keyboard letter (such as Ctrl+S) to save a document to disk.

Alt stands for Alternate. It's a long story. As computers got more and more capable, people began to want a second Shift key, to be able to enter special characters besides the ones on the keyboard. Figuring that it's an alternate to the old shift keys, someone decided that this one should be called "Alternate," or Alt for short. In Windows, the **Alt** key is used as a keyboard shortcut to open menus. We'll deal with that happy fact in the next section.

Caps Lock shift-locks the keyboard to print uppercased letters. It does have one idiosyncrasy, however. If you have **Caps Lock** turned on and you type a shifted character, the character will be lowercased. Go figure.

Some things in a computer can be on or off; one state or another. A **toggle** moves a thing between its two states. For instance, pressing a key can type a capital or lowercase character. The **Caps Lock** key is an example of a toggle.

Backspace is one of your two big oops-protection keys. (The other one is Esc.) Backspace moves your cursor back to the left one character space, and at the same time deletes any character in its path.

Arrow keys allow you to move your cursor (whatever form it may take in a particular program) around on your screen. In Windows itself, they move the active highlight from place to place; in Excel they move the cell cursor.

Spacebar creates spaces. Duh! Did you know that the spaces between words on your screen were characters too? Yup. Remember: your computer is a stupid machine. The simple idea of "just leave a blank area between two words" is far too complicated for it. The Spacebar is a key that types a character, just like any other character, except it's invisible. Eerie, huh.

When you type a key on your keyboard, it may or may not be acted upon at once. Sometimes, your computer's microprocessor is busy with something else, and simply doesn't have the milliseconds necessary to deal with keystrokes.

What actually happens when you type a key is that your computer makes note of what keys you've just pressed and for how long you pressed them. The information of which keys were pressed is placed in a short-term storage area called a *keyboard buffer*. Your computer uses the "how long they were pressed" information to know how many of those keystrokes to put into the buffer.

Later, as it has time (not much later—this is a computer, after all), the computer takes the first keystroke stored in the keyboard buffer and acts upon it.

Ins(ert) toggles the Overtype mode on and off. In Overtype mode, text you type replaces any text that's already there. In Insert mode (the opposite of overtype), text you type makes existing text move over.

Del(ete) erases the character just to the right of the cursor, moving all the other downstream characters up by one.

Home moves your cursor to the beginning of a row or line. In Excel, if you press **Ctrl+Home**, you go to the uppermost left cell of your worksheet: cell A1.

End works with your arrow keys to move you to the last cell in a row or column. For example, if you type **End+Down Arrow**, you'll go to the last filled cell in the column; **End+right arrow** moves you to the last filled cell to the right.

Page Up and **Page Dn** scroll your worksheet up (or down) by one screenful. It's a lot like flipping the pages of a stenographer's notebook back and forth.

A Bit of Dialog

Often, you'll need to give Excel some needed information so it can do its work. To do so, you use something called a *dialog box*. Although they look different, every dialog box has in it the same kinds of elements that behave in the same way. Check this out:

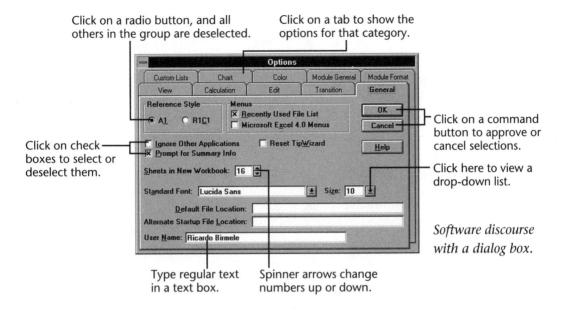

Click on a radio button, and all others in the group are deselected.

Click on a tab to show the options for that category.

Click on check boxes to select or deselect them.

Click on a command button to approve or cancel selections.

Click here to view a drop-down list.

Software discourse with a dialog box.

Type regular text in a text box.

Spinner arrows change numbers up or down.

Sometimes, it's faster to discourse with a dialog box using your keyboard rather than your mouse. After all, your fingers are already there, aren't they? Press **Tab** to move from one element in a dialog box to the next. If a letter in an option is underlined, know that you can press **Alt+<that letter>** to select that option. Here are some of the landmarks:

☛ **Option buttons** are like the radio buttons on your car—when you select one, all the others pop back out. Option buttons are usually arranged in groups of mutually exclusive options.

☛ **Check boxes** let you answer yes or no questions and toggle features on or off. Each one stands alone—unlike option buttons, they don't rely on other check boxes being selected.

☛ **Text boxes**, not surprisingly, are where you type text. For instance, if you need to enter a label or a name, a text box will often be provided.

☛ **Drop-down lists** enable you to choose from a list of items. The list drops down when you need it so it won't take up precious real estate in the dialog box unnecessarily.

☞ **Tabs** are just like regular tabs in a folder—they denote different sections. If a dialog box has several tabs at the top, clicking on a tab will bring up a different page of options to select.

☞ **Command buttons** are decision-makers. If you're satisfied with all your selections in the dialog box, choose **OK**. If you want to forget the whole thing, choose **Cancel**. If you aren't sure, choose Help to get more information.

I'm Outta Here!

Once again, I feel the overwhelming need to belabor the obvious. When we're done with Windows, we gotta turn off the software; a process appropriately called *exiting*.

There are a number of ways you can do this. Pulling your computer's plug would certainly work. I wouldn't recommend it; however, it's so inelegant what with all the bending down involved—and it can fry your computer.

Of course, you could simply turn off the computer, but that wouldn't give Windows a chance to clean itself up, computer memory-wise. You see, as it works, Windows is using a number of temporary files to hold scratch information. It's also allocating and de-allocating memory to different applications (Excel, for instance), and all that has to be kept straight. When Windows is allowed to go through its normal closing process, it has the chance to "clean up after itself," as it were.

By the Way . . .

Take a quick look at the Program Manager Control menu. It's hidden. To display it, click on the minus sign at the window's very top left corner. That minus sign is called the Control-menu box.

Notice that there's a **C**lose option, followed by **Alt+F4**. That means you can exit Windows by opening this Control menu and selecting **C**lose or by pressing **Alt+F4**. Or if you want to get speedy, you can just double-click on the Control-menu box.

The best way to exit (close down) Windows is to go to the File Manager's File menu. Click on it with your mouse pointer, and slide down to the Exit Windows option. One quick click on it turns Windows off. And for one last piece of oops-protection, Windows will ask if you are sure you want to exit. Click on **OK**, and off it goes.

I'm outta here!

The Least You Need to Know

Hokey dokey. We've had our little tour of Windows. We can turn it on and off, and even change the size of the windows. Lest we forget, however:

- ☞ You start Windows by typing **WIN** at the DOS prompt.

- ☞ The Program Manager is the Windows program that controls the other programs.

- ☞ To use your mouse, move it around on its pad (or your desk) so that the mouse cursor goes to where you want it on your computer's screen.

- ☞ To click with your mouse, press and release the left mouse button once. Click to select something, such as an icon or menu command, to be acted upon.

- ☞ Double-click (press the mouse button twice quickly) to get Windows or Excel to perform an action or command on the thing selected.

- ☞ Always use Windows to turn itself off. Don't simply pull the plug.

**RECYCLING TIP: TEAR OUT THIS PAGE
AND PHOTOCOPY IT.**

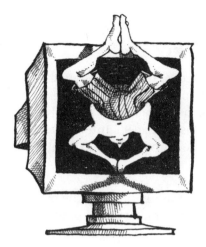

Chapter 4
Taking a Quick Plunge

In This Chapter

- Starting Excel
- Getting to know workbooks
- Creating a simple worksheet
- Adding automatically
- Dealing with the dreaded "oops!"
- Leaving Excel

The best way to learn something is often by jumping right in and doing it. That's why we're going to create a simple worksheet in this chapter. That may sound complicated for now, but it's really not. We'll take each step one at a time. When you're done, you'll have a good, basic understanding of Excel, *and* you'll be ready to tackle more advanced information in later chapters.

When the Windows user interface was invented, the computer mouse was still a novelty. Some people, thinking themselves computer "purists" decried its use, claiming that they never should have to lift their precious digits off their sturdy keyboards. Microsoft went the extra mile to accommodate these people. So to this day, if you'd rather not use a mouse, you don't have to. You can perform any menu option or window movement by using only keystrokes.

On the other hand, if you like using a little bit of both, you can do that also. To start Excel running, for instance, you can click with your mouse to highlight its icon, and then press return to load it.

The Splash (Launching Excel)

When you installed Excel 5, the setup program created a program group in Windows called Microsoft Office (if such a group wasn't already there), and put the icons for Excel 5 into it. If you're working with Excel 4, the program group is called Excel instead.

To get Excel up and running, open up the program group that holds its icon, and then double-click on the Excel program icon. (If that sentence didn't make sense to you, turn back to Chapter 3 for a Windows refresher.)

The Big Screen: A Tour

Here it is: the whole enchilada.

The first thing you see once Excel is up and running is a blank workbook with its first page open. See the following figure for an example of what your screen shold look like. A workbook is Excel's basic *document*—the thing that holds all the other things. It's a lot like a three-ring binder, or a ledger book, that can hold worksheet pages. The other buttons, bars, and menus are support staff for the worksheets you create.

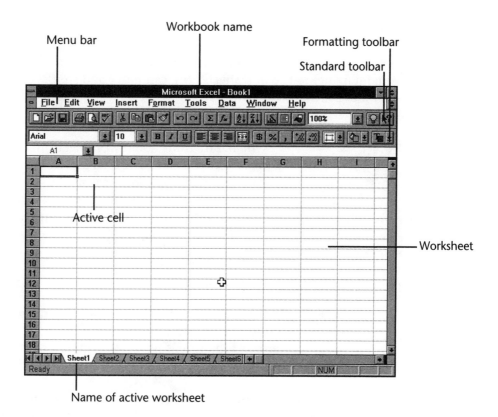

Menu bar — Workbook name — Formatting toolbar — Standard toolbar — Active cell — Worksheet — Name of active worksheet

Worksheet Workout

The big area in the middle with all the gridlines is the *worksheet*. The gridlines form rectangles called *cells*, which you may remember from Chapter 2.

Just as a three-ring binder can hold more than one sheet of paper, a workbook can hold more than one worksheet. The tabs at the bottom are there to help you go from one worksheet to another in your workbook. You keep track of which worksheet is the active one by noting which tab's title is bold.

Although you start out with only sixteen worksheet pages in a workbook, you can add more, up to 256, or delete all except one. You can keep the default names (Sheet1, Sheet2, and so on), or you can assign more meaningful names to the worksheets. You can move and shuffle any of them around by simply dragging the tab. You'll learn to do this later in the book.

The worksheet that's "on top" (in view) at a given time is the **active sheet**. Only one sheet can be active at a time, and you can input data only into the active sheet.

Being able to repeat values from one cell in another cell is a great feature. For example, say you are tracking expenses or bills. You could have one worksheet for each month of the year. You could have one more worksheet (summary) that draws the data from the appropriate cells in the monthly worksheets, adds up the numbers in them, and displays the total for you.

One handy thing about worksheets in a workbook is that you can share data among them. For instance, you can perform a calculation on Sheet1 based on some data on Sheet5. When you get more acquainted with Excel, you'll find that it's a snap to get them to "talk" to each other.

A Cellular Affair

In Chapter 2, you learned that a cell is the rectangle at the intersection of a numbered row and a lettered column. Cells hold pieces of data. Some of the types of information a cell can hold include:

A **number** representing a value (like money), the position of an item in a list, or even a date (which is nothing more than a number in a special series, displayed in a more familiar format).

A **label** (text) to describe the numbers in nearby cells. Unless you're going to use Excel as a quick, one-time calculator, you should *always* include a label for every number in your worksheet.

Formulas where numbers in other cells are manipulated to derive the answer you seek. Some formulas, such as summing a series of cells, can be done with a simple mouse click; others require that you write them much like in high school algebra class.

Data from other cell(s). You can copy the number or label from one cell to a different cell, or use the contents of another cell in a formula. The other cells can be on other worksheets, even! When the content of the first cell changes, the content of the other cell changes automatically, too.

A Fashionable Address

As you learned in Chapter 2, Excel assigns *cell addresses*, or names, to each cell by combining the column letter and row number. For example, the cell at the intersection of column C and row 12 would be called C12. There are ways to assign more descriptive names to individual cells (and groups of cells, called ranges); you'll learn to do this later in this book.

A **formula** is a mathematical equation, such as 2+2. Formulas are often constructed with variables, such as **principal+interest** or C1–C2 (the contents of cell C1 minus the contents of cell C2).

Active cell's address appears here.

Column letters

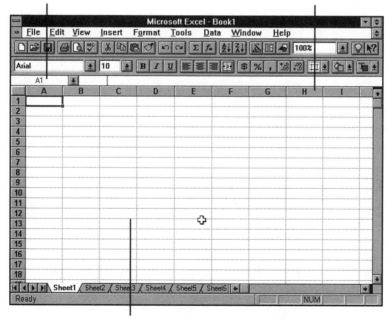

A whole lotta cells.

Cell C12, at the intersection of row 12 and column C.

By the Way . . .

People who are former Multiplan users may be a bit confused at first by this cell addressing scheme. Instead of the referring to cells by a letter/number address, Multiplan uses a Row number/Column number addressing scheme. For example, what Excel users know to be cell A1, Multiplan would call cell R1C1. If you're a former Multiplan user, or if you're simply curious, select **O**ptions from the **T**ools menu, click the General tab, and select the R1**C**1 reference style.

An **address** is a letter or number combination that uniquely identifies each individual cell, and by which cells are referred.

Menu Mania

Almost all Windows-based programs have menus, and Excel is no exception. Some menus, such as the File and Help menu, are Windows standards; you can always rely on them to offer you a way to start a new file, open an old one, print, exit the program, and get help. Other menus are unique to Excel. Here's a quick rundown:

The **File Menu** is what you use to act on entire files at once. Here are options for you to open new workbooks, save workbooks with which you're done working, and to print entire workbooks or individual worksheets.

The **Edit Menu** helps with the cell housekeeping. You can cut and copy, find and replace, clear, and delete individual cells or groups of them.

By the Way . . .

My personal favorite **E**dit Menu option is the very first one: Undo. Not that I use it very often, you understand. Still, it's nice to have the oops protection for the rare occasion when my 2 + 2 ends up to be 4 $\frac{1}{2}$.

The **View Menu** lets you act on what you see on your computer's screen. You may want to zoom out or in (kind of like a zoom lens on a camera), or tell Excel what tools you want to show on-screen (such as the status bar, formula bar, and toolbars).

The **Insert Menu** enables you to rearrange and reorder the structure of your worksheet. You can insert or delete entire rows or columns, insert a brand-new worksheet at the beginning of your workbook, or even insert an illustration, sound, or equation.

The **Format Menu** is where you find options that allow you to vary the look of a part, or all, of your worksheet. You can make text bold or italic, change its font or size, add graphic lines, and modify the width of columns.

The **Tools Menu** brings "helpers" into your Excel workbook. These mini-applications can audit your worksheet for logical mistakes, create, record, and run macros, check your spelling, and perform many other useful functions.

The **Data Menu** is your gateway to Excel's rather extensive database capabilities. Besides calculating numbers, Excel can do a fine job keeping track of things on lists, such as names and addresses or inventories. Part III of this book shows you all you need to know about Excel's database capabilities.

The **Window Menu** appears in most Windows applications. It lets you switch among the open workbooks and arrange them on your screen.

The **Help Menu** has so much going on that we've devoted an entire chapter to it: Chapter 6.

The Right Toolbar for the Job

Menus are okay, as far as they go. But they can be so awkward in a graphical environment such as Windows. It's a lot easier to point and click—especially to perform common tasks such as printing and saving. That's where the toolbars come in.

By default, Excel starts up with two toolbars visible: the Standard toolbar and the Formatting toolbar. The standard one's on top, and the formatting one directly beneath it.

> ## By the Way . . .
> Excel includes a number of other toolbars and toolboxes, each of which you can easily add to your display by choosing **Toolbars** from the **View** menu and picking among them. The only difference between a toolbar and a toolbox is that a toolbar sits atop your worksheet window, while a toolbox appears in a movable window. You can make a toolbox into a toolbar by dragging it up into the toolbar area.

The two default toolbars: Standard and Formatting.

Standard toolbar

Formatting toolbar

On the Standard toolbar, you'll find buttons that do all the common worksheet tasks. Some of them, such as save or print, are things that you might do many times during a single work session. To use a button, simply click on it.

Button	**Use**
	Opens a new, empty workbook.
	Opens an existing file.
	Saves the active workbook to disk.
	Prints the active worksheet.
	Previews the printout on-screen.
	Checks spelling.

continues

continued

Button	Use
	Cuts the selected data to the Clipboard.
	Copies the selected data to the Clipboard.
	Pastes the contents of the Clipboard onto the worksheet.
	Copies the format of the active cell to another cell.
	Reverses the last action.
	Repeats the last action or command.
	Adds a list of values.
	Helps you create a formula.
	Sorts data from A to Z.
	Sorts data from Z to A.
	Helps you create a chart.
	Creates a text box for explanatory notes.
	Displays the drawing toolbox.
100%	Adjusts the view at which your worksheet is displayed.
	Shows or hides tips for more efficient Excel use.
	Helps you interpret various parts of the screen.

On the Formatting toolbar, you'll find buttons that act on the active cell or selected range. Rather than affecting the actual content of the cells, these buttons simply decorate the cells with some formatting. If you change the contents of the cells, the formatting is applied to the new contents.

> ### By the Way . . .
> You may notice that most of the Formatting toolbar buttons duplicate the features on the Format menu. It's nothing more than a bit of handy redundancy.

Button	*Use*
Lucida Sans	Applies any installed font to the selected cell(s).
10	Changes the type size in the selected cell(s).
B	Turns the bold attribute on and off.
I	Turns the italic attribute on and off.
U	Turns the underline attribute on and off.
	Sets left-alignment in the selected cell(s).
	Sets center-alignment in the selected cell(s).
	Sets right-alignment in the selected cell(s).
	Joins several cells into a single cell.
$	Formats numbers as currency.

Button	Use
%	Formats numbers as percentages.
,	Separates thousands with commas.
+.0 .00	Displays one more digit to the right of the decimal point.
.00 +.0	Displays one less digit to the right of the decimal point.
	Adds or removes a border or shading from the cell.
	Changes the background color of a cell.
	Changes the color of a cell's text.

By the Way . . .

From time to time in the text of this book, you'll read something like **move to A1**. This means that you should move your mouse cursor to cell A1. Once there, you can expect to be told to input numbers or text into that cell, or to manipulate its contents in some way.

Doing Something Real

Enough talk; let's create a worksheet of our own. This fine example will help with that all-too-common fiscal scourge of businesses and homes alike: monthly bills! The worksheet we create here will add up the bills and subtract the total from our paycheck amount, to arrive at the amount that's left over to spend.

SPEAK LIKE A GEEK

When text in a cell moves down from line to line so that it fits into the space available, the text is said to **wrap**.

Identification, Please!

The first thing to do with our worksheet is to put in our labels.

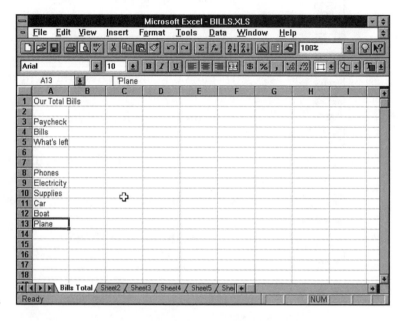

First come the labels.

1. Start Excel, if you haven't already. (Remember, to start Excel, double-click on the **Excel 5** icon in the Microsoft Office program group, or if you're an Excel 4 user, on the **Excel** icon in the Excel program group.)

2. If the workbook on your screen is not totally empty (that is, if you've been messing around with Excel), click on the **New Workbook** button. That way, you'll have a blank worksheet with which to work.

3. Move to cell A1 on Sheet1, and enter a title for this worksheet. Type **Our Total Bills** and press **Enter**.

4. Now let's give the worksheet a real name. Move the mouse pointer down to the worksheet tab that says "Sheet1." Click your right mouse button, select **Rename**, type **Bills Total** in the dialog box, and select **OK**.

5. Move to cell A3, type **Paycheck** and press **Enter**. The cell cursor moves on down to cell A4, which is exactly where you want to be.

6. Type **Bills** in cell A4 (you should already be there), and press **Enter**. This moves you down to cell A5.

7. Type **What's Left** in cell A5, and press **Enter**.

8. Starting in cell A8 and going down, enter **Phones**, **Electricity**, **Supplies**, and **Car**. If you're successful or optimistic, you can enter **Boat** and **Plane** under those four.

9. Now for something *really* important: *save your work*. Select Save **As** from the File menu, type **Bills** under File Name in the dialog box, and select **OK**. If you're prompted with a summary box, fill out the info it asks for. (Chapter 7 has more details about this box.) You can watch Excel doing its work saving the file by looking at the little save-o-meter at the bottom of your screen. When it's full, Excel's done.

And the Number Is . . .

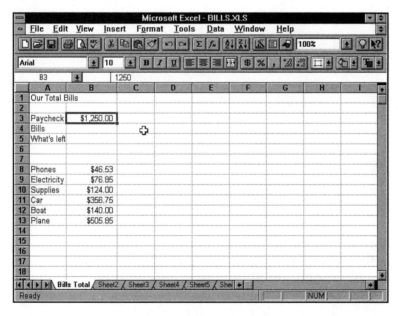

Next come the numbers.

Once you've put in the labels, your worksheet has its basic organization. Now it's time to enter some numbers.

1. Move to the cell to the right of the one that says **Paycheck** and enter in the amount you usually take home. When you type in the number, first type a dollar sign ($) so that Excel will know that it's a money amount you're entering.

2. Next, move down to the cell next to **Phones** and enter what you think a normal month's phone bill might be.

3. In the same way, enter money amounts for the other bills. If you'd like to add more labels and bill amounts, feel free to do so.

Tis What's Worth

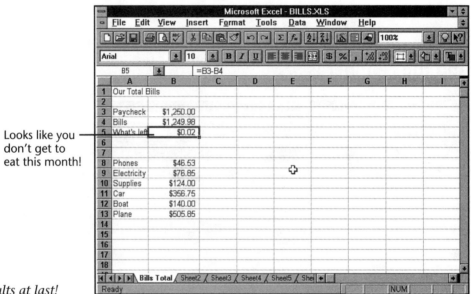

Looks like you don't get to eat this month!

The results at last!

Simply entering numbers into your worksheet doesn't usually answer any important questions. To get the answer you seek, you'll need to enter a formula that assesses the damage. Here's how:

1. Move to cell B4 and make sure it's highlighted.

2. Click on the **Autosum** button on the Standard toolbar. It's the one with the Sigma (Σ) on it, and it causes the beginnings of a formula to be placed into B4.

3. To tell Excel which cells it should add, move to cell B8 (the phone bill), press and hold your mouse button as you move down to the last bill amount, then release your mouse button. (Be sure you include only the cells in a single column that contain numbers.)

4. Press **Enter**. Excel puts the addresses of the cells you highlighted into the formula in cell B4, and does the arithmetic.

There'll be a time when you look at your worksheet and see one or more cells filled with nothing but #######'s. That's Excel's way of letting you know that the contents of those cells are too wide for them to fit.

The quick and easy fix is for you to widen the columns in which the cells fall. To do so, "grab" the line separating the column heading letter from its neighbor and move it to one side. Do this by clicking and holding the left mouse button on the line while you move the mouse.

The only thing left to do now is find out what—if anything—you've got left. And that simply requires us to subtract the bills from our paycheck. Follow these steps:

1. Move to cell B5.

2. Press the equals key (=) on your keyboard to "tell" Excel that a formula is coming. Then, click on cell **B3**, type a minus (-), and click on **B4**.

3. Press **Enter** to let Excel know you're done entering the formula.

4. Read the **What's Left** number and weep.

That's all there is to it! If you want, you can go to any of the bill amounts and change them. At the very instant you do, Excel will automatically resum the bills total and subtract that number from your paycheck amount, letting you know what's left. Pretty slick, huh?

Adding Sideways

One thing new about Excel 5 is how the cell highlight moves down when you press **Enter** after entering a number. But what about when you want to add numbers across columns?

What you do is highlight the row of cells into which you want to type, starting with the first one you're going to use. With them highlighted, you move to the first one, do your thing, and press **Enter**. Each time you do, Excel moves the current cell highlight over one. One caveat, though: when it reaches the end cell and you press **Enter**, the highlight moves over to the first cell. If you enter something into it, you'll be typing over what's already there. Yup, even "smart" computer software like Excel can be a bit dense sometimes.

The Dash

Well, you've come this far and nothing's broken. With all of your new knowledge, it would be a shame not to also know how to get out of Excel; something we call *exiting* the software.

First though, you've saved your work, haven't you? Actually, if you forget, Excel will double check before turning itself off. But it's more elegant to have taken care of that little chore before you go.

You can exit Excel several ways:

- ☞ Press **Alt+F4**.

- ☞ Click on the Excel **Control-menu** box, and select **Close**.

- ☞ Double-click on the Excel **Control-menu** box.

Whatever you do, don't simply turn off your computer while Excel (or Windows) is still running! It'll work, of course, but it won't give Windows and Excel a chance to clean up after themselves (deleting temporary disk files, and such). By far it's best to shut down Windows and wait until you see a DOS prompt (like **C:>**) before you turn off your computer.

The Least You Need to Know

When it's all said and done, creating a good Excel workbook isn't all that complicated. Keep in mind, however:

- ☞ To start Excel, find the program group in which it's located, and double click on its icon.

- ☞ Label everything! Never get caught having to guess as to what a number or figure means.

- ☞ Save early and often. That way, even if the power goes out, you won't be completely out of luck.

- ☞ Use the menu bars and toolbars to work efficiently.

- ☞ Always remember your friends: the Undo and Repeat buttons.

- ☞ Once you're finished, exit Excel using the **Exit** command from the **File** menu (or press **Alt+F4**). Don't simply turn off your computer.

SPECIAL BONUS PAGE!

Chapter 5
Taking Control of Your Workbook

In This Chapter

- ☞ Scrolling around a worksheet
- ☞ Moving from sheet to sheet in a workbook
- ☞ Arranging Windows
- ☞ Looking at a worksheet in more than one way
- ☞ Hiding and showing individual worksheets

It's a little-known historical fact that worksheets have been around for a long time. Archaeologists have even found parts of one in Rome, written on velum (what else?) and apparently used to keep track of finances at the coliseum. It seems that Emperor Nero was angry because the place wasn't doing better than breaking even. He clearly didn't realize that the lions were eating up all the prophets! Ahem.

Unlike the simple worksheets of antiquity, those of Excel can be quite convoluted. In this chapter, we're going to look at how to move around on one worksheet. We'll also move from worksheet to worksheet within a workbook, and try our hand at looking at more than one part of a worksheet at one time.

Going Mobile

You can move to various parts of your worksheet with either the keyboard or the mouse. It's totally up to you. I'll tell you about both methods, and let you make the final decision for yourself.

Moving Around with the Keyboard

There are a host of special key combinations you can use to move from place to place in a workbook. Here's a summary:

Key	Moves
Arrow	One cell in the arrow direction
Tab	To the next unlocked cell in a protected worksheet
Home	To leftmost cell in row
Ctrl+Home	To top left cell in worksheet
Ctrl+End	To bottom right cell in worksheet
Page Down	Down one screenful
Page Up	Up one screenful
Alt+Page Down	Right one screenful
Alt+Page Up	Left one screenful
Ctrl+Page Down	To next sheet in workbook
Ctrl+Page Up	To Previous sheet in workbook

Scrolling Around with the Mouse

Moving the cell cursor to a cell with the mouse is easy; just click on it. If the cell isn't on the screen at the moment, you can use one of the keyboard shortcuts you just learned about to move it into view, but an easier method is to use the scroll bars.

There are two scroll bars for your use, as in most other Windows-based programs. The vertical one on the right edge of the worksheet lets you scroll up and down through the rows. The horizontal one at the bottom right of your worksheet allows side to side movement.

You can go directly to any cell or range of cells by pressing the keyboard shortcut, **F5**. When you do, Excel displays a dialog box in which you type your destination. When you click on **OK** or press **Enter**, Excel whizzes you right there.

Each scroll bar has three parts, which will be familiar to you if you're an experienced Windows user:

The scroll bar is, of course, the long narrow bar with an arrow button at each end.

The arrow buttons scroll your screen one row or column at a time each time they're clicked. Click and hold on an arrow button to scroll quickly.

The scroll boxes are like handles. You drag them along the scroll bars to move swiftly to another part of the worksheet. You can also use scroll boxes to help determine your position in the worksheet.

When you open a new worksheet, the vertical scroll button is at the top of its bar. Likewise, the horizontal scroll button is at the extreme left of its travel. As you move around to various parts of the worksheet, the scroll boxes move also. When you see them at the middle of their travels, you'll know that you're pretty near the geographical center of your worksheet.

Shuffling Through the Sheets

Moving from worksheet to worksheet is a snap! Click on any tab at the bottom of your screen to call up that worksheet. If you can't see the worksheet tab you want, click on one of the tab scrolling arrows that you'll find just to the left of the tab names until it comes into view. Keyboard fans can press Ctrl+Page Down and Ctrl+Page Up to move from sheet to sheet just as easily.

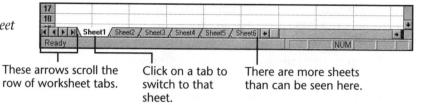

Switching from sheet to sheet.

These arrows scroll the row of worksheet tabs.

Click on a tab to switch to that sheet.

There are more sheets than can be seen here.

Zooming Around

Normally, when you look at an Excel worksheet, it's displayed at the size that the programmers thought would be easiest on your eyes. Of course, they had no way of knowing that you've got super VGA while Irving Schmaltz down the hall is stuck with something less. Fortunately, like that famous purveyor of dead cows, carefully prepared: you can have it your way.

You use the Zoom command on the View menu to vary the magnification at which your worksheet is displayed. Select it, and then click on one of the options, or type in a number in the Custom field. Numbers greater than 100% magnify the text; numbers smaller than 100% decrease the size of the text. Also, you can highlight a group of cells and choose **Fit Selection** to magnify just those cells.

A New Arrangement

With Excel, you can see several workbooks at once on the screen, or several worksheets within a single workbook. The key here is the Window menu.

You can open up to nine workbooks at once in Excel, and arrange them on your screen so you can see at least a small piece of each one. (With nine windows open, you won't be able to see very much of any of them!) Or if you prefer, you can open a single workbook that has many sheets, and arrange several of the sheets on-screen so you can view them simultaneously.

TECHNO NERD TEACHES

The size at which the worksheet displays on your screen depends on several factors. One, of course, is the Zoom discussed here. Another is the video driver you're using. Unless you have made a special point of installing a Super VGA video driver, Windows is probably running in regular VGA mode on your computer, which is 640 by 480 pixels at 16 colors. If you run Windows at 800 by 600 with a special driver, the worksheet, and everything else, will appear smaller, allowing you to see more of your woorksheet on-screen at a time.

Whether it's multiple sheets or multiple workbooks you're seeking to see, here's how to manage it:

1. Open the workbooks you want to see, if you want to view multiple workbooks. (Use the **Open** command on the File menu, or the **File Open** button on the Standard toolbar.)

2. Select Arrange from the **Window** menu. The Arrange Windows dialog box appears.

Zoom to change the view or magnification with which you see your worksheet. Zooming out is like the view of the earth that Wiley Coyote gets as his rocket flies up. Zooming in is like what he sees as he falls toward the canyon floor.

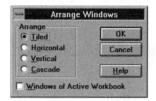

3. Pick an arrangement:

   Tiled so that they each take up an equal amount of screen space.

   Horizontal split so they appear stacked up from top to bottom.

   Vertical so they stand next to each other, side by side.

   Cascade so the windows are stacked neatly one on top of the other, slightly overlapping.

4. Select **OK**. The windows arrange themselves in the manner you chose.

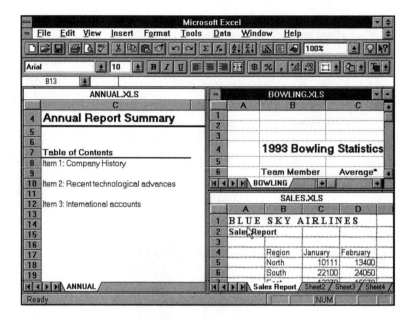

Tiled windows.

The Big Split

In the last section, you saw how to arrange different worksheets and workbooks on the screen. But what if you want to see several parts of the same worksheet at once? No problem. Just split the window. Once you've split a window, you can move to a different spot in one pane while still viewing the original spot in the other.

SPEAK LIKE A GEEK

In Excel you can **split** (break into parts) a screen in up to four parts. The split is for on-screen appearances only; the worksheet itself is still a whole. When you print it, the split has no effect.

When you split a window, a split line appears in the window. A complete copy of the worksheet is accessible from each split pane, and edits you make in one pane will immediately affect the copy in the other pane.

1. Select the row or column below or to the right of where you want the split to occur.

2. Select **S**plit from the **W**indow menu. A split bar appears.

3. Use the normal methods of moving the cell cursor you learned earlier in the chapter to move to a different location in a pane.

If you want to make the split semi-permanent, select **Freeze Panes** from the Window menu. Excel replaces the split bar with a single line to let you know that the panes in that window are split. When you choose unfreeze Panes, also from the Window menu, Excel reinserts the regular split bar.

Put It to Work

Here's a quick way to isolate those titles you have running along the top of your worksheet.

1. Insert a horizontal split line in your worksheet.

2. Drag the split box until it's just underneath your column titles.

3. Switch to the lower split pane (click there), and move to the rows you want to see. Your column titles stay firmly in view.

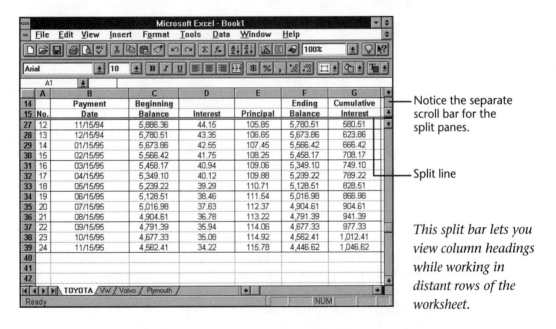

Notice the separate scroll bar for the split panes.

Split line

This split bar lets you view column headings while working in distant rows of the worksheet.

When you isolate the titles, you'll still be able to keep track of which column means what when you scroll your data up and down. You can split your window vertically in much the same way. The only difference is that you grab the split box that is just to the right of the horizontal scroll bar.

Moving and Copying Entire Worksheets

In lesson 10, you'll learn to move and copy cells and ranges from place to place, but what if you want to move or copy a whole worksheet? This is a job for the Move or Copy Sheet command.

There are a number of reasons you might want to move a worksheet within an Excel workbook. It might not be in a logical order with its neighbors. Or perhaps its information is of lower priority, and you'd like things to be a bit more organized. Or you might be making another workbook and want to move this worksheet into it.

Moving gets done through the Edit menu. First, select the worksheet you want to move. If it's only the current one, fine. Otherwise, **Ctrl+click** the tab(s) of the worksheets you want to act upon.

Next, select the Move or Copy Sheet command from the Edit menu to call up the Move or Copy dialog box. Here's where you have to make some decisions!

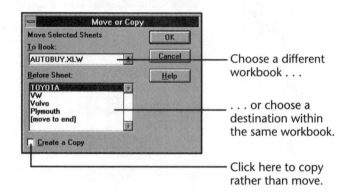

The many moving and copying options available.

Choose a different workbook . . .

. . . or choose a destination within the same workbook.

Click here to copy rather than move.

First, you need to decide whether you want to move or to copy. When Excel moves a worksheet, it copies the worksheet to the new location and then erases the original. When Excel copies, the original is not erased. If you want to copy, make sure you select the Create a Copy check box. Otherwise, Excel assumes you want to move.

Next, you need to specify where the sheet is going. If the destination is another workbook, enter its name in the To Book field. On the other hand, if you're just rearranging things within a single workbook, highlight the appropriate worksheet name in the Before Sheet list. When you're done, click on **OK** to get outta there.

Renaming Worksheets

When you first open Excel, the default work-book includes sixteen worksheets. Each one has its own name; in this case, **Sheet1** through **Sheet16**. You can, of course, change any sheet name to just about anything you'd like it to be. If you need more, you can add another 239.

The only reasonable way to keep track of that many worksheets is to name them. Fortunately, that's simple. Double-click on a worksheet tab to open the Rename Sheet dialog box. Type a name for the worksheet under Name, and press **Enter**. Your worksheet name can be up to 31 characters long, and it can include spaces.

This might seem like cheating, but it's not. You can "move" a worksheet by simply renaming it. Double-click on a tab, and enter a new name in the dialog box. Then drag the newly named tab to a different part of your workbook.

Keeping Out the Snoops

Don't you just hate it when people look over your shoulder at your work? With worksheets, the situation's worse! They don't have to even be in the same room with you to know what you've been doing. All they have to do is to look at cells you'd rather be hidden.

In Excel, you hide an entire row or column at a time. (For now, there's no way to hide an individual cell.) Select the row or column you want hidden by clicking on its number or letter. Then choose **Row** or **Column** from the Format menu, and click on **Hide** from the submenu. You'll find the **Unhide** option on that same submenu.

Hiding columns is useful for making print-outs of sheets without showing all the infor-mation. When you're wary of onscreen snoops, it's not as effective, because the astute snoop will notice that a row or column is

Instead of going through all those menus, try this: With a row or column selected, leave your mouse pointer there, and click the right mouse button. Excel displays a formatting menu from which you can click on Hide or Unhide.

hidden and will be able to unhide it just as easily as you hid it. For security problems such as this, you should investigate the **P**rotection command on the **T**ools menu, as covered in Chapter 7.

While you can't hide a cell in the sense that it "looks" empty (or not there), you can hide any formula associated with it. With the cell highlighted, click your right mouse button. Select Format Cells to call up the dialog box by that name. When it comes up, click on its Protection tab. Finally, click on the Hidden check box. Note that you have to protect the worksheet (the dialog box tells you how) before the cell's formula is hidden.

By the Way...

Although you can't hide a single Excel cell, you can make it so unobtrusive that nobody would notice it. All you have to do is to format its text color to be the same as the background color. Highlight the cell, and click your right mouse button. Select the Format Cells option from the pop-up menu that appears. What you're actually going to do is change the color of the text font, so click on the **Font** tab of the dialog box. You'll find a list of available shades in the Color list box. From it, choose one that is the same as the cell background.

The Least You Should Know

Okay, now you're a worksheet pro—or at least a functional beginner. Don't forget these important points:

- ☞ Use the keyboard shortcuts or the scroll bars to move around in a worksheet. Click on a different tab to change to a different sheet in the workbook.

- ☞ Zooming your view and then working on a portion of the worksheet has no effect when it comes time to print. Excel will make sure it comes out the right size.

- ☞ Large worksheets are less confusing if you keep their column or row titles visible. You do so by splitting the window at the titles.

- ☞ When you move something, you end up with only one of it. When you copy something, you've got two of it.

- ☞ You can hide a column or a row completely. The best you can do with a cell is to hide a formula it might contain.

Chapter 6
Rats! I Need Help, Now!

In This Chapter

- ☛ Getting instant help
- ☛ Help for Lotus 1-2-3 converts
- ☛ On-line demos
- ☛ Excel's Wizards
- ☛ Tips

Don't you hate it when a computer program starts beeping at you because you've done something wrong, but won't tell you what offensive act you've committed? It's like having a fight with a significant other who says, "if you don't know what's wrong, I'm not going to tell you!" You feel kind of helpless. If only there were a quick way to get some guidance. . . .

Well, it may not help you in your other relationships, but this chapter will show you how to get help with Excel quickly and easily. We'll also take a look at Excel's built-in tutorial. No longer should you ever feel helpless—with software, anyway.

A Menu of Help

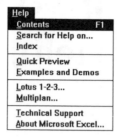

There's all kinds of help for you.

The most straightforward, no-nonsense way to get help in Excel is to open the Help menu. Not very flashy, but it works. The Help menu has quite a range of things to chose from:

Contents   The beginning of Excel's built-in help system. From here, you can get to the first help screen on any of Excel's parts. If you aren't in the middle of any task, pressing **F1** is the same as choosing Contents. (F1 does other wonderful things if you need help in the middle of a task, as you'll learn shortly.)

Search for Help On   For when you have an idea of the information for which you're looking.

Index   Like an index you'd find at the back of a book.

Quick Preview   This should be one of your first stops when you're new to Excel; especially version 5. You'll find four quickie tutorials on getting started, what's new with version 5, getting help, and switching from Lotus 1-2-3.

Examples and Demos   Focused tutorials covering most of the relatively common, but potentially unclear, things you can do while working with Excel.

Lotus 1-2-3   If you're coming to Excel from the world of Lotus, you may not have to learn anything new (for now). For the most part, Excel obeys Lotus 1-2-3 commands, translating them into Excel commands as you watch.

Multiplan   While not very big in North America, Multiplan is almost the cat's pajamas in France (just like Jerry Lewis). Use this option to get information on Excel's equivalent to Multiplan commands.

Technical Support   If nothing else works, here are the numbers to call anywhere in the world.

About Microsoft Excel   Check to see how much memory and hard disk space you still have available.

Many of the options on the Help menu can be accessed through different means. For example, pressing **F1** at a blank worksheet is the same as choosing Help Contents, and clicking on the **Search** button at the top of the Help Contents window is the same as selecting Help Search for Help On. This may seem a bit confusing, but you'll appreciate this flexibility later.

Memory is the part of your computer that stores what you're working on, while you're working on it. Your computer has two kinds of memory: *Read-only memory* (ROM) that holds permanent information, and *random-access memory* (RAM) that holds programs and data.

Contents: Your First Stop

If you have no clue where to begin, select Contents from the Help menu. A list of general topics pop up. When you pick a topic, Excel displays a narrower list. You keep picking from the lists until, at last, you come to the specific steps for the procedure you're interested in. It goes something like this:

1. Open the **Help** menu, and select **Contents**.

2. Select **Using Microsoft Excel** (the first icon on the list). A list of broad topics appears.

3. Choose the topic that the procedure you want falls under. If you are not sure, guess; you can always try a different one if it doesn't work out. The first one, **Essential Skills**, is a good place to start.

4. Keep choosing additional subtopics to narrow down the search until the procedure you want is displayed.

When you're in **Help** and your mouse cursor turns into a pointing finger, that's your clue that there's more help available about that particular topic.

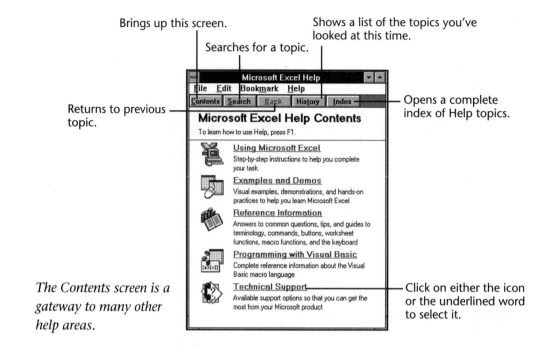

Brings up this screen.

Searches for a topic.

Shows a list of the topics you've looked at this time.

Returns to previous topic.

Opens a complete index of Help topics.

The Contents screen is a gateway to many other help areas.

Click on either the icon or the underlined word to select it.

By the Way . . .

As you saw in this procedure, words underlined with a solid green line take you to other topics or lists when you select them. Words that have a dotted underline pop up definitions when you select them.

You can click on your worksheet to get back to it. The Help window remains open, off to one side, until you close it. There you can refer to it as you perform the procedure. Once you're done, click on the **Close** button and it goes away.

Searching for Help

If you don't know which menu command accomplishes a certain task, how can you know how to get help on it? This is where the Search option comes in handy. To use it, select **S**earch for Help on from the **H**elp menu, or if the Help window is already open, click the **Search** button.

Enter the topic you want to search for, and then click on the Show Topics button.

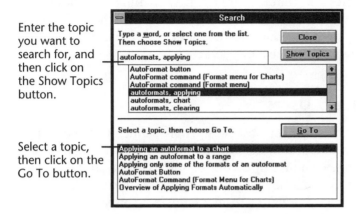

Select a topic, then click on the Go To button.

You can search a large list of keywords to find out if Excel's help system offers anything on a particular subject.

Once you're in the Search dialog box, type the subject you need help on in the text box at the top, or select it from the list. Then select Show Topics. A list of topics that contains the word you typed appears in the bottom part of the dialog box. Select the topic you want from that bottom list, and then click on the **Go** To button.

Using the Help Index

If you're not quite sure what you're looking for, choose **Index** from the Help menu. Excel displays the index screen. Click a letter button to jump from the index directly to the topic of your choice. You can display the same screen from anywhere in Excel's help system by pressing on the **Index** button.

All of the available Help topics are listed alphabetically, from A to Z. You can scroll down the (rather long) list, or a better plan would be to click on the letter button at the top of the Help screen. That will take you directly to that part of the index, narrowing down your search considerably.

Just Follow the Example

Excel examples and demos are mini-tutorials that show you how to do specific tasks. They aren't designed to be comprehensive lessons. They are more like having a friend sitting next to you, showing you how to do something.

Choose **Examples** and **Demos** from the Help menu. Excel shows you a listing of what's available. Each option can have several choices. Click on one option to display it on your screen. From there, you can follow a step-by-step demonstration, or take a little practice.

Help for Lotus 1-2-3 Users

Excel is not everyone's first spreadsheet software—much to Microsoft's dismay, I'm sure. Many people started with Lotus 1-2-3. As a matter of fact, 1-2-3 has made an enormous impact on the software industry. For a long time, 1-2-3 was the standard by which the genre was measured. Realizing that, Excel makes it very easy for a former Lotus 1-2-3 user to make the change.

If you're more familiar with 1-2-3 than you are with Excel, you can use Lotus commands to control Excel. Press the Lotus command key, slash (/), and then type in a Lotus spreadsheet command. Excel displays a series of dialog boxes that demonstrates both softwares' equivalent commands.

By the Way . . .
Use **Ctrl+macro letter** to run Lotus 1-2-3 macros under Excel.

Excel will also perform those commands, translating them into its own "language." You can even adjust the performance speed to make it easier for you to follow along.

Help for Multiplan Users

Multiplan help is a holdover from Excel's very earliest days. It's not help in the sense that it uses the Windows Help engine to call up an information screen. Instead—and I hope this isn't too technical—when you type the first letter of a Multiplan command in the dialog box, Excel looks up a number that corresponds to a Help Topic. It then calls up the help engine and displays the appropriate Multiplan Help topic.

You can get help on Multiplan topics just as you can any other topics. It's just that you call them up a bit differently.

A Technical Question

When you call Microsoft with a question about Excel, you're asking for *Technical Support* (*tech support* for short). Even if your question has to do with how something looks, it's technical (because it has to do with something on a computer).

The problem is, what number do you call to get that kind of personal help? You get that kind of information when you select—what else?—Technical Support from the Help menu.

> Be sure you only type in the one, first letter of a Multiplan command. If you type in an entire Multiplan command word, Excel won't know where in its help system to find an appropriate topic. This is one rare example of brain damage in Excel.

A variety of tech support is available from on-line computer services (such as CompuServe) to speaking on the telephone with a Microsoft employee. Scroll down the tech support list, and click on an option that seems like it will lead you to the help you need.

Read All About It

Under the About Microsoft Excel option, you'll find two useful things. The first is the copyright information screen. It might sound boring at first, but from this screen you can see your serial number and the amount of available memory on your computer. When you call technical support (see above), you'll need that serial number to get your foot in the door.

The second important thing here is the System Info button. Sometimes, enough things go wrong that you don't know if it's the software or your computer. To help you out, Excel has available a diagnostic program that can analyze your hardware, which you can run by clicking on the **System Info** button.

For Instant Help, Press F1 Now

Help in Excel is available any time you press **F1**. Here's how: As you work with Excel, it keeps track of where you are, what button you've just selected, which cell you have highlighted, and what menu option you've chosen. That way, when you call for help, Excel tries to supply you with just the information you need at that point. In computer jargon, we call this capability *context-sensitive* help. (If you aren't doing anything at all that Excel can discern, F1 brings up the same generic help box as when you select Contents from the Help menu.)

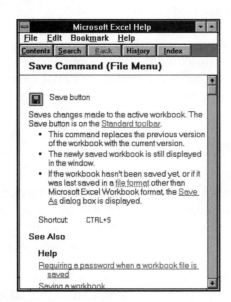

Here's the context-sensitive help screen for Save. There are dozens of them; one for every occasion.

Using the Toolbar's Help Button

Of all the help available to you in Excel, I think the Help button on the Standard toolbar is probably the most useful for beginners. Say you have a question about the button with what looks like a floppy disk on it. Click on the **Help** button. Your mouse cursor turns into an arrow with a question mark next to it, like this:

Putting the finger on just what ails you.

Go ahead and try it. For example, place that cursor on the floppy disk button and click to get a screenful of how to save your Excel workbook.

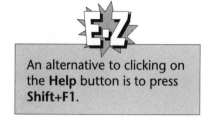

An alternative to clicking on the **Help** button is to press **Shift+F1**.

Have I Got a Tip for You!

In the beginning, when you're just getting familiar with a piece of software, something that "holds your hand" can be useful. Excel has Tip Wizards to do just that.

You toggle Tip Wizards on and off by pressing the **TipWizard** button. It's the one with a light bulb on it, almost all the way to the right on the Standard toolbar (next to the Help button). Excel then displays tips on how to accomplish your current task more efficiently. When they're on, you'll also see a different Tip of the Day each time you start Excel.

Putting It to Bed

Once you've received what help you need, you'll want to "blow away" the Help window.

☛ To close a Help window completely, select Exit from the File menu, or press **Alt+F** and then **X**.

☛ To put the Help window away for a while, but keep it close enough so you can quickly call it up again, click your mouse cursor on your screen someplace outside of the Help window. To return to Help, press Alt + Esc, to view its open window.

The Least You Need to Know

Excel isn't hard to use—even at first. But it can be a bit confusing, so keep the following in mind:

☞ Almost all of Excel's help features can be accessed through the **Help** menu.

☞ Don't be shy about pressing **F1** any time you want context-sensitive help.

☞ If you have a question about a command, click on the **Help** button on the Standard toolbar or press **Shift+F1**, and then click on the command.

☞ Toggle tips on and off using the **TipWizard** button.

☞ Excel's demos and examples make good refreshers when you haven't done a particular task in a while.

☞ If you're more familiar with Lotus 1-2-3 than with Excel, remember that Excel responds to Lotus commands just as easily as it does to its own.

Chapter 7
I'll Be Back!

In This Chapter

- ☞ Saving a workbook
- ☞ Valid file names
- ☞ Automatic saving
- ☞ Adding summary information

There I was, early evening, and I'd been at home working on that analysis since the day before. Now it was about time to get the little darlings off to bed, but I wanted to input the last two formulas before stopping. Number one son, curious as usual, was climbing over everything, asking questions. "What's this, Daddy?" he asked, reaching for the computer's power switch. Then the screen went blank.

Fortunately, I had gotten into the habit of saving early and often just after he started to crawl. All I lost was about ten minutes of work. It could have been *a lot* worse. Time will tell if seeing his daddy bouncing off the walls and screaming did him any permanent psychological harm. Although at the time, he seemed quite unduly amused, "Do it again, Daddy!"

In this chapter, I'm going to show you how to save your workbooks. We'll look at file names, at how Excel can automatically save your work, and how to make it easier to find your files later.

Picking Valid File Names

Before you can save a file, you have to decide what name you're going to assign to it. Excel workbook file names have three parts: eight characters for a name, a period for separation, and three letters for a name extension. When you type a file name, Excel adds the period and the XLS (for Excel spreadsheet—get it?) on its own. You can use something different if you want to, but that wouldn't make much sense. Excel uses this extension for a reason, namely so that when you look at a directory of file names, you'll know that the ones ending in .XLS are probably Excel spreadsheets.

You can use any letters or numbers in the file name, but you can't use any spaces. You can also use these non-alphabetical characters: _, @, #, $, %, –, &, and !—but no others. All in all, your best bet is to name your workbook file something as descriptive as is possible in the eight letters allowed.

Here are some examples:

AUTOBUY.XLS

MY_PLAN.XLS

BUDGET94.XLS

FISCAL.XLS

BOING!.XLS

BANKRUPT.XLS

On second thought, try not to use these last two examples. They could be distressing to a client.

The **file name** is the designation under which a workbook is saved on disk. An Excel file name comprises up to eight letters, a period, and an extension (usually XLS).

What's Wrong with This Picture

Question: Herman Feeblebottom down the hall is saving his first Excel workbook. Being a former Mac user and wanting to make sure he'll be able to find his file again, he gives it the name MYSPECIALANALSYS.XLS. What did he do wrong?

Answer: 'Ol Herm used too many letters; he's only allowed eight (as well as three letters for an extension) here in the DOS world.

Question: Well, so he changes the name to ANALYSISXLS. What's wrong with the picture now?

Answer: Silly him. He forgot to use a period to separate the file name from its extension.

How to Save a Workbook

When you save an Excel workbook, you're saving a computer file. Intuitively, you'd expect to find the **Save** command on the **File** menu, and that's where it is. Excel offers three save choices:

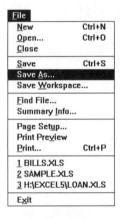

The File menu is where you start your save.

Save is your general, all-purpose, make-sure-I-don't-lose-it command. This is the one you'll use most often. If you haven't already saved this workbook, however, Excel goes through its Save As process. If the document has been saved before, Save resaves it quickly and tidily, with no input required.

Saving stores the contents of your file onto a hard or floppy disk. Excel does this automatically, if you specify for it to do so. Excel also prompts you to save your work when you exit the program.

Save As gives you the opportunity to make some decisions about the way you want the file saved. It comes up automatically the first time you save a file, even if you choose Save instead of Save As. Later, if you want to change any of the file details, such as its name, type, and summary, you can choose Save As to save it differently.

If you look at the **S**ave option on the **F**ile menu, you'll notice that you can use **Ctrl+S** as a shortcut to save your file. There's also another shortcut: **Shift+F12**. They work the same.

Save Workspace comes in handy when you're good with Excel and you find that your projects require more capacity than even a workbook gives you; you'll want to work with several workbooks at one time! A workspace is basically that: a collection of workbooks. When you save your workspace, you save the contents of all its workbooks (which means all their sheets) at one time.

Saving (the First Time)

Each time you start Excel, you are presented with a new workbook full of blank worksheets. Although you can jump right in and start crunching numbers with them, if you want to use the same workbook next time, you have to save it.

Saving a workbook the first time is only a bit more involved than doing it subsequently. Choose **Save** or **Save As** from the File menu to get the process started. (Since you're saving for the first time, these two commands do the same thing.)

Replace this generic file name with a more descriptive one.

Put it away for a rainy day.

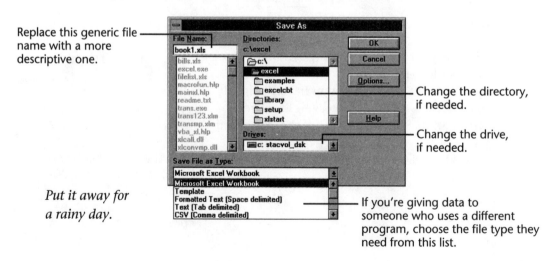

Change the directory, if needed.

Change the drive, if needed.

If you're giving data to someone who uses a different program, choose the file type they need from this list.

First, of course, you'll have to give your workbook a name. By default, the workbook has the name **BOOK1**, and the spreadsheets are called **Sheet1** through **Sheet16**. Not very descriptive. For that reason, they're not very useful, either. Type a better name in the File Name field at the top of the Save As dialog box. If you want to save the workbook on a different drive or in another directory, select those from the drop-down list boxes.

By default, Excel suggests that you save this workbook in its own native workbook format. If you click the **OK** button at this point, that's all there is to it; your file is saved to hard disk.

On the other hand, you may want to share this workbook with a person using other software. Excel automatically translates its workbooks into a number of different formats, everything from simple ASCII text files, through other spreadsheet software brands' formats, to database formats. You indicate your format choice under the Save File as Type drop-down list box. Excel keeps intact as much of your file as it can. This includes any formulas, macros, names, and formats in the workbook.

The easiest way to save a file—first time, and every time—is to click on the **Save** button on the Standard toolbar. Working exactly like the **Save** command on the **File** menu, the Save button takes less effort to get to.

What Are My Options?

Take a moment and click on the Options button in the Save As dialog box to bring up the Save Options dialog box. There is a check box that lets you have Excel create backup files automatically.

It's usually a smart idea to keep this option selected.

More bells and whistles to enhance the saving process.

What happens is this: When you load a workbook, Excel actually copies what is stored on your hard disk into your computer's RAM. When you choose to save the workbook later, Excel doesn't copy it out to the hard disk right away. It first renames the original file, using the file's current name, but with the extension .BAK instead of .XLW or .XLS. Then Excel goes ahead and stores the latest workbook using the name you've given it, including the normal .XLS extension.

If this sounds like a good thing to you, keep Always Create Backup selected. If, on the other hand, you are very short on disk space and can't afford to have those pesky .BAK files taking up space, turn this feature off.

> ## By the Way . . .
> I'd strongly recommend that you click the Always Create Backup check box. It's cheap and easy insurance: one mark of a true professional, as well as the intelligent amateur.

A Bit of Protection

There are two password text boxes in the Save Options dialog box. The first one, **Protection Password**, enables you to assign a password for both reading and changing the file. Without knowing this password, a person will not be able to even open the file.

The other kind of protection is **Write Reservation**. If you choose to use this kind of password, anyone may open the file but only those who know the password can make changes to it.

Summary Information

Before Excel saves your workbook the first time, the Summary Info dialog box is displayed. The information you enter is extremely useful when you later want to find this workbook among many others. You can change this information at any time by selecting Summary Info from the File menu.

Saving Again

After the first time you've saved your workbook, each time you save it again with the Save command, Excel simply stores it out to the hard disk using the same name each time. Thus, the file is effectively updated with the latest information.

Later, if you want to save the file under a different name, change its type, or change any of the other options, use the Save As command. You go through the exact same process that you went through when you saved the file the first time.

When Should I Save?

Most professionals use this rule of thumb when deciding when to save:

Early and Often!

I don't mean to belabor this idea, but you haven't lived until you're on deadline and you ruin the work you've done because something has gone wrong with your computer. Even if the information lost isn't "important," it's still a major and avoidable frustration.

Saving on Time

Excel includes an add-in called Autosave. Add-ins are special mini-programs that add functionality to the basic Excel product. As you might have guessed, Autosave is a kind of clock that automatically saves your workbook at specified time intervals. For example, you can have your work saved every two, five, or ten minutes.

You'll find Autosave by selecting Add-Ins from the Tools menu. Click on the check box next to Autosave to activate it. Excel prompts you to specify how long it should go between saves, just what it should save, and whether you should be reminded about the save each time.

You can tell in two ways if Autosave is on: First, you're being inter-rupted in your work every now and then as the workbook is saved. Second, the Autosave command on the Tools menu has a check mark next to it.

Be careful when you click on a Control-menu box. There are two of them, one on top of the other. The lower one controls the current spreadsheet; the other is for Excel, itself. If you double-click on the one for Excel itself, the whole program will close.

Au Revoir

Excel knows whether you've made changes to a file since you last saved it. When you're done with your work, click on the workbook's **Control-menu** box, and select **Close** (or simply press **Ctrl+F4**, or double-click the Control-menu box). If necessary, Excel will prompt you as to whether you want the now-changed workbook to be saved.

The Least You Need to Know

Saving your workbooks is as basic as typing numbers into them. Here are a few good ideas:

☞ Use as descriptive a name as you can get into eight letters, but don't use spaces.

☞ Save early and often.

☞ The easiest way to save a file is to click on the **Save** button on the Standard toolbar.

☞ It's extra insurance for you to always create a backup file.

☞ Take the time to fill out the Summary Info dialog box. Finding old workbooks will be much easier.

☞ When you want to share your workbook informa-tion with someone who uses a different spreadsheet program, save the file in a different file format.

Part II
Doing Something Useful

Now that you can navigate your way around the workbook, it's time to start the real work—entering your data and making it look right.

In this part, you'll learn about entering formulas and functions, making changes to a workbook, formatting it nicely, and printing out a copy. It may sound like a lot of work, but these are important skills! If you can master the tasks in this part, you'll have conquered almost everything a beginner absolutely needs to know.

Chapter 8
A Range by Any Other Name

In This Chapter

- ☛ Naming a cell
- ☛ What is a range?
- ☛ Selecting and naming ranges

You and I have something in common: we each have a given name. For example, in my lifetime I've been variously called Ric, Daddy, You Creature (by my sister), Adonis, and Stud Muffin—okay, maybe not Adonis. The point is, when someone wants to get my attention, they call my name. Because it's reasonably common, they usually have no problem remembering it. For that matter, if I were the same person, they wouldn't care if my name happened to be Bill or Joe.

Excel cells are something like that. Each cell has a name based on its position in the worksheet, such as A1 or B2. You can also assign more descriptive names to cells, like Price or Total. If you're working with several cells at once (a range), you can name the entire range, too. In this chapter, you'll learn how to assign names to cells, select ranges, and assign names to ranges.

Home on the Range

Before we get started with the names, you need to understand *ranges*. A *range* is a rectangular block of cells, which can be as small as one cell in the same row or column, or as large as an entire worksheet. The range's default name consists of the top left cell's name and the bottom right cell's name, separated by a colon, as in A1:C5. Here are some examples of ranges:

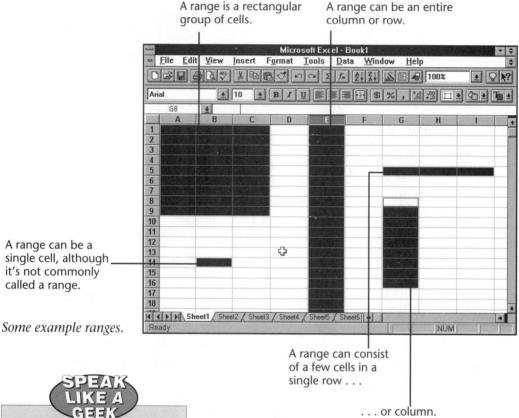

A range is a rectangular group of cells.

A range can be an entire column or row.

A range can be a single cell, although it's not commonly called a range.

Some example ranges.

A range can consist of a few cells in a single row . . .

. . . or column.

It's easiest to select a range with the mouse. Just click and hold the left mouse button on the top right cell of the range you want to select, then drag the mouse pointer to the bottom left cell in the range. When you release the mouse button, the range is highlighted, and you're ready to act upon it. In later chapters, you'll learn many things that you can do to a selected range, such as move it, copy it, sum it, and delete it.

To select a range with the keyboard, move the cell cursor to the top right cell in the range. Hold down the **Shift** key while you press the arrow keys on the keyboard to extend the range. When you release the Shift key, the range is selected.

Naming Cells and Ranges

Now that you know what a range is, you're ready to enter the wonderful world of naming cells and ranges. It may seem like a lot of trouble up front to assign names, but later you'll appreciate how easy these names make your calculations.

Why Should I Name Things?

And now, back to our regularly scheduled lesson. You already know that every cell has its own unique address or *cell reference*, such as A1 or C3. But these names are not always satisfactory. For one thing, while A1 makes perfect sense to a software program like Excel, to a human it doesn't stand out well when combined with all the other cells in a worksheet. For example, what if cell A1 contained a value representing a car payment? Wouldn't it make better sense to us as human beings to call that cell something like Car_Payment instead? Of course it would. That's where assigning a name to the cell can come in handy.

Ranges can also benefit from names. Take a moment to look at our Acme Products inventory worksheet in the following figure. Suppose you wanted to work with all the cells in column B: the ones under the heading **Number on Hand**. Perhaps you want to do something as simple as add them all up. You could deal with each cell individually— B4, B5, B6—of course. But that would be cumbersome. Instead, you can give that range of cells a name: **Number_On_Hand**, perhaps. Then you can simply refer to that name instead of each cell when you want to deal with those cells collectively.

	A	B	C	D	E	F	G	H
1				Acme Products				
2				Inventory				
3	Item	Number on Hand	Cost Each	Cost Total	Price Each	Price Total	Profit Potential	
4	Floppy disk	4060	$0.68	$2,760.80	$0.98	$3,978.80	$1,218.00	
5	Printer paper	500	$11.45	$5,725.00	$21.99	$10,995.00	$5,270.00	
6	Fax modem	43	$89.90	$3,865.70	$179.95	$7,737.85	$3,872.15	
7	Data modem	38	$67.45	$2,563.10	$122.95	$4,672.10	$2,109.00	
8	Printer ribbon	84	$8.60	$722.40	$12.95	$1,087.80	$365.40	
9	Power cable	36	$4.50	$162.00	$7.75	$279.00	$117.00	
10	Serial cable	25	$5.50	$137.50	$8.95	$223.75	$86.25	
11	Parallel cable	24	$5.60	$134.40	$9.25	$222.00	$87.60	
12	Wrist rest	18	$3.25	$58.50	$4.50	$81.00	$22.50	
13	Mouse pad	13	$2.75	$35.75	$4.85	$63.05	$27.30	
14		4841	$199.68	$16,165.15	$374.12	$29,340.35	$13,175.20	

Naming the range of cells in column B would make life simpler.

Deciding on a Name

You can either decide upon a name yourself or have Excel create a name for you, as you'll learn shortly. But before you start making up names, take a moment to learn some basics so you can understand what's going on.

There are two things you need to know to create a named cell or range:

The name you're going to assign. The name must be a single word (no spaces). If you want to trick Excel into accepting a multi-word name, separate the words with the underscore character (_) as in **total_on_hand**. The name must start with either an alphabetical letter (A to Z) or an underscore (_), and can be up to 255 characters long.

The cell(s) to which the name refers. You'll need to know which cell or cells are to be included in the name.

> **By the Way . . .**
>
> No matter what you name a cell (or cells), it always remembers its old name, too (Excel's column letter/row number address).

There are several ways you can tell Excel which cell(s) to assign the name to:

- ☞ If there's only one cell to be named, click on it to highlight it.

- ☞ If you want to include a range of cells, select the range using the technique you learned earlier in the chapter.

Assigning the Name

Defining a name in Excel is the hands-on method. You tell Excel which cells to include and what to call them. Here's how:

1. Highlight a cell or range to be named.

2. Choose **Name** from the Insert menu, and then choose **Define**. Excel displays its Define Name dialog box. As it does so, Excel looks at the cells you've highlighted. It's trying to find something that it might suggest to you for a name. If you've highlighted part of a column, and if that column has a label in it, that's what Excel tries to use. You'll see its suggestion in the Names in Workbook field.

> Here's another way to select a range. First, click a corner cell in the group. then hold down the shift key while you click a cell in the corner diagonally opposite to the first one. Excel highlights the cells, leaving the next step up to you.

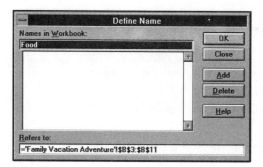

The Define Name dialog box lets you assign names to cells and ranges.

3. To accept Excel's name suggestion, click on **OK**, and off you go. Or if you want to be more original, change the name before clicking **OK**.

By the Way . . .

In the Define Name dialog box, you see the cell(s) you selected in the **R**efers to text box. But what's wrong with them? Why are there dollar signs and other odd punctuation? Let me decipher it for you.

The *worksheet name* appears, in single quotes, to orient you to the correct sheet in which to find the cells being named. Remember, every sheet in a workbook has a cell called A1. If you don't include the worksheet name, how would you or Excel know which cells hold the name?

A *colon* is Excel's way of saying "and all the cells until and including." In the present case, it's like saying, "cell B3 and all the cells until and including B11."

A *dollar sign* is Excel's way of being explicit and *absolute*. Most Excel cell references are merely *relative*. What looks to you like cell B3 may actually mean "two cells over and one cell up." Excel does this because it makes it easier for you to rearrange cells and formulas as your worksheets change. In an Excel cell name, a dollar sign means "this cell absolutely." In other words, a cell reference like B3 means "B3 and only B3."

I'm sure you have questions about relative and absolute cell addressing. It's a bit beyond what I wanted to cover in this chapter, however. We'll get more into the subject in the next chapter, "Calculations for Non-Rocket-Scientist Types."

Making Excel Assign the Names

Having Excel create names for you is a bit more indirect. It's also a very quick and efficient way to generate and assign a bunch of names quickly.

> When the $ (dollar sign) is used with a money amount the cell is automatically formatted as being currency. When used in a cell reference, it denotes an absolute cell reference.

1. Highlight the cell(s) you want to name. You can create several names at a time with this method, so if you want to assign individual names to each of four columns, for instance, you can highlight all four columns at once.

2. Choose **Names** from the Insert menu, and then select Create. Excel looks at the cells you've highlighted, trying to make sense of them. If they're in columns like our illustration, then Excel assumes that you want the cells named by columns.

3. To avoid confusion, Excel displays the Create Names dialog box. Indicate what words you want it to use for the names. For example, if you click on Top Row, as in the illustration, then it takes the text labels and imitates them for the names.

The Create Names dialog box helps Excel name the selection intelligently.

4. Press **OK** to accept Excel's names.

Naming Scattered Cells

You can name a group of cells that aren't in a normal rectangular range if you want. Here's how:

1. Press and hold the **Ctrl** key as you click each cell to be included in the name.

2. Choose **Name** from the Insert menu, and then select **Define**. Excel displays its Define Name dialog box. As it does so, Excel looks at the cells you've highlighted, noting their designations in the **Refers to** field. Type a name for these cells under Names in Workbook.

3. Click on **OK**, and there you are.

You may wonder when this might be helpful. Say you want to bring certain cells to the attention of one client (a doctor) and others to the attention of another client (a lawyer).

Select the cells for the doctor, and give them the name **Doctor**. Do the same thing with the cells for the lawyer. Then before you show the worksheet to the doctor, shade the **Doctor** cells using Excel's formatting capabilities. When the lawyer comes around looking for his information, you can unshade the doctor's cells and shade the lawyer's.

An Expanded Name

Once you've given a bunch of cells a name, you can still manipulate them. For example, say you've named cells B4 though B13 as **Number_on_Hand**. Later, you want to insert a row somewhere between them. When you do, Excel expands its definition of Number_on_Hand by one cell to include B14. You'll learn to insert rows and columns in Chapter 10.

I've Changed My Mind!

Once you've created a name, you can delete it at any time. Choose **Name** from the Insert menu, and then select **Define**. Click on the name you want deleted, then click on **Delete**.

This is something you want to do only judiciously. If you ever delete a name, other names or cells may be affected. If any of them use this name in a formula, for instance, chances are that formula won't continue to work correctly.

What Can I Do with a Name?

I'm glad you asked that question. You've already had one example with the doctor and lawyer above. In reality, just about anything you can do with one cell, you can do with a name.

As well as formatting them, you can perform any arithmetic on names, multiplying Number_On_Hand by Cost_Each to arrive at a Cost_Total, for instance. As a matter of fact, that's exactly what I did in the Inventory worksheet. We get more into that kind of thing in the next chapter, "Calculations for Non-Rocket-Scientist Types."

But there's more!

Okay, Move It, Buster!

Perhaps you want to rearrange your worksheet, moving a bunch of cells from here to there. Press **F5**, and double-click on the name you want to move. With the name highlighted, press **Ctrl+X** to cut the named cells. Move your mouse pointer to highlight the name's destination, and press **Ctrl+V**.

As Excel moves the cells, it keeps track of any other cells they affect, or which are affected by them. No matter what name you've given a cell, Excel knows it internally by its Column letter/Row number designation.

Here's an even easier way to move a name from one place to another. Highlight the name you want to move and click on the **Copy** button on the Standard toolbar. Then move your mouse pointer to the new location for the name, and press the **Paste** button.

Let's Go There

Say you want to move your mouse pointer to the name. Press **F5** (the Goto key). When Excel displays the Go To dialog box, double-click on the name you want to go to. Excel takes you there and highlights all the cells in the name.

The Least You Need to Know

A single Excel cell can be pretty darn useful. And to manipulate it alone is not too confusing even when using its built-in designation. But give the cell a name. Or combine the cell with its cohorts and give the entire range a name, and it becomes very effective. In this chapter, you learned:

☞ To select a range of cells, drag the mouse pointer over them, or hold down the **Shift** key while you press the arrow keys to expand the range.

☞ You can assign any name to a cell or range, up to 255 characters, but do not include any spaces.

☞ Excel can create names for your cells and ranges, using its best guess at the names.

☞ A dollar sign ($) tells you that the cell is placed absolutely, not relatively.

☞ Once a name has been assigned, that name can be used in place of the cell address in formulas and references.

Chapter 9
Calculations for Non-Rocket-Scientist Types

In This Chapter

- ☞ Working with formulas
- ☞ How to use functions
- ☞ Winning arguments
- ☞ Excel's Function Wizard

Number two son was rummaging around in my desk drawer. (I *love* it when they do that.) "Hey Dad, what's this?" he asked, holding an old plastic slide rule. As I looked at it, images from the past danced in my memory.

Me, slide rule strategically placed in my shirt pocket, going to high school. I was trying to appear intelligent to the incomparable Julie, a ninth grade beauty who—rumor had it—was attracted to "brains." Sitting in class one day, I was asked to answer a problem; one that I thought would remotely justify my using this powerful tool.

Brow furrowed and scales sliding, I furiously worked the problem. I was about to speak up when Hubert, the class rich kid who had one of those new-fangled calculators, called out the answer. Julie, who until then hadn't even noticed him, brightened, much to my dismay.

Operator is short for "arithmetic operator" and is the +,–,*, or / placed between numbers and used to manipulate them.

Well, time moved on. Julie's dad was transferred, Hubert got in trouble for something he claimed he didn't do (heh heh), and I saved up for my own new-fangled calculator.

In this chapter, I'm going to show you how Excel can help you get answers to all kinds of mathematical questions, and to do so faster than any Hubert you may know.

The Formula for Success

By now, you know that you can take any Excel cell and type numbers or text into it. There's also something else you can type into an Excel cell, something that will make your life even easier: the formula! Writing an Excel formula is simple:

- ☛ First, move to an empty cell and type an equal sign(=). This tells Excel that what this cell contains is not merely a number (or text, of course), but rather something that will calculate an answer. You move to an empty cell because you don't want to inadvertently overwrite the value in another cell.

- ☛ Next, type the first number in the formula, or a cell reference of a cell that contains the number.

- ☛ Type in an arithmetic operator.

- ☛ Enter another number, or the cell reference containing the second number.

Here's an example of a formula that adds the contents of several cells:

=A1+A2+A3

If you put the formula into an empty cell and press **Enter**, you get the answer immediately. (This assumes, of course, that there are valid numbers in cells A1 through A3.)

> ## By the Way . . .
>
> Do you remember algebraic notation, where you use paren-theses to combine terms to be manipulated? You can do the same thing in Excel:
>
> **=(A1+A2+A3)–A4**
>
> As you can see, this formula sums the contents of the first three cells and then subtracts the contents of the fourth from them.

Here's a real time-saver: you can choose the cells to be included in a formula with your mouse. Just type the equals sign (=) to signify the beginning of a formula, then click on the first cell you want to refer to. Its name appears next to the equals sign. Type in one of the mathematic operators (such as a plus or minus), then click on the next cell to be included. Keep repeating this until your formula is complete.

Easing into Functions

Although this works, there's an easier way—we're working with computers, after all—and that's to use the AutoSum function. Say you've got some numbers in cells A1, A2, and A3. (If you don't, then type some in.) Move to cell A4, and highlight it by clicking there. Then click on the **AutoSum** button on the Standard toolbar.

Notice that Excel automatically enters something that looks like this in cell A4:

=SUM(A1:A3)

When you press **Autosum** once again, that formula-looking thing goes away and is replaced by a number: the sum of the contents of those three cells. What you've done is to use a *function* (the sum function) in a for-mula.

Functions: Excel's Power Tools

Excel functions are like power tools. For example, you might have a hand saw and a power saw. Both cut wood, but one does it "automatically" and much more easily.

In Excel, you have tools like the SUM() function we just used to add a series of numbers, or AVERAGE(), with which you can find the arithmetic mean of some numbers. Although you can accomplish the same tasks "by hand" with regular formulas, the functions work much like a power saw to make doing the same thing easier.

If you click on the **Autosum** button the second time too quickly, all you'll see in the cell is the answer. But never fear! You can see the SUM() function in the formula bar any time that cell is highlighted.

What a Function Looks Like

An Excel function has three parts:

The *function name* that identifies it to you and to Excel. There are a couple of things you'll want to remember about the function name: First, you must make sure that you spell it correctly as you type it in. Second, although you can type in lowercase, when Excel accepts your entry as being correct, it converts the function name to uppercase. Nice little double check, isn't it?

A *pair of parentheses* that immediately follow the name, with no space between them and the name. They are there to enclose the function's arguments.

One or more arguments allow you to give the function the information it needs to do its calculation. Each argument is separated by a comma. Arguments can be numbers, a cell reference, a name, text, or another function. You enclose text arguments in quotation marks. That way, Excel can know that this is text and not the name of a cell (or group of cells) or a cell reference.

As you start working with functions, they may seem complicated. I've found it easiest to scrutinize a function part-by-part to understand how it works. I look at the arguments, noting how many there are, and what data each needs to do its work. Like most of life's little problems, Excel functions aren't too difficult once broken down into their constituent parts.

**=FunctionName(Argument1,
Argument2, ..Argumentn)**

A *function* is a self-contained routine that accomplishes some task. Most Excel functions take information from your worksheet in pieces called arguments, which they use in their work.

A *parameter* is a value (or values) that is passed to a function so that it can accomplish its task. Excel parameters are the words held within function parentheses, and separated by commas.

It Takes All Kinds

Excel contains approximately 320 built-in functions. They're arranged logically in categories:

Arguments are independent data-holding items that are used to pass values into and out of functions. The value of a function depends upon the value of its arguments. Roughly synonymous with parameters.

Financial   Functions that cover most of those kinds of things you might need to do as a financial analyst. Here you'll find the tools to do depreciations, figure the time value of money, and more specialized stuff like determining the Macauley modified duration for a security.

Date & Time   Functions that help you convert numbers in cells to their date and time equivalents and vice versa.

Math & Trig   All those kinds of operations you'd find on a fancy pocket calculator. They run the gamut from taking sines and cosines to converting Arabic numbers to Roman—useful if you're taking your computer with you to Italy.

Statistical   Just the cat's pajamas the next time your boss wants you to take a very close look at those sales figures. Here you'll find everything from AVERAGE to the ever-popular GAMMAINV (which returns the inverse of the gamma cumulative distribution).

Lookup & Reference   More functions you'd use when you're using Excel to do database kinds of tasks. For example, you can choose or look up a value from a list, or find out in which column a cell is located.

Database   Functions you can use to automate database chores. They do things, such as get a record, connect with external data sources, and statistically analyze your data.

Text   Allows you to manipulate the content of cells that contain text rather than numbers (things like converting a number to text, finding parts of words, or removing nonprintable characters).

Logical   Known in the trade as Boolean functions—after George Boole, who invented a kind of algebra. They let you compare numbers or parts of numbers, and make decisions based on the results of those comparisons.

Information   For when you want to check on some characteristic of a cell's contents. This would mean things, such as what is the location or contents of a cell, whether it is blank, or if it contains an odd number. (That's an uneven value, not something that looks peculiar.)

By the Way . . .

You can get a list of all of Excel's functions. From the **Help** menu, choose **Contents** (or press **F1**). Click on **Reference Information**. It has a list of a number of general areas of information, displayed in green text. The one you want is Worksheet Functions. From the Worksheet Functions help topic, you can get an alphabetical or categorized list of all of Excel's functions. Each one is pretty well explained, with examples of how to use it.

Ask for It by Name

In Chapter 8, we talked about cell and range names, and how you can assign them. Now you're about to see the elegance of that, and you'll have a chance to actually do something useful with a formula.

Let's say you want to find the average of a list of numbers.

1. First you need to enter a label and the numbers. Move to A1 and type **My Numbers** and press **Enter**.

2. Enter some numbers to be averaged in the six cells below A1 (in other words, in cells A2 through A7). It doesn't matter to Excel what numbers you use. If you like, you can even enter fractions and decimals.

3. Next, you'll want to name those cells. Highlight all the cells from A1 through the last cell into which you entered a number. Choose **Name** from the **Insert** menu, click on Create, select Top Row and **OK**. Excel automatically names those cells, **My_Numbers**. It takes the name from the label you put in A1. (Didn't I tell you labels would be useful?)

4. Move down two cells to A9 and type **Average:** to use as a label for your answer.

5. Finally, move to the cell just to its right, to B9, and enter the following:

   =AVERAGE(My_Numbers)

   and press **Enter**.

Voilà! Excel figures the average of all those numbers and displays it in the cell before you. If you want to play with it, you can change any of the values in My Numbers and watch as Excel immediately refigures the average.

If you're feeling curious and statistical, you can move to cell A11, say, and type **Std. Dev.:** and then move one cell right, to B11, and enter the formula

   =STDEV(My_Numbers)

Then press **Enter** to see the Standard Deviation of the figures in My Numbers. Pretty cool, isn't it! (I just love doing fancy number calculations without having to work hard.)

What's Wrong with This Picture?

Let's say you want to find the arithmetic mean of My_Numbers. So, you move to an empty cell and you type in the formula **=MEAN(My_Numbers)**. But instead of getting an answer, you see **#NAME?**.

What happened is, you typed in a formula that doesn't exist in Excel. Even though you and I know that an average and a mean are basically the same thing, Excel isn't that smart.

If you see the dreaded **#Name?** when working with a formula that uses a name, then perhaps you have:

- ☞ Misspelled the name or function in the formula.

- ☞ Forgotten to create or define the name.

- ☞ Enclosed the name in quotation marks.

- ☞ Forgotten to include a colon in a cell reference.

When you fix the problem, your formula should work just fine.

I Can Figure It Out by Myself

Now that you've taken an average "by hand," let me show you how to do it automatically using Excel's built-in Function Wizard.

The Function Wizard is an interactive program built into Excel. We've just seen that entering formulas into Excel isn't very hard. The Function Wizard makes it even easier because it guides you step by step through the process. You call it up by pressing the **Function Wizard** button on the Standard toolbar.

Using the Function Wizard is a two step process:

1. Select which function you're going to use.

2. Insert the arguments it needs to do its work.

Giving Function Wizard a Try

Let's re-average the numbers with which we just worked. That way you'll be able to directly compare how it is to do the same kind of thing two ways. First, make sure that you've highlighted the cell where you want the answer to appear.

Get things going by clicking on the **Function Wizard** button on the Standard toolbar. Excel displays a categorized list of its functions for you in the Function Wizard—Step 1 of 2 dialog box.

Along with its built-in categories, Excel keeps track of the last several functions you used under **Most Recently Used**. That way they're handy and ready for reuse. Of course, you can also find those functions under their normal categories as well.

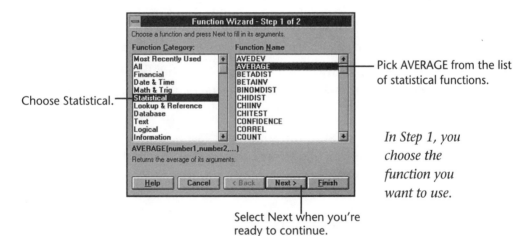

Choose Statistical.

Pick AVERAGE from the list of statistical functions.

In Step 1, you choose the function you want to use.

Select Next when you're ready to continue.

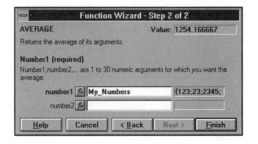

Excel displays the Function Wizard—Step 2 of 2 dialog box. This is where you set up AVERAGE to do its work.

Click on the Function Category with which you want to work. In our case, click on **Statistical** because that's where you'll find AVERAGE. Excel displays all its statistical functions alphabetically in the Function Name list. Click on **AVERAGE** to select it, and press the **Next >** button.

It sounds kind of circular, but before you can average numbers, you must have numbers to average. (Say *that* three times fast!) That's where function arguments come in. You enter arguments in the blank text boxes provided in the dialog box.

The arguments you type there can be:

☛ The numbers themselves.

☛ The cell references of the cells that hold those numbers.

☛ A name of a cell or group of cells.

☛ The result of another function (up to seven levels deep).

Because we've already created the name My_Numbers (to contain the cells holding the numbers we want to average), you can simply type that into the number1 text box.

When you click on the **Finish** button, Excel takes over to do two things: First, it places your function into the current cell. Second, it does the calculation so it can show you the answer in that same cell.

A Function Within a Function

If you need the result of another function to do the calculation in this one, press the **Fx** button next to the argument text box. Excel will step you through the same process to define the other function, and then return you to this point.

The Least You Need to Know

Well, by now, you should be able to understand that it doesn't take the intellect of a rocket scientist to do sophisticated number crunching with Excel. As you get better at it, keep the following in mind:

- ☞ Always start your formulas (formulae?) with an equal sign (=).

- ☞ You can define a formula by typing in numbers or cell references, or by selecting cells with either the mouse or the keyboard.

- ☞ Use names for cells and ranges whenever possible. The extra few moments it takes you to define them pays off big time when you later face figuring out a function's arguments.

- ☞ Functions are built-in "power tool" formulas that enable you to perform complicated calculations without having to enter complex formulas.

- ☞ The Function Wizard button on the Standard toolbar opens the Function Wizard, the easiest way to enter formulas into Excel.

VIRTUAL TEXT PAGE—VIRTUALLY NO TEXT ON IT.

Chapter 10
Tidying Up the Place

In This Chapter

☞ Copying labels and values

☞ Copying formulas

☞ Moving labels, values, and formulas

☞ Erasing cells

The spreadsheet software genre has been around for the better part of two decades now. In that time, software developers have gotten a lot of feedback from users, telling the programmers what most want to be able to do.

While sophisticated, analytical tools are requested every now and then, they are not what people mostly want. Believe it or not, the most often requested "features" are those that simply make it easier for people to use their software.

In this chapter, I'm going to show you some of those handy little things that will make your workbook life more pleasant: things like how to move a cell's contents from here to there, or to copy it. We'll also look at one of my favorites: Excel's Autofill. By the time we're done, you'll have that extra bit of polish on your Excel skills.

Moving (and Copying) Made Easy

Anything you put into one cell, you can also put into another. That sounds obvious, but think about it for a moment. What would it be like, for instance, if you couldn't copy a formula from one cell to another? If you had to type it again into each new cell? I'd go back to pencil, paper, and calculator in a heartbeat.

When we say that we are "moving or copying a cell," it's actually the cell's *contents* that we manipulate; the cell itself never goes anywhere. When you *move* a cell, you're actually taking out the contents of the first cell, and putting it into another. By the same token, when you *copy* a cell, you're actually duplicating the contents of the first cell in the second.

The Easy Way to Move or Copy

If you need to move cells from one place to another on the same worksheet, you're in luck. There's a really easy way to do this. It's called *Drag & Drop*.

First, highlight the cells to be moved or copied. Notice how along with the highlight, Excel puts a thick border around the cells. Put your mouse pointer tip on the border and drag it to the new location. To copy, do the same thing but hold down **Ctrl** while you drag.

As your mouse pointer moves, Excel displays a replica border as a kind of place marker that moves along with it. It helps keep you oriented as you move around on your worksheet. Move the replica border to where you want the cells placed, and release your mouse button.

Multi-Sheet Moves and Copies

What if you want to copy some cells from one worksheet to another? Believe it or not, that's just as easy.

1. Highlight the cells you want to copy.

2. Do one of the following:

   ☞ Click on the **Copy** button (to copy) or on the **Cut** button (to move) on the Standard toolbar.

   ☞ Right-click on the cells to pop up the Quick menu, and then select **Copy** (to copy) or **Cut** (to move).

3. Click the tab of the second worksheet to open it.

4. Click on a cell to highlight a destination for the first worksheet's cells.

5. Do one of the following:

   ☞ Click on the **Paste** button on the Standard toolbar.

   ☞ Right-click on the destination cell to pop up the Quick menu, and then select **Paste**.

Autofill 'Er Up!

Quite often you'll create a worksheet that contains a series of numbers. Rather than fill in the entire series by hand, Excel lets you put in only the first two numbers. It looks at those numbers, figures out what the series interval should be, and then enters the rest of the series into the cells you indicate.

For example, suppose you want to handle your check book using Excel. You'll need columns to hold such data as check number, date, Payee, Amount, and Balance.

Set up a worksheet with column headings, as shown on the following page.

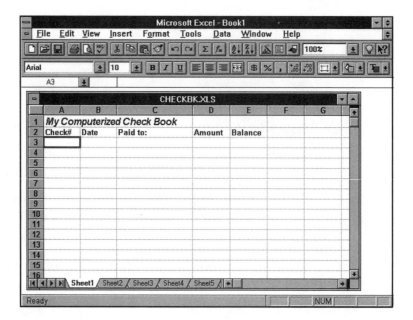

Type in these column headings to get started.

Move to cell A3 and enter a first check number, such as **1001**. Press **Enter** to move down one cell. Into it, enter a second check number, **1002**.

Now, you've got enough of a series that Excel can figure out what you want done from it. Highlight a range of cells, including the first two to A16. With them highlighted, select Fill from the Edit menu. Then select Series from the menu that pops up. Excel displays its Series dialog box. You want Excel to fill in the series numbers automatically, so click on the **AutoFill** radio button under Type, and press **OK**.

Excel automatically figures the series interval.

Excel fills in the check numbers for you into the cells you highlighted. Now all you need to do, is to make sure there's money to cover the checks you're going to keep track of.

> ## By the Way . . .
> You can use Excel's AutoFill feature to enter just about any kind of serial data. For example, if you enter **Jan** and **Feb** into two cells as column headings, Excel will know that you want the rest of the headings to continue **Mar** through **Dec.**

Painting a Format

Every now and then, you will want to copy only a cell's format, not its contents (they're different, remember). Highlight the cell that's formatted the way you want the others to be, and then click on the **Format Painter** button on the Standard toolbar. (It's the one that looks like a paintbrush.) Move your mouse pointer over to the cells you want formatted like the first one, and drag over them to highlight them. Excel copies the format over once you release the mouse button.

Shooting Blanks into a Sheet

Here's a situation: you're setting up a worksheet when you realize you need another row or column right in the middle of it! No need to panic—it's easy to add more.

Inserting rows and columns are so similar that if you know how to do one, you know how to do the other. For now, however, let's say that you want to insert a new row.

First, slide over to the row letters and below click where you'd like one inserted. Notice how Excel highlights the entire row. Next, move up to the menu bar, and choose **Rows** from the Insert menu. Excel inserts a row above the row letter you highlighted. You can insert several rows at the same time, if you like; just highlight more than one row letter.

If you want to insert one or more columns, then do the same thing; only remember to highlight a column and to choose **Column** from the Insert menu. The new column(s) will be inserted to the left of the column(s) you highlighted.

A Squeeze Play

To insert a single cell (or group of cells) is only slightly more involved that doing the same thing with rows and columns. First highlight a cell. Then choose **Cells** from the Insert menu, and Excel displays the Insert dialog box.

The Insert and Delete dialog boxes look much alike. Be sure you're working with the right one!

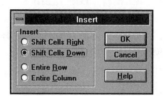

Now you've got a decision to make. Whenever you insert cells, you necessarily have to move others to make room. By default, Excel will shift those cells down in the same column. If you'd rather, however, you can have Excel shift the other cells in that row to the right. In the dialog box, click on the radio button that shifts the cells in the direction you want.

Away with You

To delete cells in Excel, whether individually or by row or column, do the opposite of inserting them. Something you'll need to keep in mind is when you delete cells in Excel, they go away leaving only a memory. Excel, abhorring a vacuum, needs to replace them with cells shifted from some-where nearby.

First highlight a cell (or row or column), and then choose **Delete** from the **Edit** menu. If you did not select an entire row or column, Excel displays the Delete dialog box. You indicate from where Excel should shift cells to replace the deleted ones by clicking on the radio button in the Delete dialog box.

It's unfortunate that Excel's Insert and Delete dialog boxes look the same except for their title. If you do something with one—when you should have used the other—remember that you can cancel your action by using the **U**ndo command on the **E**dit menu.

A Built-In Spelling Bee

As you crunch numbers in Excel, you can be pretty sure that the math will be correct (assuming that you've put in the right figures, of course.) That fact is a real confidence builder for the people who look at your work. Wouldn't it be embarrassing if your spelling was wrong?

To check the spelling of words on your worksheet, choose **S**pelling from the **T**ools menu. Starting from the currently active cell, Excel checks each word it encounters (ignoring all numbers), comparing it with an internal dictionary that holds literally thousands of words.

Excel spell checks all of your worksheet's cells that it can. These include hidden cells or cells in collapsed outlines. Because it has no way of knowing what's a "word" in a formula, it does not check cells that contain them.

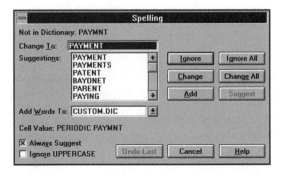

With spell check, your words can be as accurate as your numbers.

When it finds a word that's not in its default dictionary, Excel displays it to you in the Spelling dialog box. It also gives you a list of words it thinks you might have meant, displaying the most likely word in a Change To box, (with the rest in a suggestion list). If the one in the Change To box is correct, then click on Change. Otherwise, you can scroll through the suggested words looking for the right one. When you click on Change, Excel replaces the misspelled word with the one you selected.

Here's a shortcut to get a spell check going: simply press **F7**. To Excel, it's exactly the same thing as going through the menu.

Your Own Little Dictionary

Often you might have a name, or some technical jargon, that appears in your worksheet. When it runs across a word like that, Excel may wrongly decide that it's misspelled. If that's the case, you can tell it to ignore that word for this occurrence or all occurrences.

You can also have Excel add the word to a custom dictionary. This dictionary is called CUSTOM.DIC. It is a list of words that you want Excel to disregard whenever it checks your worksheets.

Excel shares CUSTOM.DIC with other Microsoft products, like its Word for Windows word processor. That way, a word that is correct for one is correct for all.

Find & replace to look for an occurrence of specific characters in a cell, and to exchange them for other characters. In Excel, you can **Find** (without replace), in which case you simply look for a cell containing the characters you specify.

Find It! Fix It!

Excel offers you two ways to search your worksheet when you need to find specific formulas or text: Find simply looks for the text or formula you indicate. Replace, on the other hand, lets you change what you've found to something else.

Choose Find from the Edit menu to start your search. Enter the specific characters in the Find What text box for which you want Excel to look. By default, Excel checks your worksheet row by row. If that's okay, click on Find Next, and Excel commences its search. If not, select **By Columns**, and click on Find Next for Excel to perform the search.

Excel wends its way though your worksheet, comparing each cell's contents with the characters you've specified. When it finds a match, Excel displays it for you. At that point, you can press **Esc** to close the dialog box, or click on Find Next to continue your search.

If you decide to replace those characters in that cell, press **Replace**. Excel changes the Find dialog box into its Replace counterpart—the same dialog box that Excel displays when you choose Replace from the Edit menu.

Type the new characters into the Replace with text box. To actually perform the replacement, either click on **Replace** to change that one occurrence, or click on Replace All to change all such occurrences in your worksheet.

I Hate it When a Dentist Says "Oops!"

Unlike yourself, Every now and then, I make a mistake. Not often, you understand—just when it's most inconvenient. For people like me, Excel includes an Undo command on the Edit menu.

As you work with it, Excel notes and re-members each action you take to see if it's something that can be undone. If so, you select Undo from the Edit menu, and Excel cancels what you've just done. At the same time, Excel changes the Undo command to Redo—just in case you become wishy-washy. (If you're starved for entertainment and want to look like you're working until your coffee break, you may try doing, undoing, and redoing stuff in Excel. It's not very aerobic, but then it's not fattening, either.)

TECHNO NERD TEACHES

As you're doing your search, you might want Excel to look for patterns of text rather than for specific characters. For example, you may be looking for Smith and Smyth. Not a problem.

Use a question mark (**?**) to replace the variable letter. In this case, search for **sm?th** to find either name. Use an asterisk (*****) replace multiple variable letters, starting at that position.

I know this probably should be in an E-Z box, but if you like, you can press **Ctrl+Z** to undo mistakes. Oh yes: it also works to redo what you did in the first place.

A Matter of Style

A style is a typographical definition for a cell; a way of grouping types of cell by "look." It encompasses such things as the name of the cell's text font, how big it is, whether it is bold or italicized, and how the text is aligned in the cell. If the cell contains a value, the style defines its number format. Finally, the style incorporates cell border, shading, and protection information.

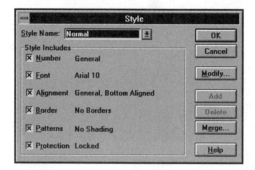

Styles are Excel's way of giving certain cells their own look.

Every cell automatically has the style called Normal applied to it. To apply a different style, choose **Style** from the **Format** menu. Select the name of the style you want from the **Style Name** list box.

It's One of Your Own

If you want, you can also create your own styles. With the Style dialog box open, type a name for your new style in the **Style Name** list box. Check the boxes denoting the parts of the style (font, alignment, and so on) that you want it to include. You change any of those items by clicking on the **Modify** button. Excel displays its Format Cells dialog box, with which you can make any adjustments you'd like. When you press **OK**, Excel incorporates your style into the workbook.

Deleting Styles

You can get rid of a style by deleting it. With the Style dialog box open, choose the name of the style you want to delete, and press the **Delete** button. Excel removes the style's name from the list, and changes any cells of that style to Normal.

One thing you need to be aware of here: if you had reformatted a cell after applying the style to it, the cell will retain that reformatting information.

If you try to delete the Normal style, you're in for a disappointment. Excel needs it as a default, and so will not allow you to get rid of Normal.

Copying Styles Between Workbooks

You can copy styles from one workbook to another. You'll have to move all the styles at once, however; Excel doesn't allow you to copy them piecemeal. Copying the styles is a process called *merging*.

Make sure both workbooks are open. If not, click on the **Open** button on the Standard toolbar, choose the name of a workbook from within the Open dialog box, and press **OK**. This process is easier if you can see them both at the same time. Unfortunately, Excel opens the second workbook on top of the first one. Select **Arrange** from the **Window** menu, and then choose Tiled. Excel displays the two workbooks next to each other.

Click on the window into which you will be copying the styles. You're moving styles, so select **Style** from the Format menu. Click on the Merge button in the Style dialog box. Excel displays the Merge Styles dialog box.

Double-click on the name of the workbook from which you want the styles copied. If you have styles on both workbooks that have the same names, you'll be prompted with a warning dialog box. Your choices are whether or not to overwrite the like-named styles, or to cancel.

The Least You Need to Know

As you can see, the essence of Excel's sophistication is the fact that it's actually very easy to use. Especially, if you remember the following:

☞ When you move or copy cells, you're actually moving and copying their *contents*.

☞ The easiest way to move cells from one place to another on the same worksheet is to slide them around. Highlight the cells you want moved, grab their collective border, and move it to its destination.

☞ Use Excel's AutoFill feature whenever you need to enter a series of numbers into a worksheet.

☞ Copy only a cell's format by using Excel's Format Painter button on the Standard toolbar. Highlight the pattern cell, press the **Format Painter** button, and then click on the cells you want to have the same format.

☞ When you need to find patterns of characters instead of literal ones, use a question mark (**?**) as a place holder for single characters, and an asterisk (*) to stand for any number of characters.

☞ Use styles to quickly format a group of cells with their own "look."

Chapter 11

A Thing of Beauty

In This Chapter

- ☞ Changing number formats
- ☞ Using different fonts for a new look
- ☞ Shading and coloring parts of your worksheet
- ☞ Using the Format Cells dialog box
- ☞ Operating the Format toolbar

By this time, you know how to type a number or some text into Excel. You also know that the numbers and text go together to make up a worksheet. You even know how to fix your occasional mistake.

In this chapter, we're going to work more closely with a worksheet. We'll start by looking at different kinds of numbers and how Excel handles them. Then, we're going to format the worksheet containing those numbers and their associated text labels. We'll also play with toolbar buttons that make the whole process even easier (if that's possible).

The Wonders of Number AutoFormatting

TECHNO NERD TEACHES

When you have a cell that appears to contain nothing but pound signs (######), don't lose heart. It's just Excel's way of telling you that it doesn't have enough room to format the contents of that cell properly. Increase the cell's column width and everything should look fine. Highlight the column in which the cell sits and choose **C**olumn from the **F**ormat menu, and then select **A**utoFit Selection. Presto, chango! Excel does its stuff and off you go.

Most Excel worksheets are mostly made up of numbers. Some cells might contain dates. Others may show how much money you have to send in from each paycheck to retire a loan. Each number in every column can be important in its own way.

When we view those columns of numbers, the format makes a tremendous difference in the way we perceive them. For instance, to an American, 12, 25, and 93 separated by slashes (/), means a date that is also a Christian holiday. A number like 123.45 by itself can be most anything. But put a dollar sign ahead of it, and you have $123.45—the price of a trendy pair of tennis shoes.

Excel tries its best to interpret numbers as a human might. As it reads your input, Excel assumes that if you enter numbers in date format, it must be a date you're entering. If it ends with a percent sign, it must be a percentage value.

The way it works is kind of neat: Excel examines what you've just typed in. If the first character is an equal sign, Excel knows that the cell contains a formula, and so behaves appropriately. On the other hand, if the cell contains only letters, Excel assumes that it is a label to be associated with a number-containing cell adjacent to it. And if the cell contains digits and certain punctuation marks (and perhaps a space), Excel manipulates the cell based on its built-in rules of how numbers near those kind of punctuation marks should be handled.

Here are some things you can try to get a better grip on the concept:

To enter a "plain" number, move your cursor to any cell and type in a number, say **123.45678**, and then press **Enter.** Notice that Excel aligns the entire number to the right side of the cell and leaves it as is. Excel will try to fit in as many decimal numbers as it can; usually enough so that 10 digits are displayed.

To enter a currency amount, move your cursor to any cell and type in a dollar sign (**$**) and then the amount. If you type in more than two decimal places, Excel will round off the value of what you've typed. But never fear! Excel keeps track of the entire amount internally, and uses that number in its number crunching.

To enter a percentage, move your cursor to any cell and type in a number immediately followed by a percent sign (**%**). Just like it does with money, Excel rounds off your number to two decimal places, keeping track all the while of its "real" value.

To enter a fraction, move your cursor to any cell and type in a number, followed by a space, and then type the numerator, a slash, and finally the denominator. Whew! This reads kind of complicated, but it's actually the very same way we write fractions by hand, isn't it? Notice up in the formula line (just above your worksheet) how Excel translates the fraction into an equivalent decimal that it can use in calculations.

To enter a date, move your cursor to any cell and type in a two digit number, a hyphen (-), another two digits, another hyphen, and a final two digits. Notice that Excel indicates its acceptance of your date by changing the hyphens to slashes (/). Of course, you could have entered slashes in the first place, and Excel wouldn't have minded it a bit.

By the Way . . .

Excel keeps track of dates (and times) by serially counting the days from January 1, 1900. It continues this for 65,380 days to December 31, 2078. That means two things: First, you can easily add and subtract dates by simply adding and subtracting their serial numbers. Secondly, the only difference to Excel between something that looks like a date and something that looks like a serial number is in its format.

For example, type **19313** in any cell. With that cell highlighted, click your right mouse button. Choose **Format Cells** from the pop-up menu, and click on the **Number** tab to bring it to the front. Then select **Date** from the Format Cells dialog box. Voilà! It's a normal-looking date!

Although you could go through the menu rigmarole to call up the Format Cells dialog box, it's easier for you to use Excel's built-in short cut: **Ctrl+1**. Works just as well, and even a bit faster!

A Cellular Format

Let's say you don't feel like formatting a cell as you input numbers. You're feeling peckish, and would rather format a bunch of cells all at once (although this method works just as well with one cell).

Highlight the cells you're interested in, and then choose Cells from the Format menu. What appears on your screen is the Format Cells dialog box. This is an all-purpose container for all the kinds of formatting you might want to do on the contents of cells in your worksheet.

The Format Cells dialog box is like the Grand Central Station of cell formatting.

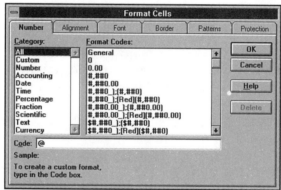

It contains six tabs, each of which is a kind of mini-dialog box within a dialog box.

Number   Contains all the formatting possibilities for numbers broken down into logical number type categories.

By the Way . . .

Notice that there's a Text format for numbers. Text is for those occasions when you want to treat numbers as though they were words rather than as numerical values (ZIP codes, for instance).

Alignment   Places the cells' contents in a certain position within the cell.

Font   Specifies the type of lettering in which your text appears. You can choose a typeface and size, and make it bold, italic, underlined, colored, superscripted, subscripted, or struck through. Whew. To make it easier for you to select just that right font, Excel displays a sample of your current choice in a little preview box.

Border   Helps lay out lines around your cells. You have your choice from among eight built-in styles. Your border can even be colored.

If you'd rather, you can type a bunch of numbers into a group of cells straight—without formatting them. Then, later, you can highlight the group of cells, click on a formatting button on the toolbar, and so apply the format to all the cells at once. We'll cover the formatting buttons later in this chapter.

Patterns   Lets you add color and texture to the cells. Excel displays an array of colors from which you can make your selection. You can also specify a pattern for the color. You can have a bit of fun with it, as you see your current selection displayed in a sample window.

Protection   Gives you two options: to lock a cell, and to hide its formula. In the first case, when a cell is locked, you can't type in it. The second case has to do with formulas. While any cell can display a number, that number may be the result of a formula—one you'd rather keep from prying eyes. When a formula is hidden, while its resulting value appears in it, its underlying formula is not displayed in Excel's formula bar.

I'm sure you still have a question or two about the tabs in the Format Cells dialog box. But not to worry: we'll be looking at them in more detail as the chapter moves along.

Put It to Work

Let me share with you a real-life use for Excel that I found recently. Number one son looked up at me with his big brown eyes and a grin. "Could you help me with my homework, Daddy?" quoth he, "We're multiplying fractions."

continues

Now this kid is an honor student, who rarely needs help with *anything*, let alone homework, and who delights in finding gaps in the old man's knowledge. It was the grin that tipped me off.

"Sure, son," sez I, while quickly looking over his shoulder at the math book problem. "Give me a moment to finish what I'm doing and I'll be right back."

Surreptitiously dashing to my computer, I typed in the problem: 2 15/38 times 1 19/24. In a trice, I was sauntering nonchalantly back to my son, where I told him, "That looks like, um, 4 2/7."

If you'll swear yourself to secrecy, here's how I did it. I put my cursor in any cell and typed:

=(2 15/38) * (1 19/24)

As soon as I pressed **Enter**, Excel was back with the answer.

The equal sign tells Excel that this cell contains a formula (see Chapter 9) rather than simply numbers comprising text. The two parentheses pairs are there to group the two numbers algebraically, thus helping to keep Excel from being "confused."

I knew that Excel changes fractions into decimals to keep track of them internally, rounding them as necessary. So I simply formatted the cell to "Fraction" using the **Number** tab of the Format Cells dialog box I called up from the Format menu. Shazam!

Pretty clever, huh? In any case, Daddy got to show his stuff, and number one son was suitably impressed. Seems to me like a win-win situation in the "Great Saga of Family Life."

AutoFormatting a Whole Sheet

Now that we've worked with individual numbers, let's take a look at formatting a worksheet as a whole. Here's a plain one that tracks some family trip expenses. It's functional, but pretty uninteresting.

Our Worksheet
before.

Clearly the worksheet needs to be spruced up a bit. And rather than doing it all by myself, I'll let Excel format most of it for me. Watch, because what comes next is nothing short of magical!

Our Worksheet
after.

Boy, this was simple. Excel includes a bunch of built-in formats. All I had to do was to highlight the cells I had typed in, select AutoFormat from the Format menu, and then click on **Simple.** (I could have clicked on any of the formats there.) Excel did the rest!

Put It to Work

Here's a handy way of centering your worksheet titles across several columns:

1. Highlight across the columns over which you want to center the titles. (Make sure you've included the cells that actually contain the text.)

2. Choose Cells from the Format menu.

3. Click on the **Alignment** tab.

4. Click on the **Center across** selection button.

Excel, in its clever little way, will maintain the title's centering even if you change the width(s) of the columns under it.

One constant thing to keep in mind about how to get Excel to do what you want it to, is that you almost always "first highlight and then do." If you want to type numbers into a cell, you highlight that cell first. If you want to change the format of a cell, or group of cells, you highlight them before making the modification. And so it goes. . . .

I Want to Do It Myself!

Autoformatting is cool, but you want to know enough about it so you can change things around to suit yourself precisely. Not a problem.

Let's think for a moment about some of the elements of formatting: lines (also known as borders), colors and shading, and different looks for text.

On the Border

In Excel, borders and lines are basically the same thing. In fact, a border is nothing more than four lines that surround a cell or group of cells. Both are great for separating or emphasizing certain areas of your worksheet. And if the columns are really long—more than six or eight rows—thin lines across them are the most efficient way you have of keeping your reader's eyes from losing her place.

Excel treats every cell as a whole. So when you modify the appearance of text in a cell, *all* the text in that cell is changed at the same time, and to the same thing.

Here's how to put in a border: Highlight the area in your worksheet that you want to emphasize, and then open the Format menu and select Cells. Click on the **Border** tab in the Format Cells dialog box.

If you click on **Outline** in the dialog box, Excel will draw lines around the entire outside of the highlighted area. Clicking on **Left**, **Right**, **Top**, or **Bottom** causes Excel to put a line only on that side of *each* cell you've got highlighted. With the Border tab active, you can select the line style and color by clicking on one of the sample Styles there.

A Bit of Shade

Another way of emphasizing a part of your worksheet is to shade some cells. You'll have to watch this, though. It's easily overdone to the point where your worksheet starts to look messy. More embarrassingly, shaded text often doesn't print very effectively because numbers and text in shaded cells seem smudged.

Dither is a process where colors or shades are approximated by varying the intensity and spacing of individual dots.

You shade a cell (or area) in the same way as you put a border around it. When you have the Format Cells dialog box displayed, click on the **Patterns** tab. Click on the pattern of shade Excel should use, as well as the color in which the shade should appear. Excel adds the shade to whichever to-be-bordered cells you have selected. You can keep track of your choice by looking at the sample Excel provides next to the selection pick list.

SPEAK LIKE A GEEK

A **font** is a collection of letters in a single typeface and that is given a name like Century Gothic or Engravers Bold or Felix Titling. (Sounds a lot like a posh horse race, doesn't it?)

TECHNO NERD TEACHES

The typefaces available depend on your currently installed printer. There are two ways for you to change the current printer. First, you can do it from the Windows Control Panel by selecting **Printers**. In Excel, you can open the File menu, click on Print, and then select Printer (from the lower right corner of the dialog box). For more information about this stuff, see Chapter 12.

Trying on a New Font

Almost more than anything else, the fonts you choose for your worksheet have the greatest impact on how your information comes across to your audience. There are two aspects to fonts: the typeface (like Helvetica, or Times New Roman, or whatever) and the attributes (bold, roman, or italic). Well, actually there are three aspects; there's also the size of the type.

To select a new font, just highlight the cells you want the change to affect, then drop down the list of fonts from the Formatting toolbar, and choose a new one. To bold or italicize the text, click on the bold or italic button on that same toolbar.

For less common text formatting, you'll need to select cells from the Format menu, or press **Ctrl+1**, and then click on the **Font** tab for the full range of options.

Color Me Dotted

Colors are also good for emphasis, especially if you have a color monitor and printer. If you're working with a black-and-white display (like on a laptop), however, they're something less than impressive. The same goes for printing colors on a black-and-white dot-matrix or laser printer. The best those printers can do is to print a dot pattern that simulates various degrees of shading. A cyan border comes out as a light, dotted line when printed with a laser printer. Cyan text is almost unreadable. Red, on the other hand, becomes a more dense dotted line, while green is darker still, and blue prints almost solid.

One of the most effective uses of text color in Excel is to highlight negative currency values in red. You can do this semi-automatically by selecting either the **$#,##0_);[Red]($#,##0_)** or **$#,##0.00_);[Red]($#,##0.00)** format code under **Currency** in the **Number** tab of the Format Cells dialog box.

Using the Formatting Toolbar

The simplest way to change the appearance of your text is to click on buttons on the Standard toolbar. In Chapter 4, you saw a complete list of the buttons and their functions; turn back there now if you need a quick refresher.

When you click a button, Excel immediately changes the appearance of the text in the highlighted cell, or group of cells. As for "oops protection," some of the buttons (bold and italics, for instance) are toggles that turn a feature on or off; just click on the same button again to undo. Other buttons are paired sets, for example, to reverse the effects of the Enlarge Text button, click on the **Reduce Text** button. (And don't forget the regular Undo button on the Standard toolbar, too!)

You can change the text color using the **Text Color** tool on the Formatting toolbar. (It's the last button on the right.) Click the arrow to see an array of colors from which to choose. Click on the color, and that's what the text in the highlighted cell will be.

If you forget what a tool does, click and hold the mouse button on it, and a description appears in the status bar. Move the mouse pointer away from the tool before releasing the mouse button if you don't want to use the tool at the moment.

Put It to Work

This is one thing you've gotta try. Type in some numbers into a group of cells in a new worksheet. Highlight that group of cells, and then click on several of the Format Toolbar tools. You won't find a faster way to understand exactly what these tools do. And more importantly: it's fun!

A **serif font** is a font whose letters have a line or curve projecting from the ends of their ascenders and descenders (the vertical strokes).

A **sans serif font** is a font whose letters don't have a line or curve projecting from the ends of their ascenders and descenders. Uses the French word "sans" which means "without." Want an example? The headings in this book are sans serif, as is the type in this box. The regular text is serif.

Some Basic Design Rules

Although the formatting you end up using is largely a matter of taste, most designers agree on a couple of loose rules:

- ☞ Use no more than two faces, one *serif* and the other *sans serif*.

- ☞ Use no more than two or three sizes of each; the fewer usually the better. For example: a large serif for the worksheet heading, a matching serif for column or row labels, and then a same-sized sans serif for the numbers themselves.

The Least You Need to Know

It's been a hoot, but now you're ready to step out on your own formatting gangplank. Before you hit the water, try to keep the following in mind:

- ☞ When you enter numbers into a cell, you can format them "automatically" by using punctuation: slashes or hyphens for dates, % for percentages, or $ for money amounts.

- ☞ To format a cell or group of cells using a menu option: "first highlight, then do."

- ☞ Formatting a worksheet is largely a matter of taste coupled with common sense. As with most of the elegant things in life: "less is often more."

☛ Keep the same kind of things the same. For example, the text in cells that label columns should all be the same font. The text in the columns should also be alike in a different font.

☛ One of your very best formatting friends is the Formatting toolbar. It has the buttons to take care of most of your everyday formatting tasks.

☛ If you can't find it in one of the tabs on the Format Cells dialog box, you don't need to do it—well, as far as formatting goes, anyway.

NO, IT'S NOT A PRINTING ERROR.

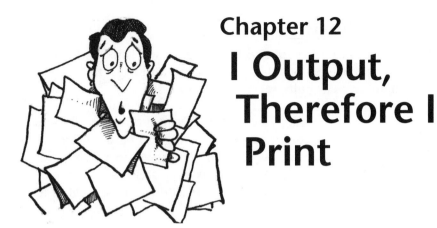

Chapter 12
I Output, Therefore I Print

In This Chapter

- ☞ Instant printing using Excel's defaults
- ☞ Printing your worksheet with more control
- ☞ Printing only parts of your worksheet
- ☞ Making sure your printer is ready
- ☞ Avoiding common problems

There is some satisfaction to be taken in simply crunching numbers, I suppose. But the whole idea behind working with Excel is to turn numbers into meaningful information. Unfortunately, without putting your worksheets on paper, the only people who'd ever gain anything from them would be those who could peer over your shoulder.

In this chapter, I'm going to show you how to print your worksheets and charts. We'll look at some of the subtleties involved, and at how to avoid some of the more common problems.

Pushbutton Printing

Of all the things you can do with Excel, the very easiest is to print out a worksheet. All you have to do is click on the **Print** button on the Standard toolbar. Excel, using its defaults, takes care of the rest.

If you've got a worksheet up, go ahead and click on that **Print** button. You won't break anything, and it's fun to see what you've got.

When you select the **Print** button, Excel prints the current worksheet using its built-in defaults. That means, depending on the fonts you're using or to what dimensions the margins are set, the whole thing may not print on a single sheet. If it doesn't, Excel prints any "extras" on subsequent printer pages.

Talk About Printing!

While simply pressing the Print button can get the job done, more often you'll want to have greater control over the operation. That comes when you select Print from the File menu. Excel pops up the Print dialog box, as you see here.

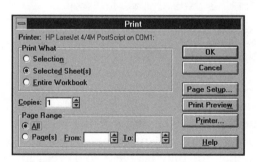

The Print command lets you print all or part of your workbook.

The Print dialog box is the nerve center of Excel's printing capabilities. You have a choice of what and how much of your workbook you want Excel to print. From this point, you can branch out to control how your printed page should look, to take a sneaky peek at what's likely to print (given Excel's current settings), and to configure your printer.

We'll get into each of those branches shortly. For now, let's take a closer look at the Print dialog box.

Print What contains options that enable you to specify which particular part of your workbook Excel should print. You click on an option to activate it.

Selection is for printing only a selected area. This could be a name, for instance, or only certain cells. If you tell Excel to print nonadjacent areas or cells, each one is placed on a different sheet.

Selected Sheets causes the print areas of the current worksheet to be printed. If you haven't specified a print area, then Excel prints the entire worksheet.

Entire Workbook lets you print the whole tomato—everything on every page—unless you've defined print areas on each worksheet. In that case, only they will be printed.

Copies is the number of duplicate pages you want to print. You can type a number in the text box, or you can press the spinner arrows to have Excel increment or decrement the number for you.

Page Range lets you specify which of the sheets you want Excel to print.

All causes Excel to print every one of the sheets you've selected.

Page(s) prints all the pages that you've specified in the From and To text boxes, starting with the From page number and including the To page number. You can specify up to 254 pages to print.

There's one Excel printing caveat you'll need to keep in mind: Make sure you've got something in your worksheet to print (sorry if that seems obvious). If you click on the **Print** button without anything on your worksheet, however, never fear. Excel knows the difference between something and nothing—which is comforting in software that crunches numbers. All you get is a warning dialog box and a chance to cancel.

The *print area* is a defined group of cells that you want printed. You define the print area using the **Sheet** tab of the Page Setup dialog box. If you don't define a specific print area, then Excel prints your entire worksheet.

Put It to Work

Here's how to quickly print a part of your worksheet. Highlight what cells you want printed. Then choose **P**rint from the **F**ile menu. When the Print dialog box comes up, click on Selection and then on **OK**. Finally, sit back for two minutes and watch as Excel prints only those cells. *Très util*, as my wife would say.

How the Page Should Look

Excel makes it very easy for you to get your printed page to look exactly the way you want it to. Once they're arranged, Excel uses the same settings each time you print a worksheet.

To configure your printed page, click on File and then Page Setup. Excel displays the Page Setup dialog box, with its four tabs: Page, Margins, Header/Footer, and Sheet.

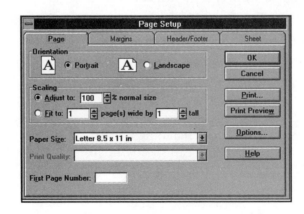

You can set up just about anything having to do with a printed Excel page.

Page Contains those pesky mechanical options you often need to set, such as page orientation and size. You can also adjust the scale at which the worksheet prints (the printing equivalent of choosing Zoom from the View menu).

Page orientation refers to the direction the letters run on the page. *Portrait* orientation means the letters run parallel to the narrow edge of the paper, and *Landscape* orientation means the letters run parallel to the wide edge.

Margins Where you specify how closely to the paper's edge your worksheet should be printed. By default, Excel sets margins to 1" top and bottom, and .75" right and left. This works out just fine for most printers. Here's a hint: If you have a large worksheet to print on a laser printer, usually you can go to within .3" of each edge.

Header/Footer Where you can get creative with what (if anything) is printed at the top and bottom of each page. Excel includes a number of "canned" headers and footers; usually with your name, the date, and page number included.

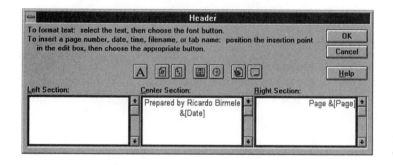

Headers and footers are formatted in the same way.

The Lowdown on Headers and Footers

Headers and footers are laid out the same, with three sections: Left, Center, and Right. If you're familiar with the old typewriter way of doing things, you can think of them as being similar to left, center, and right tabs, but with much greater capabilities.

Type the text you want to appear in any of the three sections, and Excel will print it there on every page. Also, you can include more specialized information when you place your cursor in a section and then press one or more of these buttons to put a place holder in the section:

Lets you use any font that's installed under Windows. If you want to change fonts, highlight the text involved, press this button, and select the new font.

 Puts the current page number on each page.

 Enters the total number of pages to be printed. You can use this effectively with the page number button, above, in a kind of "Page number of total pages" phrase.

 Looks at your system's calendar each time you print, and prints the date that it finds.

 Looks at your system's clock each time you print, and prints the time that it finds. This is handy for keeping track of copies when you print a worksheet now, and an updated one later.

 Takes the name of the current workbook and prints it.

 Takes the text of the worksheet tab and prints it.

Taking a Peek

I'm a visual kind of guy. I learn best visually, and to understand something, I have to see it (in my mind's eye, at least). I've found that it's a good idea, before you actually print your worksheet, to take a quick peek at what's likely to come out of your printer. To do that, select Print Preview from the File menu.

Just thought you'd like to know, there are three ways for you to get to Print Preview:

☛ Select Print Preview from the **File** menu.

☛ Press the **Print Preview** button on the **Page** tab of the Page Setup dialog box.

☛ Press the **Print Preview** button on the Print dialog box (the one you get when you choose **P**rint from the **F**ile menu.

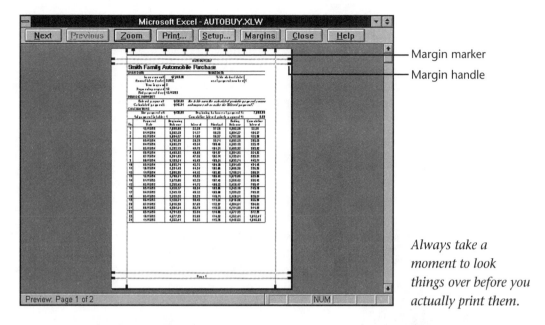

— Margin marker

— Margin handle

Always take a moment to look things over before you actually print them.

A Marginal Experience

One of the big bugaboos of worksheet printing is when the margins aren't placed where you want them, even if that's where you told the software to put them! Excel cures that problem with margin handles in print preview. You can turn them on and off by pressing the **Margin** button.

If your worksheet isn't set where you want it on the page, grab a margin handle and slide it around until the worksheet fits.

Margin handles work only up to a point. If your worksheet it simply too big to fit on a single piece of paper (assuming you've adjusted its zoom), then adjusting the margins will not save you. If the worksheet is too wide, you might try changing the page orientation to landscape, and see if that helps.

A Zoomin' View

As you can see from the illustration (or from looking at your screen for that matter), Excel does its best to show you what and how your worksheet will print. Due to the physical limitations of your screen, however, Excel has to approximate its text; a process called *greeking*.

You can get a closer look at your on-screen worksheet by clicking on the **Zoom** button. Excel enlarges the screen image. As it does so, Excel puts scroll bars at the bottom and at the right edge of your screen.

Unlike the worksheet zoom view, this zoom is an on/off affair. Your screen is either zoomed or it isn't, with no in-between.

TECHNO NERD TEACHES

When you put in your own manual page breaks, what happens to the automatic ones Excel normally inserts? If you've put in enough manual page breaks so that no automatic ones are needed, Excel removes all its automatic ones. If an automatic break or two are still needed, Excel notices and inserts them.

Breakin' Pages

If your worksheet is too large to fit on one page, Excel divides it up according to its own internal rules. Often, where Excel wants to break up your worksheet and where you would are two very different places. Fortunately, there is one sure-fire way to divide the worksheet where you want: inserting your own page breaks.

Here's a quickie lesson on inserting a page break.

1. Highlight the cell that should be at the top right corner of the new page (the page *after* the break).

2. Choose **Page Break** from the Insert menu. Excel adds a dotted line to the top and left of that highlighted cell.

Excel inserts both vertical and horizontal page breaks at the same time, with the same command. While that's good if you want to divide your worksheet both ways, it's a bummer if you only want a horizontal break. But not to worry; there's a way to work around the situation.

If you want only a vertical or horizontal page break, you'll need to remove the one you don't want. First, highlight a cell that touches the dotted page break line that you want to get rid of. Then select Remove Page Break from the Insert menu. (Excel knows that if your cell cursor is next to a page break, you may want to get rid of it.)

Your Friend, the Printer

One of the very best things about Excel, is how it uses a "built-in" Windows printer driver to actually control your printer. That takes *a lot* of the hassle out of printing your work. But there are still many things that can go wrong.

If there's a printer problem, the first thing you'll see is a Windows dialog box. It will have a message to the effect that your printer is not responding. Ask yourself:

Is my printer on? I know this sounds kind of silly, but even we terribly knowledgeable professionals occasionally get caught by this one. If it's a laser printer, you'll need to give it a minute or so to warm up. When you turn it on, your printer will seem to be exercising itself as it goes through its initialization routine.

Does my printer have paper? It's very easy to run out, especially if several people use the same printer. When you refill it, be sure you're using the right kind of paper. Most dot-matrix printers use paper with holes running along their edges. The holes are what the printer uses to pull the paper through its tractor-feed. Laser printers, on the other hand, most often use the same kind of paper you employ in your office copier.

Is the printer "on-line?" Most printers have some kind of button that allows it to communicate with your computer. They are usually labeled "Ready" or "On-line." Also, they usually have some kind of light near them that let's you know whether they're on or not. If the light's not lit, press the button.

Did you ever wonder what to call those hole-infested strips of computer printer paper? You could win a bet with this little bit of info. It seems a couple of years back, National Public Radio had a contest to name them. And what is the collective wisdom of the computer nerds of this nation? "Perfory."

Be careful when fussing around inside your laser printer. One of the last steps a page goes through is where it is heated to fuse the dark toner (powdered ink) to the paper. It takes quite a bit of heat to do the job, and the area stays hot pretty much the whole time the printer is turned on. On most laser printers, the parts that are hot are labelled CAUTION or HOT (or some such warning).

Am I printing on the "right" printer? If you're on a network, it may have several printers connected to it. You can check to which one you're connected by clicking on the **Printer** button on the Print dialog box. Windows displays its Printer dialog box, which contains a list of available printers. If *your* printer isn't already highlighted, click on its name, and then click on **OK**.

Is the paper jammed? Paper that's too thick or thin can jam a laser printer; especially the older ones. If your printer is jammed, get someone knowledgeable about your particular printer to help you fix the problem.

The Least You Need to Know

The first time you print out one of your workbooks, you're going to find out that printed output is quite an attention-getter. Whether that's good or bad depends on the quality of the output—not to mention the numbers themselves. What's important is the fact that your printed output transmits information.

As you're getting ready to print, keep the following words of wisdom in mind:

- ☞ Clicking on the **Print** button on the Standard toolbar causes your worksheet to be printed—quickly, easily, and immediately!

- ☞ You can quickly print just a part of your worksheet if you highlight what you want printed, and then choose Selection from the Print dialog box.

- ☞ A quick moment taken to use the Print Preview feature can be worth a big time savings as you find the unexpected. Select Print Preview from the **File** menu to do this.

☛ If you're having problems fitting everything on the page, try these tips:

Use the **Page** tab of the Page Setup dialog box to change the scale or page orientation at which the worksheet is printed.

Use the Print Preview Margin handles to fit more worksheet on the paper.

Put in your own page breaks.

OH, LOOK, HONEY, IT'S ANOTHER BLANK PAGE!

Part III
Data Lists Unlimited

Although Excel is billed as a spreadsheet program, it moonlights as a database program—a program that can help you store and manage information, such as phone or address lists, customer records, or inventory data. In this section, you will learn how to use Excel to store data in a list, filter and sort the list, find specific items, create reports, and summarize and analyze your data in various ways. Whew!

Chapter 13
Making a List

In This Chapter

- ☛ Typing data in a list
- ☛ Understanding how Excel treats lists
- ☛ Adding and editing records with a data form
- ☛ Getting a piece of data out of your list

For years, the computer world has had *database programs* (such as Paradox, dBASE, and FoxPro) that specialize in helping people store, manage, and analyze data. You can use a database program to keep your personal address list, track employee records, or manage your CD or video library . . . that is, if you can handle the complexity of the program. With Excel, you can do all those same things with a list: a database without the technotalk.

SPEAK LIKE A GEEK

If the list analogy trips you, and you are comfortable with "databasese," remember the following: **database**=list; **record**=row; **field**=cell; and **field name**=column label.

List Rules and Regulations

Making a list is a no-brainer. You type data into the cells to create the list. For example, to create an address list, you type each person's name, address, and other not-so-personal details. However, there are some guidelines:

☞ Keep your list on a single worksheet, one list per worksheet.

☞ Leave at least one empty row or column between your list and any other data you might include on the worksheet.

☞ Type column labels at the top of the list, and make them bold or change the font to distinguish them from the data in the list. For example, in an address book, use column labels, such as **Last Name**, **First Name**, **Address**.

You can type the list items in any order; Excel can help you sort the records later. However, if you think you might want to preserve the original order in which you entered the items, add a column that numbers the items. If you sort the items incorrectly later, you can use the numbered column to restore the items to their original order.

☞ If you have a title or some other heading above the column labels, make sure you insert a blank row between the title and the column headings. Otherwise, Excel will think that your title row is the column heading row.

☞ Do not leave a blank row between the column labels and the rows that follow. If you need to show a break between the column row and following rows, add a border to the bottom of the column labels row, as explained in Chapter 11.

☞ The cells in a given column must contain information of the same type. For example, if you have a **ZIP Code** column, all cells in that column must contain a ZIP code.

The following figure shows what a list might look like. Notice the column labels at the top of the list (bold, no empty row after them). Notice that the information for each item is in a separate row.

Column label row

No blank row

Enter the same type of data for each cell in a column.

A list has column headings and a series of items.

But Is It a Database?

Excel 4.0 was a slow learner; before it would treat your list as a database, you had to enter a command that magically transformed the worksheet data into database data. Excel has learned a little since then. Now, Excel realizes that whenever you enter a database command (cleverly placed on the **Data** menu), that you want the list treated as a database. The bottom line is that you don't have to do anything special to tell Excel that the list is a database.

Form(al) Editing

You can edit your list just as you would edit any worksheet data: go to the cell, press **F2**, and edit the data. You can add list items by typing them at the end of the list or by inserting rows. However, Excel gives you an easier way. You can have Excel display a data form that makes adding and editing records as simple as filling in the blanks.

What's a Data Form?

Remember typing the column labels at the top of the list? Well, Excel takes these labels and creates a fill-in-the-blank form that you can use to find, edit, add, and delete records (a.k.a. list items). To display the form, select any cell in your list, open the Data menu, and select Form. Here's what the form looks like for the list I showed you earlier.

The data form lets you fill in the blanks.

By the Way . . .

Now that you're working with a data form, Excel reverts to the old-time database lingo. Each text box on the form is a *field*. Each time you complete all the fields in the dialog box, you've created a record.

Using a Form to Find Data

You can use a form to quickly locate a record in your list. The easiest way is to flip through the records one at a time. With the Data Form dialog box displayed, press the down arrow key to move to the next record or the up arrow key to move to the previous record. With the mouse, you can flip records by clicking on the Find Next or Find Prev button.

Another way to flip records is to use the scroll bar inside the form box. Click on the arrow at either end of the scroll bar to move up or down one record at a time. Drag the scroll box inside the bar to move to an area in the list (for example, drag the box halfway down to move to the middle of the list). Click inside the scroll bar above or below the scroll box to move up or down by 10 records at a time.

To find a specific record, click on the **Criteria** button. Type an entry into one or more of the text boxes, and press **Enter**. Excel displays the first record that matches your entries. For example, to find the first record that has a last name entry that starts with M, type **M** in the **L**ast Name text box, and press **Enter**. You can then use the Find **N**ext and Find **P**rev buttons to flip through the records. The following table shows several wild-card characters and relative operators you can use to broaden or narrow your search:

Wild-Card Characters

Entry	What It Does
*	Stands in for any group of characters.
?	Stands in for a single character.

Relative Operators

Entry	What It Does
>	Greater Than—Finds all records that have entries greater than the one you type.
<	Less Than—Finds all records that have entries less than the one you type.
>=	Greater Than or Equal To—Finds all records that have entries that match or are greater than the one you type.
<=	Less Than or Equal To—Finds all records that have entries that match or are less than the one you type.

Adding and Editing Records with a Form

A data form makes it easy to edit or add records in your list. With a data form, you can sucker someone else into doing your data entry for you. Just bring up the Data Form dialog box, and give the person a list of what you want typed in. To add items to your list, take the following steps:

1. Select any cell in the list.

2. Open the **D**ata menu, and select **F**orm.

3. Select the New button.

4. Type an entry into each of the text boxes. You can leave one or more text boxes empty, but if you choose to filter or sort using the data in that text box, the record will be excluded from the filter or sort operation.

5. Click on **Close**.

To edit a record using the data form, display the record you want to edit, as explained in the previous section. To replace an entry, tab to the text box that contains the entry, or press **Alt** plus the underlined letter in the field name; then, type your entry. To edit an entry, click inside the text box where you want the insertion point placed, and enter your changes. Press **Enter** to accept the changes.

Deleting a Record

Say you have an address list that contains the addresses of all of your ex's friends, whom you no longer have any use for. You want to delete these records from the list. Just use the Data Form dialog box to display the record, and then click on the Delete button. When Excel displays a confirmation dialog box, click on **OK** to delete the record.

The Least You Need to Know

Okay, now that I bored you with all the details, I'll tell you what you need to know to get by:

- ☞ It's all in the list. In Excel, you type your data in a list. Excel handles the database stuff for you.

- ☞ When creating a list, make sure you have one row that contains column labels. Make the column labels bold or change their font to set them apart from the list.

- ☞ Leave no empty row between a column and its list.

- ☞ Whenever you choose a command from the **Data** menu, Excel treats your list as a database.

- ☞ As a database, your list consists of records. Each record is made up of one or more field entries.

- ☞ To find, add, delete, or edit records using a data form, select a cell in your list, and then select **Data** and **Form**.

**ANOTHER FINE BLANK PAGE, BROUGHT
TO YOU BY YOUR FRIENDS AT
ALPHA BOOKS.**

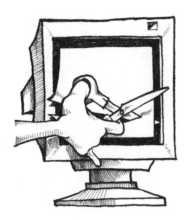

Chapter 14
Shape It, Sort It

In This Chapter

- Sorting a list by letters or numbers
- A quick way to sort
- Narrowing down your list
- Working with a narrowed list

Okay, you typed in your list, and now you have a bushel full of data on-screen. You're probably wondering how this is going to improve your life—how this list will make it easier to manage your data. In this chapter, you'll learn two data management things that Excel can do to the list: *sort* the list (from A to Z or 1 to 16,384) and *filter* (narrow) the list (for example, to show records for only those people whose last name starts with K).

TECHNO NERD TEACHES

A list can be up to 256 columns wide and 16,384 rows long. Where did they get those numbers? Programmers like to work with twos. For example, a byte is eight bits (2x2x2 or 2 to the third power). So, 256 is 2 to the eighth power, and 16,384 is 2 to the fourteenth power.

Sorting Data from A to Z ... or Z to A

Human brains were designed to perform creative and somewhat challenging tasks. Sorting a list alphabetically or numerically demands the IQ and creative skills of a grape.

Therefore, Excel includes a feature that can sort lists automatically, so you can spend your brain power on things more worthy of your time. You simply tell Excel which column contains the items you want to sort and whether you want the items sorted in ascending or descending order. Excel takes care of the rest, sorting the list according to your instructions.

Excel sorts entries that begin with numbers first and then sorts entries that start with letters. Numbers are sorted from smallest value to largest value or vice versa. If you are sorting a list of street addresses, you may want to treat numbers as text (so numbers that start with 1 always come before numbers that start with 2, no matter how large or small the value). To treat numbers as text, type an apostrophe (') at the beginning of the entry. Here's the difference in how Excel sorts numbers:

Numbers as Text	Numbers as Values
'12	12
'12356	32
'125	125
'12742	221
'221	12356
'32	12742

Sorting, Oh-So-Simply

SPEAK LIKE A GEEK

Excel is pretty good about avoiding jargon, but if you want to rub elbows with database jargonauts, you have to know what a **sort key** is. A sort key is a database field that's used to sort the records in a list. For example, if you sort by last name, the Last Name field is called a sort key.

There's a simple way to sort and a not-so-simple way. Which way is best? That depends. If you don't want any fancy sorting (for example, you want to sort a list in alphabetical order from A to Z), the simple sort is the way to go. However, if you have a special sorting need (say you want to sort by months in a year), you'll need to perform the not-so-simple sort.

Here's the easy way:

1. Select any cell in the column you want Excel to sort. Excel will use this column to sort the records in the list.

2. Open the **Data** menu, and select **Sort**. The Sort dialog box appears, as shown here.

Excel omits the column label
row from the sort.

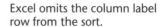

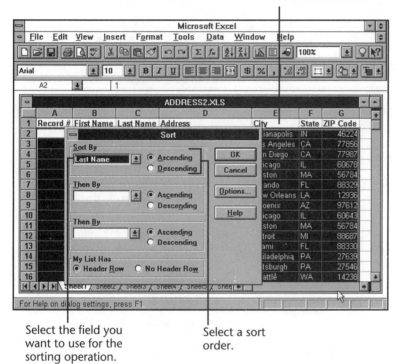

The Sort dialog box assumes you want to sort using the current column.

Select the field you want to use for the sorting operation.

Select a sort order.

3. Use the **Sort By** drop-down list to select the first column you want to sort on, and click on **Ascending** or **Descending** to specify a sort order.

4. To sort on another field, repeat step 3 for the first and second **Then By** drop-down lists.

5. Click on **OK**, or press **Enter**. Presto! The list sorts itself.

Once you have sorted your list, look at it to make sure it's what you wanted. If the sorting operation did not turn out as planned, you can undo the sort by selecting the Undo Sort command on the Edit menu, or by clicking on the **Undo** button in the Standard toolbar. To sort even more safely, you might also consider saving your list before sorting. That way, if anything goes wrong, you can open your original list.

To sort a list by a single column (say Last Names), select a cell in that column, and then click on the **Sort Ascending** or **Sort Descending** button in the Standard toolbar.

A More Complicated Sort

Sometimes, you may not want to sort alphabetically or numerically. You may want to sort by month or by category. In such a case, you can create a custom sort order.

To create your custom sort order, open the Tools menu, and click on Options. Click on the **Custom Lists** tab. Click on the Add button, and type the entries you want to use for your custom sort order; for example, type **First Quarter**, **Second Quarter**, **Third Quarter**, and **Fourth Quarter**. Press **Enter** at the end of each entry. Click on the **OK** button.

To use the custom sort order, do this:

1. Select any cell in the column you want Excel to sort. Excel will use this column to sort the records in the list.

2. Open the Data menu, and select Sort. The Sort dialog box appears.

3. Use the Sort By drop-down list to select the first column you want to sort on.

4. To specify a custom sort order, click on the Options button, select the desired sort order from the First Key Sort Order drop-down list, and select **OK**.

Select the custom
sort order you created.

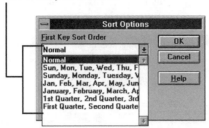

*Select your
custom sort
order.*

5. To sort on another field, use the first and second Then By options
    to specify a sort field and order.

6. Click on **OK**, or press **Enter**.

Getting Less List

So far, you've been working with your entire list. That's like opening the
phone book each time you want to find your friend's phone number. You
can have Excel filter the list for you, to provide you with the *Reader's Digest*
condensed version.

Filtering a List with AutoFilter

The easiest way to filter a list is to use Excel 5's new AutoFilter feature.
When you turn on AutoFilter, you get a drop-down list at the top of each
column. Each drop-down list contains all the entries in that column. You
select an entry, and Excel shows you only those records that have a matching entry. Here's how you do it:

1. Select any cell in the list.

2. Open the **Data** menu, select **Filter**, and select **AutoFilter**. Excel
    displays drop-down list arrow buttons at the top of each column.

3. Click on the drop-down list button for the column you want to
    use to filter the list, as shown here.

If you select Boston, Excel displays only those items that have Boston as an entry in the City column.

	Microsoft Excel						
File	**Edit**	**View**	**Insert**	**Format**	**Tools**	**Data**	**Window** **Help**

Arial · 10 · B I U · · · · $ % , · · · · · · ·

D3 · 1313 Mockingbird Lane

ADDRESS2.XLS

	A	B	C	D	E	F	G
1	Record	First Nam	Last Nam	Address	City	Sta	ZIP Cod
2	1	William	Kennedy	5567 Bluehill Circle	(All)	IN	46224
3	2	Marion	Kraft	1313 Mockingbird Lane	(Custom...)	CA	77856
4	3	Mary	Abolt	8517 Grandview Avenue	Boston	CA	77987
5	4	Joseph	Fugal	2764 W. 56th Place	Chicago	IL	60678
6	5	Gregg	Lawrence	5689 N. Bringshire Blvd.	Detroit	MA	56784
7	6	Lisa	Kasdan	8976 Westhaven Drive	Indianapolis Los Angeles Miami	FL	88329
8	7	Nicholas	Capetti	1345 W. Bilford Ave.	New Orleans	LA	12936
9	8	Allison	Milton	32718 S. Visionary Drive	Phoenix	AZ	97612
10	9	Barry	Strong	908 N. 9th Street	Chicago	IL	60643
11	10	Chuck	Burger	6754 W. Lakeview Drive	Boston	MA	56784
12	11	Carey	Bistro	987 N. Cumbersome Lane	Detroit	MI	88687
13	12	Marie	Gabel	8764 N. Demetrius Blvd.	Miami	FL	88330
14	13	Adrienne	Bullow	5643 N. Gaylord Ave.	Philadelphia	PA	27639
15	14	John	Kramden	5401 N. Bandy	Pittsburgh	PA	27546
16	15	Mitch	Kroll	674 E. Cooperton Drive	Seattle	WA	14238

Sheet1 / Sheet2 / Sheet3 / Sheet4 / Sheet5 / Shee

Ready

To see a select set of records, choose an item from the list.

4. Select the entry you want to use to narrow your list. You can use the arrow keys to scroll through the list, or type the first character in the entry's name to quickly move to it. Press **Enter**, or click on the entry with your mouse. Excel filters the list.

You can continue to narrow the list by selecting specific entries from the drop-down lists at the top of the other columns.

It never fails, as soon as I filter a list, I realize that it's not exactly what I want. To stop filtering on a given column, pull down the column's drop-down list, and select (All) at the top of the list. To unfilter the whole shebang, select **Data Filter Show All**. To turn the AutoFilter feature off, select **Data Filter AutoFilter**.

Filtering for Those with Special Needs

So far, you have filtered a list by using exact matches. AutoFilter filtered out any records that did not exactly match the entry you chose from the drop-down list. However, what if you want to view a range of records? Say you wanted to view a list of addresses for those people whose last name was between Kasdan and Strong, or you wanted to view the records of employee's who had a hire date between January and May of 1993? In such a case, you need to create a custom filter. Here's how you do it:

1. Click on the drop-down list button for the column you want to use to filter the list.

2. Select (**Custom...**). The Custom AutoFilter dialog box appears.

3. Enter your AutoFilter criteria, as shown here. (You can type criteria or select it from a drop-down list.)

This entry tells Excel to display records that have a last name entry between Kasdan and Strong.

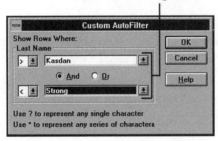

*Create a custom
filter.*

4. Click on **OK**.

5. You can repeat these steps to filter the list using another column.

Copying a Filtered List

When you filter a list, Excel hides any records it filters out. Don't worry, the records are still there; you just can't see them. If you plan on doing a lot to the filtered list, it's a good idea to copy it to a different worksheet or a different location on the current worksheet. For details about copying and pasting, refer to Chapter 10.

The Least You Need to Know

If all you want to do is sort a list from A to Z (or 1 to 10) or filter out a few records, you don't need to know a whole lot about the sort and filter options. Here's what you need to know to get you through the first day on the job:

- ☞ To sort a list, select any cell in the list, and then click on the **Sort Ascending** or **Sort Descending** button in the Standard toolbar.

- ☞ As long as you formatted the column labels using a different font or character attribute (bold, italic), Excel excludes the column label row from the sort.

- ☞ You can unsort immediately after you sort by clicking on the **Undo** button in the Standard toolbar.

- ☞ Filtering a list means displaying only a subset of records from the list.

- ☞ To filter a list, select any cell in the list, and choose **Data Filter AutoFilter.** Use the drop-down lists at the top of the columns to select the entries you want the records to match.

- ☞ To unfilter a list, select any cell in the list, and choose **Data Filter Show All.**

Chapter 15

Summing Up a List

In This Chapter

- Understanding automatic subtotals
- Subtotaling your list
- A quick look at the bottom line
- Using subtotals to create a report

If you're a bottom-line kinda guy (or gal), you're going to love Excel's automatic subtotals feature. With automatic subtotals, you can get totals, grand totals, and averages in a list without entering a single formula or function. You simply sort the list (to group all the items you want subtotaled, or averaged), and then unleash Excel. Excel inserts the required formulas, does the math, and spits out the results, as shown in the following figure. You can then collapse the list to show only the results.

If you're looking for more advanced tools for summarizing and analyzing data, skip ahead to the next chapter, in which you'll learn about the PivotTable Wizard.

You can use these controls to hide
detail or show more detail.

	File	Edit	View	Insert	Format	Tools	Data	Window	Help		
1 2 3		A	B	C	D	E	F	G	H	I	

	A	B	C	D
1			Budget	
2				
3	Month	Date	Expense	Amount
4	Jan	1/1/94	Mortgage	663
5	Jan	1/3/94	Auto	256.89
6	Jan	1/11/94	Daycare	150
7	Jan	1/20/94	Utilities	45.56
8	Jan	1/23/94	Utilities	67
9	Jan	1/25/94	Clothes	22.94
10	Jan	1/25/94	Entertainment	34.98
11	Jan	1/28/94	Groceries	54.67
12	Jan Total			1295.04
13	Feb	2/1/94	Mortgage	663
14	Feb	2/3/94	Auto	43.76
15	Feb	2/4/94	Groceries	123.98
16	Feb	2/4/94	Clothes	24.78
17	Feb	2/8/94	Misc.	32.98
18	Feb	2/9/94	Entertainment	64.32
19	Feb	2/23/94	Utilities	67
20	Feb	2/28/94	Groceries	62.37
21	Feb Total			1082.19
22	Grand Total			2377.23
23				
24				
25				

Sheet1 / Sheet2 / Sheet3 / Sheet4 / Sheet5 / Sheet6

Excel calculates the
subtotals for each
month.

The grand total shows
the total spent in
January and February.

*Excel gives you a
quick look at the
bottom line.*

Subtotaling Your List

Subtotaling a list is fairly simple. You sort the list to
group the items in the list you want to subtotal,
and then you use the Subtotal dialog box to tell
Excel which columns to subtotal and which operations you want it to perform.

Preparing Your List

You can subtotal a list in a number of ways. For
example, in the figure above, I subtotaled the
expenses for each month. This gave me a total of
how much money I had spent in January and
February. But say I was trying to decide whether it

would be less expensive for me to buy a new car, and I wanted to find out how much I had spent in January and February for auto repairs (Auto). In that case, I could have sorted by expense.

The moral of the story is that you have to decide what you want to know before you subtotal. Once you've decided that, sort your list to group the things you want to subtotal (refer to Chapter 14).

Doing It

Once you have your list sorted, you can tell Excel to create the subtotals. Here's how you do it:

1. Select any cell in the list. (To subtotal a portion of the list, select the column label row and any rows you want included in the subtotal operation.)

2. Open the **Data** menu, and select Subtotals. The Subtotal dialog box appears, as shown here.

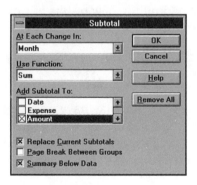

Use the Subtotals dialog box to tell Excel what to do.

3. From the At Each Change In list, choose the field whose items you want to subtotal. For example, if you want a subtotal for each expense, you would choose the Expense field.

If you added a title at the top of your list (in addition to the column label rows), you may get a dialog box saying that there is a header at the top of the list and asking if you want to extend the selection over the header. Answer **No**. If you answer Yes, Excel assumes that the title is a column label, and you'll never get subtotals to work.

4. From the Use Function list, choose the mathematical operation you want to perform. For example, you can choose Sum to determine totals, Average to determine averages, or Count to determine how many items you have in the list.

5. In the Add Subtotal To group, choose every column for which you want a subtotal. For example, to have Excel determine the total dollar amount of each expense, I chose **Amount**.

6. Select any other options as desired, and click on **OK**. Excel subtotals the list, and provides a complete summation of the data.

To use more than one function in the list (for example, to create a subtotal and average), repeat the steps, and select the second function you want to use from the Use Function list. Select Replace Current Subtotals to remove the X from its check box. When you click on **OK**, Excel recalculates the list adding the new results but not removing the old results.

Showing More or Less Detail

Now that you have a subtotaled list, you may have noticed a few funky buttons off to the left side of your list. These buttons (a.k.a. outline symbols) allow you to collapse the list to show only the subtotals and grand totals (thus eliminating the petty details), or expand the list to see all the numbers.

The easiest way to expand or collapse the list is to click on any of the numbered buttons at the top of the outline area. For example, click on **1** to see the least detail (a single level), **2** to see two levels of detail, or **3** to see three levels. You can also use the hide detail and show detail buttons to hide or show detail for a specific data group, as shown here.

Click on 1 to see the least detail, or
on 3 to see the most detail.

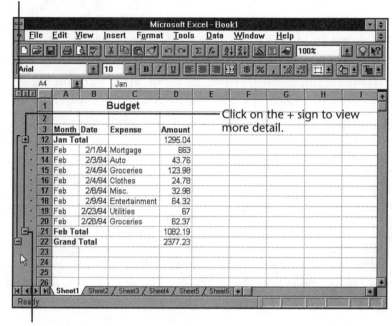

Click on the + sign to view
more detail.

*Use the outline
symbols to collapse or
expand the list.*

Click on the – sign
to view less detail.

Using Your Subtotaled List as a Report

A subtotaled list makes an excellent addition
to a report. Before you use your list as a report,
however, you should format it. The easiest
way is to use the AutoFormat feature. Here's
how you do it:

1. Select any cell in your list. Excel will
    select the entire list, including
    column labels and titles.

You can use your subtotaled
list to quickly sort groups of
data. Collapse the list, and
then sort it as you normally
would. Excel sorts the rows
displayed on-screen, mov-
ing the associated (hidden)
rows as a group.

2. Open the Format menu, and choose AutoFormat. You get the AutoFormat dialog box.

3. In the Table Format list, choose the predesigned format you want to use. When you select a format, Excel shows you what it will look like in the Sample area.

4. To exclude certain elements from the AutoFormat, click on the Options button, and choose the formats you want to turn off.

5. Click on **OK**. Excel formats your table to make it look like the one in the sample area.

By the Way . . .

When you format a collapsed list, Excel applies the formatting to the entire list, even the hidden parts. When you print a collapsed list, however, Excel prints only what's displayed. If you want to print the hidden data, use the outline symbols to expand the list before printing.

In addition to making great-looking reports, subtotaled lists are excellent for creating charts. You simply collapse the list to show only the subtotals, and then graph the subtotals. For information on creating charts, skip ahead to Chapter 18.

The Least You Need to Know

This chapter had a lot of information about creating lists, collapsing lists, and using lists to create reports and charts. If we were to collapse this chapter, we might come up with the following:

- ☞ Subtotaling a list takes two steps: sorting the list and entering the subtotal command.

- ☞ When you sort a list, you must group all the items for which you want subtotals.

- ☞ The Subtotal dialog box lets you specify three things: the column that contains the items you want to subtotal, the mathematical operation you want performed, and where you want the subtotals place.

- ☞ When you subtotal a list, Excel displays the list as an outline. You can show less or more detail in the list by clicking on the outline symbols. Click on – to hide detail or + to show detail.

- ☞ The easiest way to format a list for use as a report is to use **Format AutoFormat**.

- ☞ To create a quick graph, collapse your list, and then graph only the subtotals.

CAUTION: BLANK PAGES CAN BE HAZARDOUS TO YOUR HEALTH.

Chapter 16

Pivot Tables: Some Assembly Required

In This Chapter

- ☛ What is a pivot table?
- ☛ Summarizing and analyzing data with a pivot table
- ☛ Creating a simple pivot table
- ☛ Rearranging data in a pivot table
- ☛ Customizing a pivot table

Picture this: You're the area manager for a chain of music stores. You have four stores under your jurisdiction with several sales people at each store. You have a list that contains gobs of sales data. For stocking purposes, you want to find out whether any of your stores sell more or less of a particular musical instrument.

Sound like a nightmare? It's not. With a pivot table, you simply (well, somewhat simply) tell Excel to display the stores in rows and the sales figures for the musical instruments in the data area. Excel creates a pivot table, like the one shown here, that answers all your questions.

Data area shows sales figures.

Stores in rows

Store	Salesperson	Pianos	Violins	Guitars	Drums
Melody Sales West	Arial	$5,783.98	$838.49	$453.98	$785.93
Melody Sales West	Goya	$5,098.00	$765.00	$645.00	$820.00
Melody Sales West	Kribble	$3,400.00	$6,488.00	$764.98	$56.00
Melody Sales West	Tasha	$2,536.00	$887.00	$784.30	$873.98
Melody Sales East	Liza	$6,700.35	$764.65	$873.76	$875.90
Melody Sales East	Ali	$2,300.76			
Melody Sales East	Nick	$1,398.30			
Melody Sales East	Leroy	$6,589.00			
Melody Sales North	Leo	$2,398.76			
Melody Sales North	Cathy	$3,408.32			
Melody Sales North	Liz	$7,000.00			
Melody Sales North	Joe	$1,598.23			
Melody Sales South	Bill	$1,589.00			
Melody Sales South	Lisa	$3,765.00			
Melody Sales South	Sam	$1,298.00			

Data		Store	Total
Sum of Pianos		Melody Sales East	$16,988.41
		Melody Sales North	$14,405.31
		Melody Sales South	$6,852.00
		Melody Sales West	$16,817.98
Sum of Violins		Melody Sales East	$2,764.50
		Melody Sales North	$2,397.66
		Melody Sales South	$1,874.08
		Melody Sales West	$8,978.49
Sum of Guitars		Melody Sales East	$3,083.52
		Melody Sales North	$2,704.40
		Melody Sales South	$1,382.39
		Melody Sales West	$2,648.26
Sum of Drums		Melody Sales East	$2,996.40
		Melody Sales North	$2,958.67
		Melody Sales South	$2,234.93
		Melody Sales West	$2,535.91
Total Sum of Pianos			$54,863.70
Total Sum of Violins			$16,014.73
Total Sum of Guitars			$9,818.57
Total Sum of Drums			$10,725.91

Pivot table

A pivot table lets you cross columns and rows to get the answers you're looking for.

By the Way . . .

If you are familiar with Excel 4's Crosstab ReportWizard, you'll have a general idea of what a pivot table is all about. The pivot table is a new, improved, and renamed version of the Crosstab ReportWizard.

SPEAK LIKE A GEEK

A **pivot table** is a flexible grid that lets you drag columns and rows around on-screen (pivot them) to analyze data in various ways.

The Not-So-Big Picture

Like everything else in the computer world, pivot tables are easy . . . once you know what you're doing. Before you start, it helps to have the big picture, the Goodyear blimp perspective. So here goes.

Every pivot table consists of one or more of the following four elements: pages, row labels, column labels, and data. *Pages* allow you to create a drop-down list like the AutoFilter drop-down lists explained in Chapter 14. For example, you can create a Page drop-down list that allows you to view sales data for a single sales person.

Row labels make up the left side of the table, and *column labels* make up the top. The row and column labels are typically derived from the column labels in your list. You can use up to eight rows and eight columns. The *data area* contains the values you want added for each intersection of a column or row. In the example shown earlier, the data area consisted of the sales figures for the various musical instruments.

You can also think of a pivot table as being made up of *data fields* and *field labels*. The data fields are the values that make up the core of the pivot table. The field labels make up the column, row, and page headings. The data fields remain fixed in position, but you can pivot the field labels around the core to view the data in different ways.

Doing Your Own Pivot Table

Now that you have the big picture bouncing around somewhere inside your gray matter, you're probably itching to find out how to make your own pivot table. The how-to varies depending on whether you're creating a pivot table out of data in a single list on a lone worksheet or using data that is scattered around one or more worksheets.

In either case, however, you will run the **PivotTable Wizard**, and use it, as shown here, to set up pages, rows, columns, and the data area for your pivot table. The magical, mystical Wizard takes care of the rest, arranging the data and performing the required calculations.

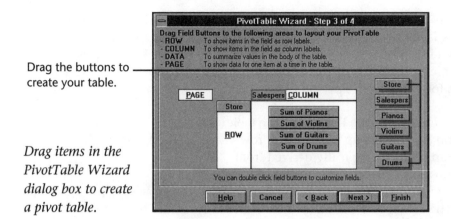

Drag the buttons to create your table.

Drag items in the PivotTable Wizard dialog box to create a pivot table.

Making a Table Out of Neighboring Cells

If all the data you want to use in your pivot table is in a single list on a single worksheet, you're in luck; creating a pivot table is fairly easy. You just run the PivotTable Wizard and answer all the questions:

1. Select any cell in your list.

2. Open the Data menu, and select PivotTable. Excel displays the PivotTable Wizard Step 1 of 4 dialog box, offering four choices. You want the choice that's already chosen (Microsoft Excel List or Database), so don't choose anything.

3. Click on the **Next** button. The PivotTable Wizard Step 2 of 4 dialog box appears, asking you to select the range of cells you want to transform into a pivot table. Excel shows a blinking dotted box that indicates what data it thinks you want to use.

4. Type the cell addresses that define the range, or drag over the desired cells with the mouse pointer.

5. Click on the **Next** button. The PivotTable Wizard Step 3 of 4 dialog box appears. (See figure at top of page.)

6. Drag the buttons on the right to where you want the row headings, column headings, or data to appear. You must drag at least one button into the data area.

7. Click on the **Next** button. The PivotTable Wizard Step 4 of 4 dialog box appears, asking you to specify additional preferences and a location for the Pivot Table. (If you don't specify a location, Excel inserts a new worksheet before the current one, and sticks the pivot table on the new sheet.)

8. Enter your preferences, and then click on the Finish button. The PivotTable Wizard creates the table according to your specifications.

If you're wondering where your original data went, it's probably on the next worksheet. To see your original data, click on the tab just to the right of the current tab.

Using Multiple Ranges or Worksheets

If you have data on several worksheets, or several separate ranges on the same worksheet, you have some work to do. You have to type or select the ranges that contain the data you want included in the pivot table. To do so, run the **PivotTable Wizard**, and select Multiple Consolidation Ranges from the PivotTable Wizard Step 1 of 4 dialog box.

When you click on the **Next** button, the PivotTable Wizard Step 2a of 4 dialog box appears, asking if you want the Wizard to create page fields for you. That's the easiest choice, so just click on the **Next** button, and continue as if you hadn't seen that dialog box.

When it is time for you to specify the ranges, you'll see the dialog box shown on the following page that asks you to specify the data you want consolidated. Select the first range, and click on the Add button. Repeat the steps for subsequent ranges. The PivotTable Wizard dialog box stays on-screen as you flip through your worksheets and select ranges.

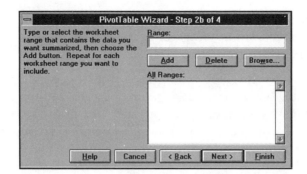

You can select more than one range from a worksheet or from separate worksheets.

When you are done selecting ranges, click on the **Next** button, and respond to the dialog boxes as explained in the previous section. Excel consolidates the data into a single pivot table.

There are three ways to enter commands for customizing your pivot table. You can use the **D**ata menu, right-click on the pivot table and use the shortcut menu, or use the Query and Pivot toolbar. The toolbar is automatically turned on when you create a pivot table. If you turned the toolbar off, you can turn it back on. Select **V**iew **T**oolbars, click on **Query and Pivot**, and select **OK**.

Customizing Your Pivot Table

The great thing about pivot tables is that they're flexible. You can drag the column and row labels around the data area, format the table, edit it, and hide or show detail to customize the table.

Pivoting Your Table

Don't worry if your pivot table didn't turn out as you had envisioned it. You can rearrange the data simply by dragging the field buttons around on-screen. This figure illustrates the effects you can expect by dragging fields.

You can also drag column and row headings to change their position in the list. To drag an item, click on it and then drag its border to the desired position.

Data	Store	Total
Sum of Pianos	Melody Sales East	$16,988.41
	Melody Sales North	$14,405.31
	Melod	
	Melod	
Sum of Violins	Melod	
	Melod	
	Melod	
	Melod	
Sum of Guitars	Melod	
	Melod	
	Melod	
	Melod	
Sum of Drums	Melod	
	Melod	
	Melod	
	Melod	
Total Sum of Pianos		
Total Sum of Violins		
Total Sum of Guitars		
Total Sum of Drums		

Drag the Data button here.

Store	Data	Total
Melody Sales East	Sum of Pianos	$16,988.41
	Sum of Violins	$2,764.50
	Sum of Guitars	$3,083.52
	Sum of Drums	$2,996.40
Melody Sales North	Sum of Pianos	$14,405.31
	Sum of Violins	$2,397.66
	Sum of Guitars	$2,704.40
	Sum of Drums	$2,958.67
Melody Sales South	Sum of Pianos	$6,652.00
	Sum of Violins	$1,874.08
	Sum of Guitars	$1,382.39
	Sum of Drums	$2,234.93
Melody Sales West	Sum of Pianos	$16,817.98
	Sum of Violins	$8,978.49
	Sum of Guitars	$2,648.26
	Sum of Drums	
Total Sum of Pianos		
Total Sum of Violins		
Total Sum of Guitars		
Total Sum of Drums		

Drag the Store button to the Page area.

Use the drop-down list to view data for one store at a time.

Store	Melody Sales East
Data	Total
Sum of Pianos	$16,988.41
Sum of Violins	$2,764.50
Sum of Guitars	$3,083.52
Sum of Drums	$2,996.40

Drag the field buttons and other items on-screen to rearrange your pivot table.

Adding and Removing Data

Remember those buttons you dragged around in the PivotTable Wizard dialog box? If you inadvertently left a button off or you decide later that you want to add a button for more detail, just select a cell in your pivot table and run the PivotTable Wizard again. Drag buttons on or off the table just as you did when you created the table.

If you want to remove a column, row or page field from your pivot table, you don't have to go through the Wizard. Simply drag the button out of the pivot table area. You'll know when you're outside the pivot table area when a big black X appears over the button you're dragging. (To drag a data field out of the data area, you have to run the PivotTable Wizard.)

You can also rearrange your table by using the PivotTable Wizard. Select one of the cells in the table, and then open the **Data** menu and select **PivotTable** (or click on the PivotTable Wizard button in the Query and Pivot toolbar). This displays the PivotTable Wizard Page 3 of 4 dialog box—the one that has the field buttons. Drag the buttons around to new positions to create the desired arrangement.

If you want to edit the pivot table without changing anything in the source worksheet, copy and paste the pivot table onto a different worksheet or different area on the same worksheet. This takes the "pivot" out of the table and transforms it into normal worksheet data, breaking the link between the pivot table and its source data.

The **summary function** is the mathematical operation that Excel performs on the values. The **calculation type** displays values as a relation of other values in the same row or column. For example, you can choose percent as the calculation type to have each value in a row displayed as a percent of the total.

Editing and Updating a Pivot Table

Before you edit any entries in your pivot table, you have to know a couple things. First, Excel won't allow you to edit any entries in the data area. To edit that data, you must go back to the worksheet you used to create the pivot table. Second, you can edit any column or row labels in the table, and Excel will retain the link between the table and its source. When you update the pivot table later, Excel will keep the changes you made to the labels.

If you edit the worksheet you used to create the pivot table, you must update the pivot table in order to incorporate those changes. To update your table, select any cell in the table, and then click on the **Refresh Data** button in the Query and Pivot toolbar (the button with the exclamation point on it), or open the Data menu and select **Refresh Data**.

Changing the Calculations for the Data Area

Most of the time, people use pivot tables to determine totals and subtotals. However, there may be times when you want to determine averages or perform some other mathematical operation on your values. Excel lets you change two things about calculations: the summary function (Sum, Average, Count), and the calculation type (difference, percent, running total).

To change the summary function or calculation type used for the pivot table, do the following:

1. Select any cell in the column whose summary function or calculation type you want to change.

2. Click on the PivotTable Field button on the Query and Pivot toolbar, or right-click on the selected cell and choose PivotTable Field. The PivotTable Field dialog box appears.

3. In the Summarized by list, select the desired summary function.

4. To select a different calculation type, click on the Options button, pull down the Show data as list, and select the desired calculation type. Select the two values you want Excel to compare. (See Table 16.1.)

5. Click on OK.

Table 16.1   Calculation Types

Calculation Type	What It Does
Difference From	Displays data as the difference that results when you subtract the value in this field from the value in the field you specify.
% Of	Displays the data as a percentage of the value in this field and the specified field.
% Difference From	Works like the Difference From calculation type, but displays the difference as a percentage.
Running Total in	Displays the data in a series of items as a running total.
% of row	Displays the values in each row as a percentage of the row's total value.
% of column	Displays the values in each column as a percentage of the column's total value.
% of total	Displays the values in the data area as a percentage of the data area's grand total.

Grouping and Ungrouping Data

Say you have all your data entered by months, and you need to whip up a report for the quarterly meeting. You have two options: you can add a new Quarter column to your worksheet, or you can have Excel group the dates into quarters for you. Excel provides you with three grouping options:

- ☛ Group text items by category. For example, you might group salespeople by region.

- ☛ Group numeric entries (such as employee numbers and product numbers) into ranges—for example, 0-99, 100-199, 200-299, and so on. (This grouping does not work for values in the data area.)

- ☛ Group dates into weeks, months, quarters, or years.

To group selected text items by category, perform the following steps:

1. Select the items you want to group.

2. Click on the Group button in the Query and Pivot toolbar, or right-click on one of the selected items, and then choose Group and Outline/Group. Excel creates a group called Group 1.

3. Repeat steps 1 and 2 for each group you want to create.

4. To rename a group, edit the name as you would edit any entry in a cell.

To group numeric entries into ranges, select any cell in the column that contains the numeric entries. Then, click on the Group button in the Query and Pivot toolbar. Excel displays the Grouping dialog box shown here. Enter the number you want to start with, the number you want to end with, and the range of numbers you want in each group. For example, if you have a list of 300 items, and you want them listed in groups of 50, you would type **1** in the Starting at box, **300** in the Ending at box, and **50** in the **By** box. Click on **OK** when you're done.

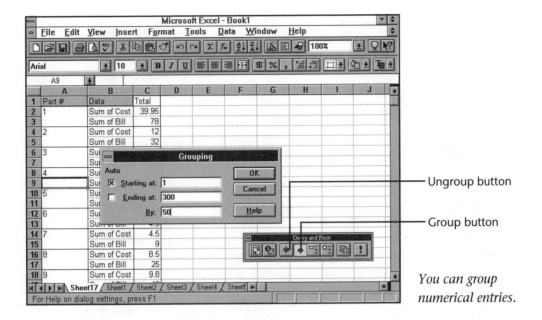

Ungroup button

Group button

You can group numerical entries.

To group dates into weeks, months, quarters, or years, you take the same steps as you would for grouping numeric entries. The only difference is that the Grouping dialog box requests different information. To group date items, you enter a starting and ending date in the Starting at and Ending at text boxes. From the **By** list, you choose a type of grouping: weeks, months, quarters, or years. Click on OK when you're done.

Hiding and Showing Detail

If you've grouped data, or if your pivot table has at least two row fields or two column fields, you can hide or show detail in a pivot table. For example, if you grouped dates into quarters, and you want to show the profit figures for the third quarter, you can hide the profit data for each date and show only the total for the quarter.

To show or hide detail, select a cell in the row or column whose detail you want to hide or show. In the example above, you might select the 3rd Quarter column. Click on the Hide Detail button in the Query and Pivot toolbar (the button with the minus sign on it). To show the detail, select the same cell and click on the Show Detail button (the button with the plus sign on it).

Although you can format your table just as you can format any worksheet, whenever you update a pivot table, Excel wipes out any formatting you may have applied. That's why it is best to use the Auto-Format feature to apply formatting.

Formatting a Pivot Table

When you create a pivot table, the last PivotTable Wizard dialog box lets you autoformat the table. If you don't like the format that was used, you can change it. Select any cell in the table, and then choose Format/AutoFormat. Select the desired format, and click on the OK button.

The one type of formatting you may want to apply yourself is the number format for your data cells. To apply a different number format, do this:

1. Select any cell in the field (column or row) whose number format you want to change.

2. Click on the PivotTable Field button on the Query and Pivot toolbar, or right-click on the selected cell and choose PivotTable Field. The PivotTable Field dialog box appears.

3. Click on the Number button. The Format Cells dialog box appears.

4. Select the number format you want to use, and click on OK.

The Least You Need to Know

Okay, I admit it—that last section on customizing your pivot table was a bit much. Unless you're doing something really complex, don't worry about those last few pages. Instead, focus on the important information:

- ☞ A pivot table is a flexible grid that lets you drag columns and rows around to analyze data in various ways.

- ☞ To make a pivot table, start with a list that has column labels.

- ☞ To run the PivotTable Wizard, select any cell in your list, open the **Data** menu, and select PivotTable. Follow the dialog boxes till you have your table.

- ☞ Once you have a pivot table on-screen, you can rearrange and analyze the data by dragging the field buttons around on-screen.

- ☞ For a quick list of pivot table options, right-click on the pivot table. You get a shortcut menu that shows you what you can do.

- ☞ To change the structure and content of a pivot table, select any cell in the table and run the PivotTable Wizard again.

- ☞ To format a pivot table, select a cell in the table, open the **Format** menu, and choose **AutoFormat**.

- ☞ If you change data in your worksheet and you want the changes incorporated into your pivot table, you must update the table. Select any cell in the table, open the Data menu, and choose Refresh.

BLANK IS BEAUTIFUL.

Chapter 17
Fetching and Merging Data

In This Chapter

- Getting data the easy way
- Joining data from two or more sources
- Asking for specific data with a query
- Running Microsoft Query
- Telling Query what you want

For some people (those with an IQ of 40 or below), typing names and numbers can be a fun and challenging experience. However, for the rest of us, it is a task to be avoided. One way to avoid the task is to use data that has already been entered. For example, if someone in your company has already typed a complete list of customer names and addresses, you probably don't need to type that information again. Instead, you use Microsoft Query to pull the data into an Excel workbook and make it your own. In this chapter, you'll learn how to get data from an existing database file and how to combine data from two or more database files.

dBASE file? If you need data that's been entered in dBASE, just open the file. Choose **File Open** and change to the drive and directory that contains the dBASE file. Pull down the List Files of **Type** list, and choose dBase Files (*.dbf). Choose the file you want to open from the File **Name** list, and then click on **OK**.

What Is Microsoft Query?

Microsoft Query is a separate program that comes with Excel. If you performed a complete installation of Excel, Microsoft Query is on your hard disk, just waiting to make itself useful.

What Microsoft Query does is allow you to pull data out of one or more previously created database files or lists and combine the data to create a new list.

For example, say someone in your company's accounting department has typed a customer list in Paradox. The list contains the account numbers, names, addresses, and phone numbers of all your customers. Somebody else, in sales, typed a list in Excel that tells what each customer bought in the last two years. You want to combine the two lists to create a new list showing the customer names, account numbers, phone numbers, and information about what each customer bought.

Query is a fancy word for question. A query might ask, "Who are my top ten sales people?" or "Which of my customers owes me money?" But of course, Microsoft Query doesn't speak in complete sentences, so you need to learn how to phrase your questions.

To perform this feat, you create a query that tells Microsoft Query which files you want to get the data from and what data you want to get. Query dips into the files and pulls out the data for you. Microsoft Query can get data from any of the following file types:

☞ Microsoft Excel (.XLS) versions 3.0, 4.0, and 5.0. That's right, you can have Query combine data from two or more Excel worksheets or workbooks.

☞ Paradox, versions 3.0 and 3.5.

☞ dBASE, versions 3.0 and 4.0.

☞ Microsoft FoxPro, versions 2.0 and 2.5.

☞ Microsoft Access, versions 1.0 and 1.1.

☞ SQL Server, versions 1.1, 4.2, NT, and Synbase 4.x).

☞ Btrieve, version 5.1

☞ ORACLE Server, version 6.0.

☞ ODS Gateway

☞ Text files

Pre-Flight Check List

You can run Microsoft Query by double-clicking on its icon in the Microsoft Office program group window or by choosing the Get External Data command from Excel's **Data** menu. The only problem is that the Get External Data command may not be on your **Data** menu. Pull down the **Data** menu, and check; the Get External Data command should be at the bottom. If the command is not there, do this to add the command:

1. Open the **Tools** menu, and choose Add-Ins. The Add-ins dialog box appears, showing you the Add-ins that are installed.

2. Click on the **B**rowse button.

3. Change to the EXCEL\LIBRARY\MSQUERY directory. This is where the Microsoft Query add-in files hang out.

Add-ins are commands and features that you can add to Excel to make it more powerful or easier to use.

4. In the File **N**ame list, choose **XLQUERY.XLA**, and click on **OK**. This puts XLquery at the bottom of the Add-ins list, and places an **X** in its check box, turning it on.

5. Choose **OK**. The Get External Data command is now on the **Data** menu.

If you still can't find the XLQUERY.XLA file, you may not have installed it. Double-click on the **Microsoft Excel Setup** button in the Microsoft Office program group, and check your installation.

> ## By the Way . . .
> Whenever you run Microsoft Query, a Cue Card window appears that can help you learn how to use Microsoft Query. If you have some spare time, poke around in the Cue Card window. It provides some good, general information about creating queries, as well as step-by-step instructions that tell you what to do. If you don't want the Cue Card displayed, click on the check box next to Don't display this card on startup. You can then close the window by double-clicking on its Control-menu box.

A Painless Extraction

Before you do anything very complicated, try something simple, such as getting a few fields of data from one or two database files. This will get you into and out of Microsoft Query very quickly and give you a taste of what it can do:

1. Open the workbook in which you want the data inserted, and select the cell in the upper left corner of the area where you want the data placed. The data you extract will be inserted into the current workbook.

2. Open the Data menu, and choose Get External Data. The Microsoft Query window appears with the Select Data Source dialog box. The data source specifies the location and type of database files from which you want data extracted.

3. Select the Other button, and do one of the following:

    ☞ Choose one of the data sources listed, and click on the Use button.

    ☞ Click on the New button, select the type of database file you want to use from the Installed ODBC Drivers list, and click on OK. Use the dialog box that appears to type a name and description for your data source, and to specify a directory where the database files are stored. Choose OK. Make sure your new data source is selected, and click on Use.

When you select a data source and choose **OK**, MS Query displays the Add Tables dialog box that lets you specify which database file(s) you want to query.

4. Change to the drive and directory that contains the database file you want to query. (If you created a new data source and specified a directory, you can skip this step.)

5. Select the database file you want to query, and then click on the **Add** button.

6. Repeat steps 4 and 5 for each database file you want to query, and then click on the Close button. MS Query displays the Query window that shows you a list of each field in each database file.

Miss one of your database files? You can add more databases later by opening the **Table** menu and selecting **Add** Tables.

7. Double-click on the fields whose data you want to extract. For example, if you want the CUSTOMER, LNAME, FNAME, PHONE data, double-click on those fields. When you choose a field, MS Query adds the data from the field to a column in the Data pane (the lower half of the Query window).

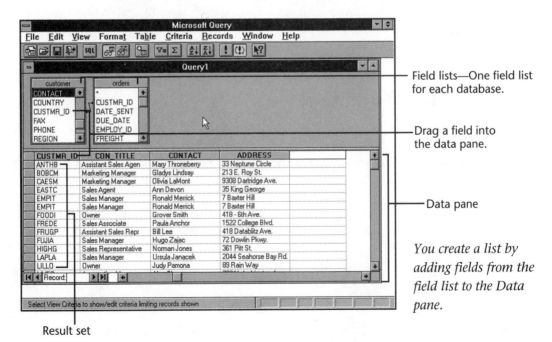

Field lists—One field list for each database.

Drag a field into the data pane.

Data pane

Result set

You create a list by adding fields from the field list to the Data pane.

You can also drag fields from the field lists to the Data pane. You can delete a column by clicking on its field name and pressing **Del**. You can move columns by dragging the field name at the top of the column.

8. To send the data to your Excel workbook, open the File menu, and select **Return Data to Microsoft Excel**, or click on the **Return Data to Excel** button in the toolbar (fourth button from the left). Excel returns you to your Excel workbook and displays the Get External Data dialog box.

9. In the **Destination** box, you can type a worksheet page number and/or cell address to specify where you want the data placed. If you don't specify a location, Excel inserts the data on the current worksheet starting with the cell you selected in step 1. Click on **OK**.

> **SPEAK LIKE A GEEK**
>
> The data list that MS Query extracts is called the **result set**. The result set is displayed in the **data pane**, in case you were wondering.

Changing a Query

If you forgot to add a data field, or you want to do more with your query as you proceed through this chapter, you can go back to Microsoft Query and edit the query you just made. Simply select any cell in the list you created, open the Data menu, and select Get External Data. When the Get External Data dialog box appears, click on the **Edit Query** button. Now you're back in Microsoft Query land.

Recycling Your Queries

Simple queries are no trouble to recreate. However, if you start using more complex queries that specify precisely which information you want to extract, you may want to save the query so you don't have to reassemble it later.

To save a query, open Microsoft Query's File menu, and choose **Save Query**. Type a name for the query (you can leave off the extension; Excel adds .QRY). Select the drive and directory where you want your queries stored, and click on **OK**. The saved query contains all of your query instructions, including the names and locations of the databases you want to query and the names of the fields whose data you want to extract.

To use a saved query, open the File menu, and choose Open Query. Change to the drive and directory that contains the saved query, and select the query file from the File Name list. Click on **OK**.

Getting More Focused

Okay, so far, you've sucked complete columns of data out of one or two databases. That's great if your sole object is to avoid retyping data. But what if you want some specific data? For example, say you want a list of all those customers who haven't bought anything from you in the last month. In such a case, you have to specify criteria that tells Query just what to look for.

The easiest way to extract a subset of records from a database is to have MS Query find only those records that have an entry that matches the entry you specify. Here's how you do it:

1. Select the cell in the data pane that contains the specific entry you want to match. For example, to extract records for only those customers who live in Boston, select **Boston** from the **City** column.

2. Click on the **Criteria Equals** button in the toolbar. MS Query filters the list to show only those records that have a matching entry.

3. To narrow the list more, repeat steps 1 and 2 for another entry in a different column. For example, if you want the list to show customers who live in Boston and buy from a specific salesperson, you might specify that salesperson.

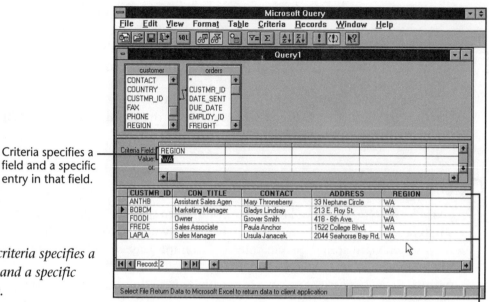

Criteria specifies a field and a specific entry in that field.

The criteria specifies a field and a specific entry.

Records that have WA in the Region field.

Exact matches don't always give you the results you need. For example, say you wanted a list of customers who live in Boston and owe you more than $3,000. You need Excel to look for a range of records. To enter this more complex specification, you could type the criteria in the criteria table. However, it's easier to have MS Query help you:

1. Select any cell in the column you want to use to filter the list.

2. Open the Criteria menu, and choose Add Criteria. The Add Criteria dialog box appears, as shown here.

3. In the Field box is the name of the database file and field that is currently selected. You can select a different field from the list.

4. Select a relative operator from the Operator list. For example, to search for records between two specific records, choose **is between**.

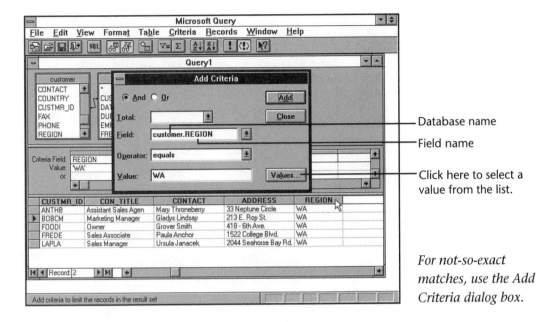

Database name

Field name

Click here to select a
value from the list.

*For not-so-exact
matches, use the Add
Criteria dialog box.*

5. In the Value box, type the specific entries you want to use as
   criteria, or click on the Values button and select the entries from a
   list. If you chose an operator that requires two entries (for example, **is between**), type two entries separated by a comma, or
   simply select the two entries from the Values list (in which case,
   MS Query inserts the comma for you).

6. Click on And if you have two criteria and you want only those
   records that match both criteria. Click on **Or** if you want the list
   to show records that match either search criterion.

7. Click on **Close.**

To remove the criteria (and unfilter the list), open the Criteria menu,
and choose Remove All Criteria.

By the Way . . .

Microsoft Query remains running after you return the data to
your Excel workbook. If you want to exit Microsoft Query,
switch back to it, open the File menu, and choose Exit.

The Least You Need to Know

We could talk about Microsoft Query well into the wee hours of the morning and still not cover all the options and nifty, little things you can do with it. However, that probably wouldn't thrill either of us. Instead, here's a list of what's important:

☞ To pull data into an Excel workbook, run Microsoft Query by selecting Get External Data from the **D**ata menu.

☞ If your **D**ata menu doesn't have the Get External Data command, open the **T**ools menu, select Add-Ins, click on the **B**rowse button, and poke around in the \EXCEL\LIBRARY\MSQUERY directory until you find a file called XLQUERY.XLA.

☞ To query a database, you have to specify three things: which database file(s) you want to query, which fields you want to extract, and which group of records you want.

☞ You can save your query and reuse it later.

☞ To edit a query, select any cell in the data area that contains the resulting data, and then open the **D**ata menu and choose Get External Data. When the Get External Data dialog box appears, click on the Edit Query button.

☞ To narrow a list, you must enter criteria. Select the column whose entries you want to use to narrow the list, open the **C**riteria menu, and select Add Criteria.

Part IV
Other Stuff You Wanted To Know

It never fails. No matter how carefully you organize things, you're always left with a couple of misfits—items that don't belong in any of the piles you've made. Such were the chapters in this section of the book.

There's some great stuff here that didn't fit anywhere else in the book, so I've grouped it all together under one roof so the individualist chapters won't feel so lonely.

Chapter 18

A Chart Is Worth a Thousand Words

In This Chapter

- ☛ Why a chart?
- ☛ What is a chart?
- ☛ Which chart is right?
- ☛ Seven steps to the perfect chart

Number two son toddled up to me and shoved a dirty piece of paper under my nose. "Look Daddy, I drew it myself!" The picture looked like an old spider with an advanced case of rheumatism. "It's a picture of you, Daddy. Do you like it?"

I must have said the right thing. As events have turned out, my son now draws a regular cartoon each week for his school's newsletter, and his pictures of me now look less arachnoid and more Homo Sapiens.

Pretty soon, you too will be creating pictures of your own. The pictures you create in Excel are called charts. In this chapter, I'm going to show you how easy it is to create them. By the time we're done, you'll be able to transmit otherwise unintelligible information to your audience, and to do it efficiently.

Why A Chart?

Many otherwise-intelligent people suddenly seem pretty dense when they are faced with columns of numbers in a worksheet. You're trying to get information across to them, but they simply can't grasp it efficiently.

There's a good reason for this. Most people don't think in terms of cold numbers; they think in terms of pictures. Pictures clearly show the relationships between the values on a worksheet—which salesperson sold the most widgets, or which division's forecast is proving "optimistic," for example.

What Is a Chart?

A *chart* in Excel is a graphical representation of the numbers in your worksheet—numbers into pictures. The way Excel turns the values in your cells into pictures is actually quite interesting.

Excel looks at a group of cells you select. It notes their labels, the values of the cells under the labels, and the geographical relationships among the cells. Excel then feeds this information into its ChartWizard, a built-in program that automates chart creation.

Creating a Chart

Let's create a chart now. Here's how:

1. Highlight the cells containing the data you want to chart. Make sure you highlight the rows and columns containing the labels, too.

2. Click on the **ChartWizard** button on the Standard toolbar. Your mouse pointer will turn into a small cross.

3. Use the cross to draw a rectangle on your worksheet. (Put the cross at the upper left corner where the rectangle should be, and drag down and to the right.)

4. When you see the ChartWizard dialog box, select the button labeled Finish, and watch the software do its stuff. Not too difficult, huh?

You've just created a very basic chart, but it's probably not exactly what you wanted. To get exactly what you wanted, continue reading this chapter.

This Is This, That Is That

Before we get too far into charts, let's take a moment to learn the parts of a chart. Here is a simple line chart showing the relationships among the amounts we spent on our vacation:

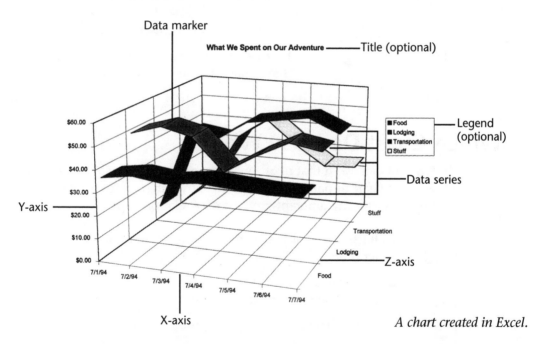

A chart created in Excel.

Here's a list of the sights you'll see on a chart:

Axis   A reference line for plotting the data. You can have up to three axes on your chart: X runs left and right, Y runs up and down, and Z runs back and forth. (The latter are found on 3-D charts only.)

Data Marker	The symbol that actually represents your data. This could be a bar, a line, a piece of pie, or single dots.
Data Series	If your chart shows data from more than one row or column, the different rows (or columns) are distinguished by different colored or patterned data points. Each color or pattern is a data series.
Gridlines	Lines that extend along the chart's axis to make it easier for you to interpolate the value of your data markers.
Legend	Captions for your data markers; it lets you know this line on the chart represents widgets, and that one represents whatchmacallits.
Plot Area	The area on your chart where the data markers are drawn to illustrate your data.
Title	A name for your chart.

Which Chart Do I Use When?

Well, I'm glad you asked that question. I mean, it would be so *gauche* to use the wrong chart in polite company. Actually, different kinds of charts are better at illustrating different kinds of data relationships.

 Line charts are what you want to illustrate trends in data occurring over time.

 Area charts are a relative of line charts. They emphasize the relative importance of the data points' value.

 Bar charts let you directly compare the value of individual data points.

 Column charts are a relative of bar charts, but oriented horizontally. Either make good histograms.

 Combination charts are used when you want to show trends (with a line chart) and absolute values (with a bar chart) on the same illustration.

Pie charts illustrate the relationship between the parts of a single data series and their whole.

 Donut charts are a more complicated kind of pie chart. The difference between them is that the latter allows you to compare two data series instead of just one.

 Radar charts are useful in engineering applications where you need to show the relationship among data points of individual numbers.

 XY or **Scatter charts** can't be beat for showing linear regressions.

 3-D charts are nothing more than fancier versions of the preceding charts.

By the Way . . .

Excel seems to offer so many chart types. Most of them, in my humble opinion, are much like the chrome fins on Detroit cars: extras that don't do much for the basic product. All in all, there are only four kinds of charts: bar, line, pie, and scatter. The rest are merely variations on a theme. For example, an area chart is nothing more than a filled-in line chart. A donut chart is only a pie chart in a pie chart.

Seven Steps to the Perfect Chart

Well, that's enough for the preliminaries. Let's jump in and create a chart for ourselves. Remember that the reason to create a chart is to transmit information; let's start with some planning.

The situation is this: we've taken a family vacation. Now we want to see how we spent our money. We want to see a representation of the absolute amounts spent, as well as relatively how much was spent each day. Because it most clearly shows the information we need, let's go with a 3-D line chart on its own sheet.

Step 1: Highlight the Data

Select the data to be included in the chart. Don't forget to select the row and column labels, too, if you want them to appear in the chart.

Before Excel can create a chart, it needs to know what data to use. You indicate what data to use by dragging across a block of data to highlight it. Notice that in this case, total figures are not highlighted and so won't be included in the chart. That's because totals numbers don't contribute to our understanding of the relationship between each day's spending.

Step 2: Start the Process

Because we're putting this chart on its own sheet, we don't want to start the ChartWizard directly. Instead, choose Chart from the Insert menu. When the pop-up menu appears, click on As New Sheet. That calls up the first ChartWizard dialog box: Step 1 of 5.

We need to make one quick check that we've highlighted the correct range of cells to be charted. Their reference appears in the Range text box in the dialog box. With everything okay so far, and with the Next> button darkened, press **Enter**.

Step 3: Choose a Chart Type

We've already decided that we're going to go with a 3-D line chart, so click on the chart type box labeled 3-D Line. If you want to use a different one, of course, you can click it here. (Check out the table a few pages back if you've forgotten your chart type options.) Excel darkens the chart type you choose to give you some feedback. With that accomplished, click on **Next >** to continue.

If you get impatient with the ChartWizard, go ahead and press **Finish**. Excel then goes through the rest of the process on its own, using its built-in defaults.

If what Excel comes up with is not to your liking, you can always change it later.

Step 4: Select a Chart Format

Our next decision is what format our chart should have. I think format number 2, with linear grid lines for all three axes, would do the job. If we had wanted logarithmic scales, we could have chosen format number 4. Call up the next dialog box in the sequence by clicking on **Next >**.

Step 5: Make Some Decisions

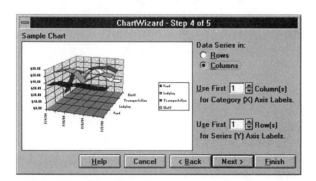

Your first look at the chart.

Here's where we get a first glimpse of what our chart is going to look like. By default, Excel assumes that data series is organized by column, and that works in this case. If our worksheet were different, we could make the adjustment by selecting Data Series in **Rows**. Change any of these options you like, and then go on to the next dialog box by pressing **Next >**.

Step 6: Add the Finishing Touches

Adding extras to the chart, such as legends and titles, makes it more meaningful.

No matter how clear your data may seem as you construct a chart, it will lose some of its immediate meaning over time. For that reason, I never create a chart without giving it a title. You type your title into the Chart Title text box. The best titles are complete sentences that summarize the information to be gained from the chart.

There is room in this dialog box to enter additional axes titles. Because the worksheet labels are complete, and because Excel uses them by default, we don't need to add anything in this case, just click on Finish.

Step 7: Sit Back and Admire Your Work

Well, there you go: one chart ready for interpretation. Mine looks like the first picture in this chapter, the one I used to show you the parts of a chart. At this point, I always like to take a bit closer look at the chart I've just created to make sure it conveys the information I intend.

Looking at this one, I can see that yes, it shows what it needs to. For example, you can tell by looking at it that food expenditures were pretty even over the entire vacation. Lodging took a dip there in the middle. I wonder if this reflects a particularly good buy on a motel, or if the data input for that day is incorrect (nice little reality check there).

The Chart Toolbar

Excel includes a handy little set of tools that lets you quickly change parts of a chart that you've already created. Choose Toolbars from the **View** menu. Click on the **Chart** check box in the Toolbars dialog box, and the chart tools appear in a toolbox. You can drag it up to the toolbar area to make it into a toolbar if you want.

There are five buttons on the Chart toolbox/toolbar:

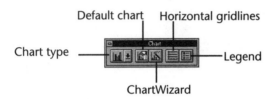

The Chart toolbox. Drag it to the toolbar area to make it into a toolbar.

Chart type   A drop-down list of chart types. Click on one to change the type of chart.

Default chart   Lets you return to start if you make a mistake.

ChartWizard   Calls up your new friend and helper.

Horizontal Gridlines   Turns them on and off in your chart.

Legend   Allows you to edit your chart's legends.

By the Way . . .

The buttons on Excel toolbars come in two sizes: small (which is the default) and large (obtained by clicking **Large Buttons** on the Toolbars dialog box). Either size do the same actions. If you're working with a laptop that employs a trackball type mouse, I'd recommend that you go with the larger size. They're also good to use if you're hung over and very nervous about that short deadline.

A Few Finishing Touches

Nothing done by machine is ever totally "right"—you know what I mean? After all, the built-in intelligence of some gadget will never compare with the artistic eye of a human.

It's the same with Excel charts. The Wizard does good work, as far as it goes. But a Wizard chart looks like a Wizard chart—not a chart done by the Great and Wonderful Ourself.

Here are some things you can do to customize the look of your charts:

- ☛ Add a legend that says something more than just what the data series are. Double-click on an entry in an existing legend to edit it.

- ☛ If a data series looks like it doesn't belong—take it out! With the chart active, double-click on the data series. When Excel changes its display to include handles (which lets you know that series can be acted upon), press **Del**. Presto, chango: Excel removes the data series from your chart.

- ☛ Depending on what kind of monitor screen you have, Excel can pick some pretty dingy colors for the chart background and floor. Click on either to activate it. Then with you mouse pointer over the area, press your right mouse button. Excel shows you its Format Plot Area dialog box. Use it to change the color and patter of the chart background.

- ☛ You can do much the same thing to change the color of data series on your chart. Move over to the legend at the side of your chart. Double-click on the one corresponding to the data series you want to modify, and then click your right mouse button.

Chart Cheating

I probably shouldn't be telling you this, but you can fudge a data series on a chart and change its underlying numbers at the same time! This works best with line charts.

1. With a chart on your screen, double-click on it to get Excel's attention. Excel responds by thickening its border.

2. In the chart proper, click on a data series to make Excel display it with handles.

3. Grab a handle, and move it up or down. Excel redraws the line and changes the value in the cell corresponding to that data point.

The Least You Need to Know

With the skills you've gained here, there's no stopping you from presenting the information in your worksheets clearly, efficiently, and in a visual, pleasing manner. Just don't forget:

- ☞ The whole reason for using charts in the first place is to convey otherwise complicated information to your audience.

- ☞ Know the strengths of the different chart types so you can select the appropriate one for your purposes.

- ☞ Before you can create a chart, you have to highlight a group of cells that contribute their data to the chart.

- ☞ You can create an instant pudding chart by first pressing the **ChartWizard** button, and then Finish on its Step 1 of 5 dialog box.

- ☞ You can use the Chart toolbar to change anything on a chart that's already been generated. Select it by choosing **Toolbars** from the **View** menu, and then clicking on the **Chart** check box.

HELP! I'M TRAPPED IN A COMPUTER BOOK PUBLISHING COMPANY! PLEASE SEND CHOCOLATE!

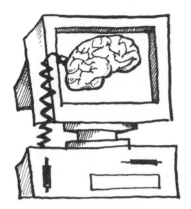

Chapter 19
Let the Macro Do It

In This Chapter

- ☞ What is a macro?
- ☞ Recording your own macro
- ☞ Running macros
- ☞ Anatomy of a macro
- ☞ Macros for 1-2-3 Refugees

I've come to the reluctant conclusion that I'm basically lazy. I know that's hard to believe, given all the hard work that I must have done, writing this book and all. I think the character flaw springs from a misspent youth. I had to spend mine working in a dark museum looking at old stuff while my more athletic friends were all working at the swimming pool looking at, um, sun-dappled water.

It was quite a pleasant revelation when I found out that in Excel, if there's something I don't want to do, I only have to do it once. If I tell it to, Excel remembers how to do it from then on. Not only that, but all I have to do is press a couple of buttons, and Excel will happily do it for me—automatically—time after time.

I like it.

You will too, friend. In this chapter, I'm going to show you how to automate just about anything in Excel that takes repetitive keystrokes to accomplish.

What, Pray Tell, Is a Macro?

A macro is a kind of tape recording you make in Excel. Just like a tape, you can rerun it any time you want to. The big difference between the two is that instead of recording music or words, a macro chronicles your keystrokes and menu selections.

To carry the tape metaphor a bit further, on some stereos today, you can put in a bunch of recordings on a changer where they remain until you want to listen to one. When that happens, you can call one up by name, and the player will perform it for you.

Here's a quickie technical question for you: What do **Ctrl+X**, **Ctrl+C**, and **Ctrl+V** have in common? If you say they are all commands associated with editing a cell's contents (to Cut, Copy, and Paste), you'd be correct. But did you know that each is also nothing more than a macro? True story. They're built into Excel itself, of course, but they're macros nonetheless.

It's a lot like that with Excel macros. They are stored in a safe place, and they each have a name. When you want to run one, you just call it up like you would a cassette tape. Easier, even. You can assign a macro to a shortcut key on your keyboard. Then, anytime you press that key, the macro runs automatically.

Let's Play Follow the Leader

Let's create a simple macro of our own. It will zoom our worksheet to 200%; we'll call it Zoom_In. The underscore character between the two words is important because macro names cannot contain any spaces; the underscore is a substitute for the forbidden space.

Choose **Record Macro** from the **Tools** menu. Then select **Record New Macro** from the submenu that Excel pops up. You'll get the Record New Macro dialog box.

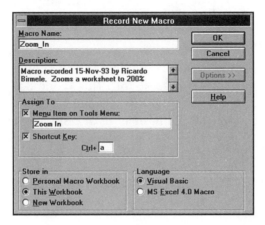

When you record a macro, take the time to fill out the blanks in this dialog box. It'll save you time and aggravation later.

Type a name for the macro into the **Macro Name** text box. In this case, let's use **ZOOM_IN**. The name can consist of any letters or numbers, but it can't include any spaces. Enter a description for the macro in the **Description** text box. In a couple of months, when you run across this macro that you've forgotten, you'll be glad that you made the description as complete as possible. (Hint, hint.)

If you want, you can have this macro appear as a menu command. To do so, select **Options**, and check the **Menu** Item on **Tools** Menu. Then enter the words for the menu command into the text box below that check box. The words you type here are what will appear in the **Tools** menu. If you want to make an underlined selection letter in the name, precede the letter you want with an ampersand (&).

Here's the menu option you added.

Well, what do you know? Our new friend Zoom In is right here on the menu.

Be careful of what shortcut key letters you use for your macros. If you pick something that Excel already uses, your macro shortcut key will supersede Excel's. You'll be able to do whatever action was associated with the Excel shortcut, of course. You just won't be able to use that shortcut key to do so.

Your safest bet is to go with whatever letter Excel offers as a default.

You can also assign this macro to a keyboard shortcut. To do so, check the Shortcut Key check box. Just below it is a box into which you type the key's letter, or you can simply accept the letter offered by Excel.

Next, indicate where you want this macro to be stored. You have a choice among a **Personal Macro Workbook**, into This **Workbook**, or into a **New** workbook. The Language choice is a no-brainer. Visual Basic is *much* easier to use than the older Excel 4.0 macro language. I'd strongly recommend that you accept Excel's Visual Basic default.

Writing the Macro

When you click on **OK** on the Record New Macro dialog box, Excel does two things: First, it sets itself up to pay close attention to what you're about to do for the next few minutes. Second, it puts up a small toolbar with only one (very important) button on it: the Stop button.

Okay, it's time to record our example macro. Here are the steps, and remember to use the keyboard for steps 1 and 2:

1. Choose **Zoom** from the View menu using the keyboard. (Press **Alt+V**, and then **Z**.) It won't work with the mouse.

2. When the Zoom dialog box comes up, tab to the 200% radio button, and then press **Enter**. Don't click on it with the mouse; you can't use the mouse to record macro actions.

3. The last thing for you to do is to stop the macro recording. Move your mouse pointer over to the Stop button and press it.

The Stop button has its own little window.

Excel stores your macro on a worksheet it names Module1. Ta-da! You have just written a macro.

Let's Give It a Try!

If it isn't there already, reset your worksheet's zoom back to 100%. Then press **Ctrl+A** (if you used Excel's default shortcut key) to run this new macro. If you'd rather, you can move up to the Tools menu, and click on **Zoom In**. Either way, Excel immediately zooms your worksheet display to 200%.

TECHNO NERD TEACHES

You may be wondering about my saying that you *wrote* a macro, when all you did was to have Excel record your keystrokes. Technical computer gurus always claim the credit for "writing code" when the program is a direct result of their actions, even if they use a tool like Excel's macro recorder to put down the actual words involved. The fancy acronym for this kind of thing is CASE, which stands for computer-aided software engineering.

Put It to Work

Now that you've seen it once, you're all ready to create a macro of your own. I even have a suggestion: how about a macro to zoom your screen back to 100%?

1. Choose **Record Macro** from the **Tools** menu, and then click on **Record New Macro** from the pop-up submenu.

2. Enter the name **ZOOM_OUT** into the Record New Dialog Box. Don't forget to also enter a description for your macro. If you want to assign this macro to a key, or to have it appear as an option in the **Tools** menu,

continues

continued

you know what to do.

3. Go through the steps to change your view back to 100%.

4. Press the **Stop Macro** button.

That's all there is to it, friend. You can sit back and congratulate yourself for having written your first macro. May you do many more.

An Anatomy of a Macro

Excel records your macro in a "language" known as the Microsoft Excel implementation of Visual Basic. This is a distant descendent of a language called the "Beginner's All-Purpose Symbolic Instruction Code," or BASIC for short.

Visual Basic is a very powerful, useful, and easy-to-use language. We won't be getting into it in detail here, but I thought you might like to at least see what it looks like. And as long as we're looking, I'll tell you a little bit about it.

Each workbook stores its own macros separately from any other workbooks. (You can copy macros from one workbook to another, however.) The macros are stored on a single worksheet called Module1. Its tab can be found after the last normal worksheet tab. Macros are stored in the order in which they are recorded.

Here's what the Zoom_In and Zoom_Out macros we just created might look like when stored in Module1. The lines that begin with apostrophes are comment lines that Excel ignores; they're just there for the user's benefit.

```
'
' Zoom_In Macro
' Macro recorded 15–Nov93 by Ricardo Birmele
```

```
' Zooms worksheet in to 200%
'
Sub Zoom_In()
   ActiveWindow.Zoom = 200
End Sub
'
' Zoom_Out Macro
' Macro recorded 16–Nov–93 by Greggy Smith
' Zooms worksheet out
'
Sub Zoom_Out()
   ActiveWindow.Zoom = 100
End Sub
```

Without getting too technical, I'd like to explain the macro to you. To do so, we'll take it piece by piece.

The Heading

A Visual Basic program reads downward going line by line. There are two kinds of lines: those that are included only for the benefit of a human who is reading the code, and those that are used by the computer to accomplish some task.

The first few lines in our macro begin with an apostrophe. The computer looks at the apostrophe and knows that these are the kind of lines that are there for human consumption only, and so ignores them. In the present case, the lines let us know the macro's name, when it was recorded, and what it is supposed to accomplish.

```
'
' Zoom_In Macro
' Macro recorded 15-Nov93 by Ricardo Birmele
' Zooms worksheet in to 200%
'
```

The Macro Itself

Because these lines don't begin with an apostrophe, Excel recognizes them as executable instructions. The words, "Sub" and "End Sub" are a way to organize the Excel's macro into computer-manageable pieces.

The line between "Sub" and "End Sub" is what actually does the macro's work. In this case, the line tells Excel that the currently active window should take on a zoom value of 200.

```
Sub Zoom_In()
   ActiveWindow.Zoom = 200
End Sub
```

It may seem like an awful fuss to have six lines of code that perform one line of action, but such is the nature of computer programming. Programmers have become resigned to it, and so must you.

Running Macros

Once you've created a macro, it is available throughout your workbook, no matter with which worksheet you happen to be working. How you actually perform the macro depends on the options you chose when you created it.

☛ If you've associated the macro with a shortcut key, you can press it to run the macro.

☛ If you made the macro a menu option on the Tool menu, then you can select and run it from there.

☛ If you have chosen not to associate your macro with a shortcut key or menu command, you have to run it using Excel's built-in macro run facility. Select **Macro** from the Tools menu. Excel displays its Macro dialog box that contains a list of all the macros associated with this workbook. Highlight the name of the macro you want to run and press **Run**. Excel hides the dialog box and performs your macro.

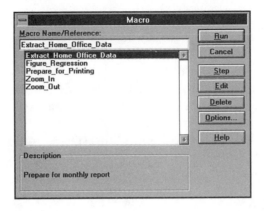

The macro dialog box gives you access to the complete list of macros in your workbook.

Anti-Macro

You delete an Excel macro using the same Macro dialog box you would employ to run it. Choose Macro from the Tools menu. Excel displays the Macro dialog box. Highlight the name of the macro you want to get rid of, and press Delete. Be careful here. Once you delete a macro, you cannot get it back again.

Macros for 1-2-3 Refugees

If you're coming to Excel from 1-2-3, you may be bringing your favorite macros with you. This shouldn't be much of a problem.

Excel runs most 1-2-3 macros that were created with 1-2-3 version 2.01 directly. Just open the 1-2-3 worksheet, and press **Ctrl+<macro letter>**. Excel translates the macro and performs it automatically. If your macro includes the 1-2-3 pause command, {?}, when Excel reaches that point, it pauses, also. Press **Enter** to continue to execute the macro.

If you have 1-2-3 macros in a version 2.2 macro library (.MLB format), you need to convert the libraries to regular 1-2-3 WK1 files before you can run the macros in Excel. You'll need to do this from the 1-2-3 program itself rather than from inside Excel. When you've converted them, you can open the new WK1 files in Excel just as you would open any 1-2-3 worksheet.

Excel doesn't support 1-2-3 add-in applications. It has no way of knowing what data they need passed to them, and so hangs up when it encounters a 1-2-3 add-in specific command.

Excel automatically runs 1-2-3 autoexecuting macros when it loads a worksheet that contains one. If you want to bypass the autoexecuting macro, then you should open the worksheet using the normal **Open** option from the **File** menu, but press **Shift+OK** as your last step.

The Least You Need to Know

I bet you didn't think you would turn into a computer programmer when you picked up this book. Welcome to the society; I hope you have a lot of fun with your new skill. As you work with Excel macros, keep the following in mind:

- To record a macro, choose **Record Macro** from the **Tools** menu, and then click on **Record New Macro** from the submenu.

- To stop recording a macro, click the **Stop** button.

- Be very careful when you assign a macro to a shortcut key. The one you choose may be already assigned to another Excel function. Your safest bet is to accept the letters that Excel offers in the Record New Macro dialog box.

- Macros are available throughout the entire workbook.

- To run your macro, you select **Macro** from the **Tools** menu. That brings up the Macro dialog box. Highlight the name of the macro you want to run and press **Run**.

Chapter 20

Beyond the Defaults

In This Chapter

- ☛ Your workspace the way you want it
- ☛ Your way at the start
- ☛ Templates
- ☛ Add-ins

Most of us like to do things our own way. Especially if we're old and crotchety, or young and stubborn, or middle-aged and set in our ways.

Fortunately, Excel accommodates us by making it easy for us to change many aspects of how it works. In this chapter, we're going to look at how that's done; how you can configure Excel to be just the software you want it to be.

Your Workspace the Way You Want It

Basic to your using Excel is organizing its workspace. To configure it, choose Options from the Tools menu. Excel displays the Options dialog box. This dialog box is organized into ten tabs, each of which control one aspect of Excel's behavior. You activate each tab by clicking on it.

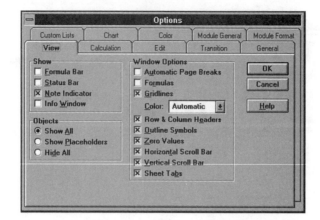

Click a tab to be able to configure Excel just the way you want it.

Click	To Configure
View	How Excel displays your workbooks. Indicate whether it should hide or show the formula and status bar, and objects like place holders. Here you control what parts of a workbook Excel should show, as well as what color they should appear.
General	What kind of cell references Excel should use (its familiar "A1" or Multiplan's "R1C1"), and whether to use the newer Excel 5.0 menu structure or that of Excel 4.0 instead. Specify what font and disk directory should be used as the default when Excel loads. Finally, here is where you enter your name as being Excel's user.
Edit	How you want Excel to handle your input. This includes whether you can edit cells directly, drag a cell to another location, and how many decimal places should be used as a general default.
Calculation	How Excel calculates the values in your worksheets. Your choices include: automatic (where Excel refigures everything any time you make a change) or manual (where you have to press **F9** to get Excel to recalculate your worksheet.)

For some kinds of figuring Excel does use brute-force methods, where it tries number after number until it arrives at the best answer it can get for the problem. You control the number of times Excel tries to find the answer, and how close it needs to get before it can accept an answer as being correct.

Transition Whether Excel should recognize its own menu commands, or use those of Lotus 1-2-3 instead.

Custom Lists This is where Excel knows what to use when autofilling cells with days of the week or months of the year.

Chart How the ChartWizard should interpret empty cells it finds, as well as how big it should make charts in the first place.

Color You can control the color of filled-in areas on charts (like columns, floors, and so on).

Module General You can specify how Excel formats macro code on module sheets. This includes such things as how many spaces to use for indents, whether to warn you if you made a mistake with syntax, and whether it should continue to execute a macro when it finds an error. You can also use this tab to specify the format of date and currency values.

Module Format You may remember from the macro chapter how Excel stores the code it generates as you create a macro. You may also remember from looking at the code you generated that it is displayed in different colors; one for comments (beginning with apostrophes), another for keywords, and so on. This is where you specify which color Excel should use for what kind of text.

Your Way at the Start

When Excel first loads, it looks into a special subdirectory called XLSTART to see if there are any workbooks in there. If there are, Excel automatically opens them for you to use. That means you can cause Excel to automatically open any of your workbooks by simply moving the workbook into the XLSTART subdirectory.

If you don't have an XLSTART subdirectory, here's one way to create it:

1. In Program Manager, open the **Main** program group and double-click on the **MS DOS** icon. This drops you into a DOS command line that looks something like **C:\>**.

2. Type **MD C:\EXCEL\XLSTART** and press **Enter**. When you do, DOS creates the subdirectory for you.

3. Type **EXIT** and press **Enter** to return to Windows.

With that done, you can move workbooks in and out of XLSTART at any time. (You can use Windows' File Manager program to move files from place to place (see your Windows manual for details). Or you can open a workbook in Excel, and then use the Save As command from the File menu to save the worksheet to the XLSTART directory.

If you like, you can use Windows' File Manager to create the XLSTART subdirectory. You'll usually find its icon (which looks like a filing cabinet) in the Windows Program Manager Main program group. Double-click on it to get it going. Then use its menu options to create the XLSTART subdirectory under C:\EXCEL. At the same time, you can move into it any workbooks you want Excel to automatically run as it starts up.

Templates

A template is a special kind of Excel workbook. You use it as a pattern for your regular workbooks. For example, you can set up a financial workbook that contains worksheets that keep track of office expenses. You can save that workbook as a template. Then you can distribute the template to all your company's offices, so that everyone works with the same basic financial data.

To save a workbook as a template, first choose Save As from the File menu. Next, enter a name for the template in the File Name text box, and select Template from the Save File as Type list. Finally, click on **OK.**

A **template** is a pattern for a workbook. Template workbooks don't actually contain data. Instead, you open a template, fill it with data, and save it as a regular workbook.

Add-Ins

As complete as Excel is, you can extend its capabilities even further by using what are called *add-ins*. Add-ins are individual sets of commands that work in Excel as if they were originally part of it.

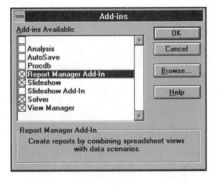

Click an Add-in name to incorporate it into Excel.

Choose Add-Ins from the Tools menu to see the Add-Ins dialog box. You incorporate an add-in by clicking the check box next to its name. Once that's done, you can use its capabilities just like they were Excel's.

Add-in	What It Does
Analysis	Provides additional engineering, financial, and statistical functions.
Autosave	Allows Excel to automatically save your workbooks at time intervals you specify.
Query	Lets your workbook database applications obtain data from external database files.

continues

continued

Add-in	What It Does
Report Manager	Controls printing reports of views and scenarios.
Slide Show	Uses worksheets and charts to create slides that you can use in a demonstration.
Solver	Lets you create worksheets that go beyond mere "what-if" to where Excel actually finds the most optimal answer to an analytical question.
View Manager	Keeps track of successive worksheet views.

The Least You Need to Know

Well, you've reached the end of the trail ride. In this chapter, you learned several non-essential but useful ways to make Excel easier to use. They include:

☛ You can change the way Excel appears and operates by selecting **O**ptions from the **T**ools menu and making changes to the dialog box that appears.

☛ Copy any workbooks that you want to load automatically each time you start Excel into the XLSTART directory.

☛ If you need the same basic workbook layout periodically to create different workbooks, consider creating a template that contains the common elements.

☛ Add-ins are extra programs that work closely with Excel to offer you special features. Load or unload them by selecting Add-**I**ns from the **T**ools menu.

Appendix A

Installing Excel

If you haven't already installed Excel, I just know that you're champing at the bit and can hardly wait to get started. Well friend, I don't blame you one bit.

Installing Excel is an easy job to do. You don't have to understand either Excel or Windows. Excel has an installation utility (that's a program that comes with Excel) that practically does the whole thing for you. Before you get started, however, there's a couple of details you need to take care of:

- ☞ You'll need to know a bare minimum about Windows: like, how to get it running and how to start a program that uses the Windows graphical user interface. I'd suggest you give Chapter 3 a quick read if you need to. You could also ask a friend to help get you going.

- ☞ Make sure you have all the disks you'll need. Excel comes on ten 3 1/2-inch high-density floppies, numbered 1 to 10. It's extremely inconvenient not to have a disk when you need it.

Well, with *that* out of the way, let's get you started on your spreadsheet adventure:

1. If your computer isn't already running, turn it on. There's probably a switch somewhere on its front, side, or back that's labeled On and Off, or 1 and 0. (Don't forget to also turn on the *monitor*: that TV-looking thing.)

2. Assuming your computer is on and running, next, you need to get Windows going. Some computers are set to have that happen automatically. If your's isn't, type **WIN** next to the DOS prompt (which looks like C> or C:\>), and press **Enter**. Oh yes, if Windows isn't already installed on your computer, you'll have to get that done first. (Go buy the program; it comes with installation instructions.)

3. Put the diskette labeled "Disk 1—Setup" into your A or B floppy drive.

4. With the Windows Program Manager running, use your mouse pointer to move to the File menu. Click on it, then move down to the **Run** option, and click on it, too. If you don't have a mouse, or you'd just rather use a keyboard, press **Alt** and **F** together, and then press **R**. Either way, Windows will show you a dialog box labeled Run.

5. Type **A:SETUP** (or **B:SETUP** if you've put the Disk 1 into the drive B), and press **Return**. If you'd like to use your mouse, click on the **OK** button when you've finished typing.

6. You'll see or hear your computer's floppy disk whir for a bit. Then Excel will show you a couple of screens that ask some simple housekeeping questions.

☛ It'll want to know which disk directory to install Excel in. Most people go with the default C:\EXCEL.

☛ Excel will need to know how much of itself it should load. There's the Complete installation which includes everything, the Custom installation which includes just those parts you want loaded (leave this one for later, once you know more about the ins and outs of Windows and Excel), and a special installation for laptop computers. Press the appropriate button: Typical, Complete/ Custom, or Laptop (Minimum).

That be about it! For the next few minutes, all you have to do is to sit back, fill out the registration card, and feed disks into your floppy drive. If you need to quit, click on **Cancel**. If not, you'll be done soon, and that's when you can jump right into number crunching with Excel!

Appendix B
Twenty Great Ideas

Here and there in this book, I've tried to give you some ideas about real-world uses for Excel, but there are many more than would fit in the chapters. In this appendix, you'll find some "brain-jogger" ideas for creating your own custom Excel worksheets.

Address Book

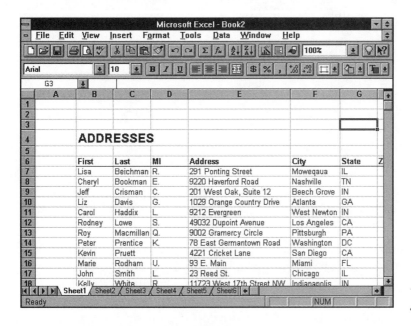

Excel makes a darned good address book.

This one we already mentioned earlier in the book; it's one of the most common uses for Excel's database features. You can keep a list of your personal and business names, addresses, and phone numbers in Excel, and never again have to tear up a perfectly good Rolodex card simply because your best friend Howard has moved again.

You'll probably want to insert the first and last names in different cells (fields). Why? So you can sort the list by last name alphabetically. Here are some fields you could include: First, Last, MI (middle initial), Address, City, State, ZIP, Phone, E-Mail, and Comments.

Emergency Phone Numbers

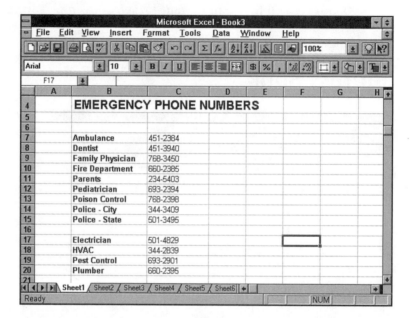

Enter the names and numbers in a clear, readable font, such as Arial.

Closely related to the address book is a phone listing. You could print this listing out and post it next to your telephone to have handy in case of an emergency. You'll want to include the names and numbers of your doctor(s), dentist, pediatrician, close relatives, neighbors, and so on. You'll also want the local ambulance, police, fire department, and poison control center.

If you really want to get ambitious, consider including the numbers of repair people who regularly work on your house. For example, having the plumber's number handy may be a real lifesaver some fateful day when your kitchen sink becomes a geyser.

Car Maintenance

Microsoft Excel - EXAMPL.XLS					
		Auto Maintenance			
		1987 Pontiac Sunbird			
Odometer	**Date**	**Service**	**Place**	**Cost**	
3500	12/14/87	Oil change	Jiffy-Quick	$19.95	
7200	2/5/88	Oil change/filter	Jiffy-Quick	$24.95	
10920	5/15/88	Oil change	Jiffy-Quick	$19.95	
12003	5/20/88	Tune-up	Dan Smith Pontiac	$58.50	
15390	9/29/88	Oil change/filter	10 Minute Lube	$20.40	
19230	1/2/89	Oil change	10 Minute Lube	$20.40	
19241	1/5/89	replaced air filter	bought at K-mart	$5.80	
23,400	4/15/89	patched hole in tire	Tire Mart	$5.00	
24,405	4/25/89	Oil change/filter	Jiffy-Quick	$19.95	
28,091	8/20/89	Oil change	Jiffy-Quick	$19.95	
30,092	9/18/89	Tune-up, oil change	Dan Smith Pontiac	$72.39	

Keep track of how much that beloved clunker is costing you.

Sure, you might love your car at the moment, but at some point, you're going to want to sell it. And when you do, there's nothing to attract a potential buyer than a complete record of all the auto maintenance and repairs that have been performed. (Buyers love sellers who appear a bit anal-retentive, because they figure if you fuss this much over record-keeping, you were equally meticulous about the car maintenance itself, which may or may not be the case.)

At any rate, if you get into the habit of recording each maintenance action, you'll not only have a tidy record, but you'll know how much the darned car has cost you over the years. If you deduct a portion of your auto expenses on your taxes, this information is particularly important.

To set it up, you'll want columns for Odometer (the number of miles on the car at the time), Date, Service, Place, and Cost. You may also want a column for Parts Replaced, in case you want to keep track of how long specific parts last before they kick the bucket. Total up the Cost column to see the total amount you've spent.

Student Grades

Forget scribbled changes and math errors in your grade book.

Teachers will absolutely love this one. By keeping student grades in Excel, you will never again have to fuss with averages or worry about math errors. You'll be able to tell at a glance how each student is performing.

To set this one up, create a column for the Student Number (#) and Name. Enter all the students under them. Then, for every grade you want to record, add a column heading for it. Unlike those cramped old paper gradebooks, you can have as much space as you want to type the description. For example, you could have a column heading **Ch. 1 Quiz**, rather than something cryptic like **C1Q**.

At the end of the semester, average each student's grades with the AVERAGE function. You can also use the AVERAGE function to see what the class average was with each test; simply average the numbers in that column.

> **By the Way . . .**
>
> You don't have to be a teacher to use this. Students of any age can keep track of their grades in various subjects using a similar worksheet, and parents can keep grade records for each of their children.

Sports Scores

Let's say your favorite football team is on its way to the play-offs. (It's a long shot, but let's pretend.) You'll want to keep track of the game-by-game stats on each player, so you can rub it in the faces of your friends who cheer for other teams during the Superbowl party. Or maybe it's baseball or hockey that's your passion. Same difference.

Just set up a worksheet for each game with the player name, player number, and whatever stats you want to keep (hockey goals, fumbles, touchdowns, or triple-plays). Print it out, and keep a pencil handy during the game to update it. At the end of the season, you can use formulas to tally up all the vital stats. If you're embarrassed by your team's poor performance in certain categories (such as fumbles), you can simply hide that column on the worksheet.

> **By the Way . . .**
>
> If you're such a serious sports fan, what are you doing watching the game on TV? Why aren't you at the stadium, with your face painted with the team colors and holding a banner?

What's that? You say you actually PLAY sports, and want to track of your stats? That's even better. An Excel worksheet is a great way to keep track of your church's bowling league or your kid's soccer team. You can even make a colorful chart that shows how each player improves over the course of the season.

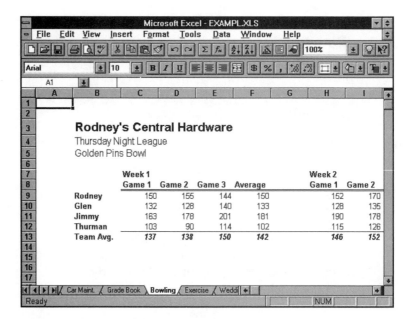

A worksheet makes even your bowling team look official.

Exercise Log

Apart from organized sports, exercise is generally a lonely business. Whether you run or pump iron, swim or aerobicize until you drop, or even ride your executive skiing machine, keeping a record of your activity will help keep you motivated in the absence of cajoling teammates.

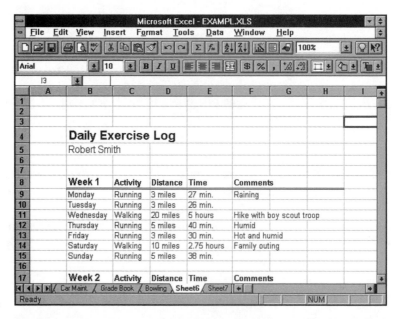

Keep motivated by tracking your progress.

It's pretty straightforward, actually. If you're tracking a motion-oriented sport (like running or skiing), make columns for Activity, Distance, Time, and Comments. If you're tracking a weight-lifting program, you'll want to set up a Date column, and then two columns for each exercise you do: one for reps and one for weight.

Wedding Planner

If you're planning a wedding (or bar mitzvah, or other major social event), you've got hundreds of little details that need your attention, each one due on a different date. How will you cope? Well, you could scream at your spouse-to-be (or substitute appropriate equivalent for your special occasion), or you could organize it all with Excel.

Plan your wedding—or any other monumental occasion.

This one is a little tricky. Set up a column for each week between now and the event. Set up a row for each detail that needs attention. Then use Excel's cell shading feature to shade the cells where the activity meets the time it's supposed to be done. You can print this out to see a time line of the work to be accomplished. When you actually complete a task, enter the date that you did it (or whatever details you want) into the shaded cell, so you can see at a glance that it's been taken care of.

> ## By the Way . . .
> If you think it won't depress you too much, add a column for each activity to track how much you've spent on it. (How about some personalized engraved matchbooks at $160 a carton? I don't think so!)

Project Manager

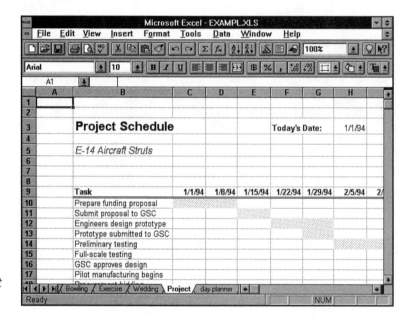

If you can plan a wedding, you have most of the skills needed to be a project manager.

If you stop to think about it, what is a wedding, anyway, if not a giant project? You can use the wedding planner approach in that last section to tackle any business or personal project. Use the shading to create time lines, then sort the activities according to date due or date completed.

Day Planner Pages

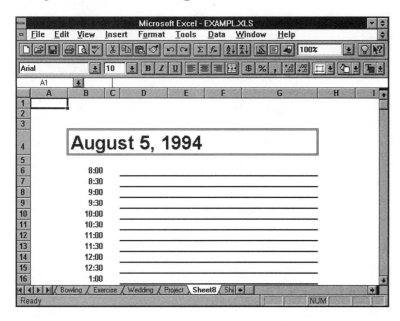

Planning your day doesn't have to break your bank account.

Lots of people spend big bucks on pages for their daily calendar notebooks, which is fine if you actually use all those little check boxes and special columns on the page. Personally, I write down my appointments and a few notes, and that's about it.

For people who don't need a fancy page, Excel can provide a cheap source of day planner pages. Just list the date across the top (as a title), and create a column for times and another column for the activity.

If you want to get really fancy, you could add another column for the location of the activity (such as Conference Room 3) and the people you're going to be meeting with (such as President and Senior Executive Officer).

You can use the Fill feature to fill in the times for you after you've done the first two.

Calendar

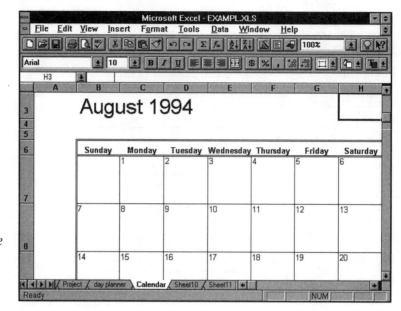

Plan your month for $25 with an executive calendar, or with Excel for free; your choice.

A natural extension of the day-planner is a month-planner, otherwise known as a calendar. This one is mostly a matter of changing the row heights and column widths until you've got a grid of squares, and then placing borders around each cell. To get the numbers in the proper corner, use the **Alignment** tab in the Cell Format dialog box. Don't forget to add the days of the week as column headings, the month across the top, and the days in the top corner of each cell.

Presentation Graphics

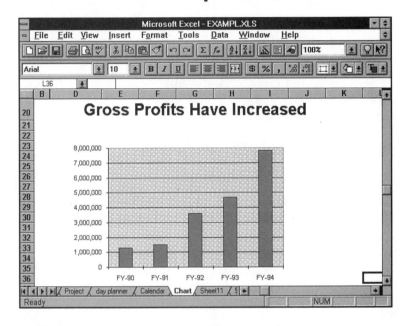

Excel can create presentation graphics that are good enough for most situations.

There are plenty of graphics packages out there that are slicker than Excel for creating your overhead transparencies, but Excel will do in a pinch. It makes lovely graphs, as you saw earlier in the book, and can knock out passable text-only slides, too. Don't forget to buy the right kind of transparency film for your printer, and learn to load it correctly BEFORE you print out the entire batch.

Although you can center titles across several cells, for a text-only chart, you might find it easier to expand the width of a single column to stretch almost across the entire page, and then center the title in that cell and left-align the points underneath it.

Read the box carefully! Transparency film that is not designed specifically for laser printers will often melt inside a laser printer, creating a horrible sticky mess inside your printer which usually requires an overpaid factory-authorized repair person to clean up.

Don't forget to turn off the gridline display before you print out; you certainly don't want the gridlines to appear on your transparency.

Household Budget

By this point, you're probably thinking, "Can't I use Excel for something useful that actually involves calculation?" Well, yes. Here's an idea: use it to map out your household budget.

	A	B	C	D	E	F	G	H	I
2	**Household Budget**								
3									
4									
5			Jan	Feb	Mar	Apr	May	Jun	Jul
6	**Income**								
7		Salary	$1,500	$1,500	$1,500	$1,500	$1,500	$1,500	$1,5
8		Child Support	$800	$800	$800	$800	$800	$800	$8
9		Total:	$2,300	$2,300	$2,300	$2,300	$2,300	$2,300	$2,3
10									
11	**Fixed Expenses**								
12		Mortgage	$900	$900	$900	$900	$900	$900	$9
13		Cable	$50	$50	$50	$50	$50	$50	
14		Car Payment	$300	$300	$300	$300	$300	$300	$3
15		Credit Card Debt	$500	$500	$500	$500	$500	$500	$5
16		Total:	$1,750	$1,750	$1,750	$1,750	$1,750	$1,750	$1,7

Budgets help you keep a lid on your spending.

You might find it helpful to design your budget in sections. First, create a column for each month in the budgeting period (usually one year). Then create the following rows: Income, Fixed Expenses, and Variable Expenses. Bold these titles so they stand out. Then insert rows under each of these three headings for each item in each category. For instance, under Income, you might have rows for Salary, Child Support, and Investments. Under Fixed Expenses would fall Rent, Cable TV, Car Payment, and Credit Card Debt. Under Variable Expenses would be the bills that are not the same every month, such as Electricity, Telephone, Medical, Dining Out, and Clothes.

Add a formula under Income in this month's column that sums the various forms of income. Then add a formula under the Expenses rows in this month's column that sums the expenses. Finally, add a row at the bottom called Difference containing a formula that subtracts the expenses from the income. This will tell you how you're doing!

After entering the formulas in the current month's column, copy them to the appropriate cells in the upcoming months so you'll be ready.

By the Way . . .

If you want to get really ambitious, you could have two columns for each month: Estimated and Actual. This might help you keep on track with your discretionary spending such as dining out.

Checkbook

Here's a classic spreadsheet use: the family checking account register.

Date	Check #	Description	Withdrawal	Deposit	Cleared	Balance
1/1/94		Opening balance			X	$500.0
1/2/94	001	Ace Hardware	$45.20		X	$454.8
1/3/94	002	Friendly Food Mart	$60.38		X	$394.4
1/7/94		ATM withdrawal	$50.00		X	$344.4
1/8/94		Paycheck		$650.00	X	$994.4
1/10/94	003	Martha Williams	$10.00		X	$984.4
1/12/94	004	Friendly Food Mart	$119.20		X	$865.2
1/13/94	005	Incentive Mortgage Company	$750.00		X	$115.2
	006	Shell Oil Company	$50.00		X	$65.2
1/23/94		Paycheck		$650.00	X	$715.2
1/25/94	007	Friendly Food Mart	$35.12		X	$680.1
1/30/94	008	Security Power and Light	$50.30		X	$629.8

Now, if you can only discipline yourself to enter the transactions in the worksheet. . . .

Set this one up just like the paper check register in your checkbook. You'll need columns for Date, Check #, Description, Withdrawal, Deposit, and Balance. Set up a simple formula to subtract the Withdrawal from the previous line's Balance, add the Deposit to it, and print the result in the current line's Balance cell.

If you like, you can add a Cleared column, and when you reconcile your register with the bank statement you can enter an X in that column. Later, if you want to see which checks have not cleared, simply sort the records by that column.

Chores List

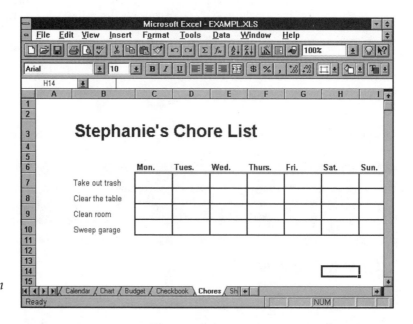

Kids and grownups alike can benefit from a list of chores to do.

Excel is great for any kind of list. If your kids are constantly forgetting to do their chores, a worksheet can help remind them.

Here's how it works. Each kid gets his or her own worksheet. Set up a column for each day of the week, and a row for each chore. Print it out—you're done! When the chore is accomplished, the kid gets to put a check mark (or a sticker, or whatever) in the appropriate cell on the printout.

Sales Contacts

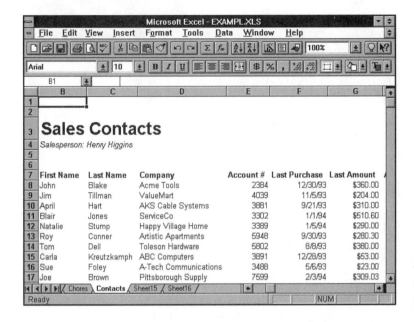

Keeping a list of sales contacts means never forgetting a customer.

Okay, let's get down to business here. If you're in the sales business, you know how important it is to maintain good relationships with your customers. You've gotta call them, schmooze them, be their friend. It takes regular contact.

Use Excel to set up your list of customers thusly. Create these columns: First Name, Last Name, Company, Account #, Last Purchase, Last Amount, Average Purchase, Last Contacted, and Call Again. Then just fill in the blanks for each customer!

Class Schedule

Students—college students in particular—have to constantly be thinking about where they have to go next. Run to this building for a class, run to that building for lunch, squeeze in a trip to the bookstore or the bathroom somewhere in there. Having an at-a-glance view of where you need to be if it's 2:55 on a Wednesday, for instance, can be a real lifesaver.

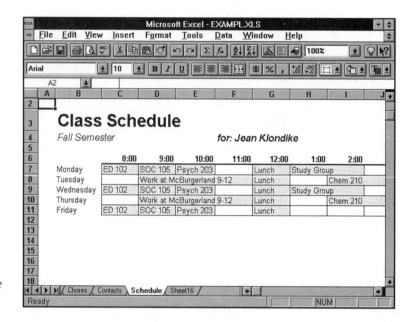

It's 10:00—do you know which class you're supposed to be in right now?

For this project, set up a row for each weekday (weekend, too, if you're unlucky enough to have a weekend class) and a column for each hour (or half-hour, if that's the way it works in your life).

Now, use Excel's Shading feature to shade the times when you have to be somewhere, so you can tell at a glance which blocks of time are already spoken for in your life. In those shaded blocks, type the place you're supposed to be.

Mortgage Amortization

Here's something you can do with Excel that actually requires real mathematics. Keep track of your home mortgage (or auto loan), so you can figure out how many payments you have left and how much you still owe.

First, at the top of the worksheet, set up your Initial Loan Amount, Number of Payments, and Interest Rate. Then create a monthly interest rate in a different cell by dividing the contents of the yearly interest rate cell by 12. This monthly number will be important in your worksheet!

Next, set up columns for Payment #, Amt. Paid, Interest, Taxes/Ins., Principal, and Balance. Under the Payment Number column, select Fill from the Edit menu, then select Series to fill in the payment numbers. Fill in the normal amount you pay on your mortgage in the Amt. Paid cell for the first payment, and then copy that amount for each payment. Do the same thing for Taxes/Ins.—they won't change either.

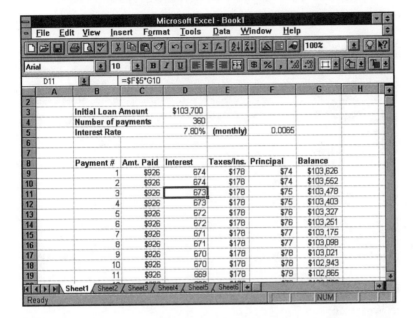

			D11		=F5*G10		
	A	B	C	D	E	F	G	H

Initial Loan Amount	$103,700			
Number of payments	360			
Interest Rate	7.80%	(monthly)	0.0065	

Payment #	Amt. Paid	Interest	Taxes/Ins.	Principal	Balance
1	$926	674	$178	$74	$103,626
2	$926	674	$178	$74	$103,552
3	$926	673	$178	$75	$103,478
4	$926	673	$178	$75	$103,403
5	$926	672	$178	$76	$103,327
6	$926	672	$178	$76	$103,251
7	$926	671	$178	$77	$103,175
8	$926	671	$178	$77	$103,098
9	$926	670	$178	$78	$103,021
10	$926	670	$178	$78	$102,943
11	$926	669	$178	$79	$102,865

Keep track of your mortgage debt—it's depressing, but you need to know.

Now comes the tricky part. In the first Interest cell (the one for Payment 1), multiply the initial loan amount by the monthly interest rate. In subsequent Interest cells, you'll want to multiply the Balance from the previous line by the monthly interest rate.

In the first Principal cell, subtract the contents of that row's Interest and Taxes/Ins. cells from that row's Amt. Paid cell. Now, for the grand total of the first line, subtract the contents of the Principal cell from the Initial Loan Amount. For all subsequent Balance rows, subtract the Principal cell from the previous line's Balance.

Watch out! When you copy this formula, you'll want it to refer to the previous line's balance, wherever the formula may be, but you won't want the reference to the monthly interest rate to change. Therefore, you'll need to refer to the monthly interest rate cell by its absolute value; for example, your formula in D11 might read **F5*G10**. When you copy the formula to D12, it'll read **F5*G11**. See?

Home Inventory

When you apply for home owner's insurance or renter's insurance, the agent will invariably want to know how much you think your valuables are worth. Most people estimate far too low, because they forget about all the little things that they've purchased.

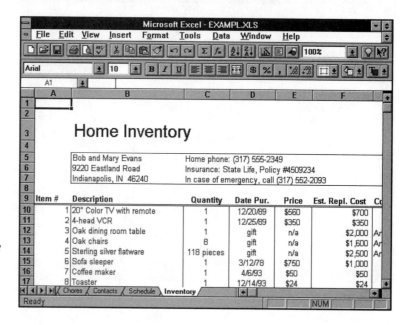

Be safe—keep a home inventory. But keep a copy in a safe place, like a lock box!

You can prepare a realistic replacement cost estimate for your insurance company by doing a thorough home inventory; and should disaster strike, you'll be glad you had the list! Just make sure you keep a copy somewhere else besides on your computer, because your computer might get damaged or stolen.

To set up a home inventory, just create columns for Item #, Description, Quantity, Date Pur., Price, and Est. Repl. Cost. You might also add a column for Comments. Then fill in the rows for each item! When you're done, sum the Replacement Cost column to find out how much your belongings are worth.

> ### By the Way . . .
> Don't expect to get all your possessions logged in one day; this is a huge (but worthwhile) project that could take weeks or even months.

CD/Video Collection

While you're logging your valuables, you might want to make a completely separate listing for your audio and video collection. This list can help you estimate your collection's worth (usually quite a bit!) and help you keep track of what you already own so you don't accidentally buy duplicates.

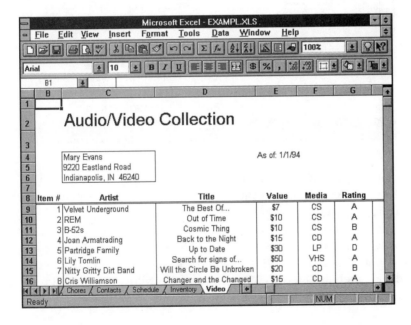

Do you have the latest Buns of Steel video tape or not? Find out at a glance.

Set up your columns with these headings: Item #, Artist, Title, Value, Media, and Comments. You could also add a column for Rating, in which you assign a rating to the item from 1 to 5 or A to F. That way, you can later sort your list with all your favorites at the top.

Invoice

If you do any kind of free-lance work, you'll need to bill your customer when you complete a job. Sure, you could scribble something out on a three-part preprinted form, but wouldn't it be much cooler to create your own?

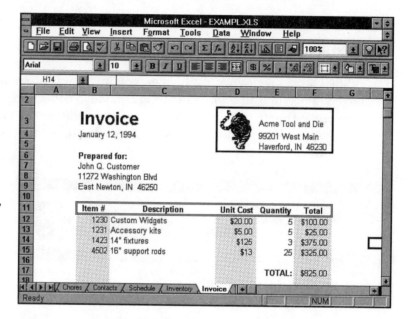

A snazzy invoice may not get you paid any sooner, but it'll impress the heck out of the accounting department.

Set up the top part of the worksheet with your company name and logo. Add a DATE formula somewhere so the current date is always displayed. Add the customer's name and address, too.

For the invoice portion itself, use the Borders and Shading features to create a neat-looking grid. Then fill in the pertinent information for your column headings, such as Quantity, Description, Unit Price, and Total Price. Add it all up, figure in the sales tax, and present a grand total.

At the bottom of the invoice, include a notice about when you expect payment, for example, "Due upon receipt" or "Net 30 Days."

Appendix C
A Function Beastiary

There are some things in life that we all have in common. For example, sooner or later, you're going to have to pay taxes—unless you die first, of course.

Taking Excel as a metaphor for life—it's a stretch, I know—you can look at it in similar terms. Sooner or later, you're going to use a function. In this section, I've given you a pretty complete list of those Excel functions I've found most useful (along with some less popular ones thrown in so you don't feel cheated).

Why Use Functions?

There are only so many ways you can solve a problem with computer software. As a result, the chances are you're not the first person to do whatever it is you're doing with Excel. Even if what you're doing is, um, unusual, somebody probably did it before you. And to belabor the obvious: before *they* did it, they had to figure out how.

Well, class, what do we do when someone's already figured out how to do something? That right! We copy it and use it ourselves. The best part of this is, we're not talking about cheating; we're talking about not reinventing the wheel.

A function is a kind of wheel built in to Excel: a wheel that lets you quickly figure something out or manipulate your data. Instead of your having to recreate a solution, you simply use one of Excel's.

Yet Another Look at an Excel Function

An Excel function has three parts:

- **The function name** identifies it to you and to Excel. There's a couple of things you'll want to remember about function names: First, you must make sure that you spell it correctly as you type it in. Second, although you can type in lowercase, when Excel accepts your entry as being correct, it converts the function name to uppercase. Nice little double-check, isn't it?

☞ **A pair of parentheses** that immediately follow the name, with no space between them and the name. They are there to enclose the function's arguments.

☞ **One or more arguments** allow you to give the function the information it needs to do its calculation. Each argument is separated by a comma. Arguments can be numbers, a cell reference, a name, or text—or another function. You enclose text arguments in quotation marks. That way Excel can know that this is text and not the name of a cell (or group of cells) or a cell reference.

Financial Functions

These functions cover most of those kinds of things you might need to do as a financial analyst. Here, you'll find the tools to do deprecations, figure the time value of money, and more specialized stuff like determining the Macauley modified duration for a security—something I stay up nights wondering about.

Use This Function	To Get This
ACCRINT	The interest accrued for a periodic interest security.
ACCRINTM	The interest accrued for a maturity interest security.
AMORDEGRC	The depreciation for a regular accounting period.
AMORLINC	The depreciation for a linear accounting period.
COUPDAYBS	The number of days from the first to last of a coupon period.
COUPDAYS	The number of days in a coupon settlement period.
COUPDAYSNC	The number of days from a settlement date to the next coupon due date.
COUPNCD	The coupon date after the settlement date.

Use This Function	To Get This
COUPNUM	The number of coupons due between the settlement and maturity dates.
COUPPCD	The coupon date before the settlement date.
CUMIPMT	The cumulative interest that accrues between two periods.
CUMPRINC	The cumulative principal on a loan that should be paid between two periods.
DB	The fixed-declining balance depreciation for an asset for a specific period.
DDB	The double-declining balance depreciation for an asset for a specific period.
DISC	A security's discount rate.
DOLLARDE	A fractional dollar price expressed as a decimal.
DOLLARFR	A decimal dollar price expressed as a fraction.
DURATION	A security's annual duration.
EFFECT	A security's effective annual interest rate.
FV	An investment's future value.
FVSCHEDULE	An investment's future value after applying a series of compound interest rates.
INTRATE	A fully invested security's interest rate.
IPMT	An investment's interest payable for a given period.
IRR	The internal rate of return for a cash flow series.
MDURATION	The Macauley modified duration for a $100 security.
MIRR	The internal rate of return of a series of differently financed cash flows.
NOMINAL	A security's nominal annual interest rate.
NPER	The number of periods for an investment.

continues

Financial Functions   Continued

Use This Function	To Get This
NPV	An investment's net present value, incorporating periodic cash flows and a discount rate.
ODDFPRICE	The price of a $100 security with an odd first period.
ODDFYIELD	A security's yield, when it has an odd first period.
ODDLPRICE	The price of a $100 security with an odd last period.
ODDLYIELD	A security's yield, when it has an odd last period.
PMT	An annuity's periodic payment.
PPMT	An investment's payment on principal.
PRICE	The price of a $100 security paying periodic interest.
PRICEDISC	The discounted face value price for a $100 security.
PRICEMAT	The face value price for a $100 security paying interest at maturity.
PV	An investment's present value.
RATE	The periodic interest rate for an annuity.
RECEIVED	A fully invested security's amount at maturity.
SLN	An asset's one-period straight line depreciation.
SYD	An asset's specific period sum-of-the-years' depreciation.
TBILLEQ	The bond-equivalent yield for a T-bill.
TBILLPRICE	The face value of a $100 T-bill.
TBILLYIELD	A T-bill's yield.
VDB	The specific period declining balance depreciation for an asset.

Use This Function	To Get This
XIRR	The internal rate of return for a series of possibly nonperiodic cash flows.
XNPV	The net present value for a series of possibly nonperiodic cash flows.
YIELD	The yield of a security paying interest periodically.
YIELDDISC	The annualized yield of a discounted security.
YIELDMAT	The annual yield of a security paying interest at maturity.

Math & Trigonometry Functions

These functions perform all those kinds of operations you'd find on a fancy pocket calculator. Operations that run the gamut from taking sines and cosines to converting Arabic numbers to Roman—useful if you're taking your computer with you to Italy.

Use This Function	To Get This
ABS	A number's absolute value.
ACOS	A number's arc cosine.
ACOSH	A number's inverse hyperbolic cosine.
ASIN	A number's arcsine.
ASINH	A number's inverse hyperbolic sine.
ATAN	A number's arctangent.
ATAN2	A number's arctangent using x- and y- coordinates.
ATANH	A number's inverse hyperbolic tangent.
CEILING	A number (in a range of cells) that is to be rounded up to the nearest integer, or significant multiple.

continues

Math & Trigonometry Functions   Continued

Use This Function	To Get This
COMBIN	The number of combinations for a given series of objects.
COS	A number's cosine.
COSH	A number's hyperbolic cosine.
COUNTIF	The number of nonblank cells that meet specific criteria and that fall in a range of cells.
DEGREES	A conversion from radians to degrees.
EVEN	A number rounded up to the nearest even integer.
EXP	The constant *e* raised to a power.
FACT	A number's factorial.
FACTDOUBLE	A number's double factorial.
FLOOR	A number (in a range of cells) rounded down to the lowest value in that range.
GCD	A number's greatest common divisor.
INT	A number rounded down to the nearest integer.
LCM	A number's least common multiple.
LN	A number's natural log.
LOG	A number's logarithm taken to a specific base.
LOG10	A number's base-10 log.
MDETERM	An array's matrix determinant.
MINVERSE	An array's matrix inverse.
MMULT	Two array's matrix product.
MOD	A number's division remainder.
MROUND	A number rounded to a multiple.
MULTINOMIAL	The multinomial of a numbers in a set.
ODD	An integer rounded to the nearest odd number.

Use This Function	To Get This
PI	(Π) The ratio of the circumference of a circle to its diameter.
POWER	A number raised to a power.
PRODUCT	The result of multiplying two numbers with each other.
QUOTIENT	The integer part of a division.
RADIANS	A conversion from degrees to radians.
RAND	A random number falling between 0 and 1.
RANDBETWEEN	A random number falling between two numbers that you specify.
ROMAN	An Arabic number converted to its roman numeral text equivalent.
ROUND	A number rounded to a specified number of digits.
ROUNDDOWN	A number rounded down to the nearest integer.
ROUNDUP	A number rounded up to the nearest integer.
SERIESSUM	A number that is the sum of a series of numbers.
SIGN	A number's positive or negative sign.
SIN	A number's sine.
SINH	A number's hyperbolic sine.
SQRT	A number's positive square root.
SQRTPI	The square root of the number multiplied by pi (Π).
SUM	Arithmetic addition.
SUMIF	The arithmetic addition of the contents of a specified range of cells.
SUMPRODUCT	The arithmetic sum of the products of corresponding array components.

continues

Math & Trigonometry Functions   Continued

Use This Function	To Get This
SUMSQ	The arithmetic sum of the squares of the contents of a specified range of cells.
SUMX2MY2	A number that is the sum of the difference of the squares of corresponding cells' values in two arrays.
SUMX2PY2	A number that is the sum of the squares of corresponding cells' values in two arrays.
SUMXMY2	A number that is the sum of the differences of corresponding cells' values in two arrays.
TAN	A number's tangent.
TANH	A number's hyperbolic tangent.
TRUNC	A number's truncated into an integer.

Database Functions

These are functions you can use to automate database chores. They do such things as get a record, connect with external data sources, and statistically analyze your data.

Use This Function	To Get This
DAVERAGE	A number that is the average of the selected database cell values.
DCOUNT	A count of the cells in a specified database range that contain numbers.
DCOUNTA	A count of the filled cells in a specified database range.
DGET	The contents of the cell that matches the current criteria.
DMAX	The maximum value from the cells in a database range.

Use This Function	To Get This
DMIN	The minimum value from the cells in a database range.
DPRODUCT	A number that is the product of the values of cells from a database range.
DSTDEV	An estimate of the standard deviation of the values of cells from a database range.
DSTDEVP	The standard deviation of all the values of cells from a database range.
DSUM	The sum of the values of cells from a database range.
DVAR	An estimate of variance in a sample of selected cells in a database.
DVARP	The variance of the values of cells from a database range.
SQLREQUEST	The result of a query to an external database.

Date & Time Functions

These functions help you convert numbers in cells to their date and time equivalents. Oh yes, some of these functions work vice versa, too.

Use This Function	To Get This
DATE	A serial number corresponding to the date.
DATEVALUE	The conversion of a date formatted as text into a serial number.
DAY	The conversion of a serial number into it corresponding day of the month.
DAYS360	The number of days between two dates, figured according to a 360-day year.
EDATE	The serial number of the date that occurs when the indicated number of months have elapsed before or after the start date.

continues

Date & Time Functions   Continued

Use This Function	To Get This
EOMONTH	The serial number of the last day of the month before or after the indicated number of months.
HOUR	The conversion of a serial number to it corresponding specific hour.
MINUTE	The conversion of a serial number to its corresponding specific minute.
MONTH	The conversion of a serial number to its corresponding specific month.
NETWORKDAYS	The number of workdays between two dates.
NOW	A conversion of the present serial number to the current time and date.
SECOND	A conversion of the current serial number to a second (as in "hours, minutes, and seconds").
TIME	The serial number of the current time.
TIMEVALUE	A conversion of a time formatted as text into a serial number.
TODAY	A serial number corresponding to the present day.
WEEKDAY	A conversion of a serial number to its corresponding day of the week.
WORKDAY	The serial number of the workday before or after the specified number of workdays.
YEAR	A conversion of a serial number to its corresponding year.
YEARFRAC	A number that is the fractional part of the amount of days between a starting and ending date.

Statistical Functions

Nothing in this life is certain. That's why statistical functions are so important. They let you make decisions (or persuasions) based on what's likely to happen. That means, the next time you get a job with a politician, you'll know enough Excel to help them lie ever-so-convincingly.

Use This Function	To Get This
AVEDEV	The average of the absolute deviations from mean of a series of data points.
AVERAGE	The arithmetic mean of a series of data points.
BETADIST	The cumulative beta probability distribution of a density.
BETAINV	The inverse of the cumulative beta probability distribution of a density.
BINOMDIST	The probability of the individual term binomial distribution.
CHIDIST	A chi-square distribution's one-tailed probability.
CHIINV	The inverse of a chi-square distribution's one-tailed probability.
CHITEST	A test for independence.
CONFIDENCE	A population mean's confidence interval.
CORREL	The correlation coefficient between two sets of data. (An alternate lingual pronunciation of the name of a Canadian software company.)
COVAR	The average of the products of deviation pairs.
CRITBINOM	The smallest possible cumulative binomial distribution value that is less than or equal to a criterion amount.
DEVSQ	The sum of the deviation squares.
EXPONDIST	The exponential distribution.

continues

Statistical Functions   Continued

Use This Function	To Get This
FDIST	The distribution of the F probability.
FINV	The inverse of the distribution of the F probability.
FISHER	The Fisher transformation.
FISHERINV	The inverse of the Fisher transformation.
FORECAST	A value that falls along a linear trend.
FREQUENCY	A frequency distribution expressed as a vertical array.
FTEST	An F-test result.
GAMMADIST	The gamma distribution of a set of data points.
GAMMAINV	The inverse of a gamma distribution of a set of data points.
GAMMALN	The gamma function's natural log.
GEOMEAN	The geometric mean of a series of data points.
GROWTH	A value that falls along an exponential trend.
HARMEAN	The harmonic mean of a series of data points.
HYPGEOMDIST	The hypergeometric distribution of the values in a series of data points.
INTERCEPT	The value of an intercept of the linear regression line.
KURT	The kurtosis of a set of data points.
LARGE	The value of the kth largest point in a set of data points.
LINEST	The parameters of a linear trend.
LOGEST	The parameters of an exponential trend.
LOGINV	A value that is the inverse of a lognormal distribution.
LOGNORMDIST	A value that is the cumulative lognormal distribution.

Use This Function	To Get This
MAX	The maximum value found in a list of arguments.
MEDIAN	A number that falls exactly in the middle of a set of values in a set of data points.
MIN	A smallest value found in a list of arguments.
MODE	A number that occurs the most often in a set of data points.
NEGBINOMDIST	A value that is the negative binomial distribution of a series of data points.
NORMDIST	A value that is the normal cumulative distribution of a series of data points.
NORMINV	A value that is the inverse of the normal cumulative distribution of a series of data points.
NORMDIST	The standard normal cumulative distribution of a series of data points.
NORMSINV	The inverse of the standard normal cumulative distribution of a series of data points.
PEARSON	A value that is the Pearson product moment correlation coefficient.
PERCENTILE	A number that is the kth percentile of the values in a range of data points.
PERCENTRANK	A number that is the percentage rank of a particular value in a set of data points.
PERMUT	The number of permutations for a given number of objects.
POISSON	A number that is the Poisson distribution of a series of data points.
PROB	A number that indicates the probability that a values in a range of data points are within two limits.
QUARTILE	A number that is the quartile of a series of data points.

continues

Statistical Functions   Continued

Use This Function	To Get This
RANK	The place rank of a number in a number list.
RSQ	The number that is the square of the Pearson product moment correlation coefficient.
SKEW	A number that represents the degree to which a distribution is skewed.
SLOPE	The slope of a linear regression line.
SMALL	The value of the *k*th smallest point in a set of data points.
STANDARDIZE	A number that represents a normalized value.
STDEV	An estimate of the standard deviation of a sample of data points.
STDEVP	A number representing the standard deviation of an entire population.
STEYX	The value of the standard error of the predicted y-value for each x-value in a regression.
TDIST	The value of the T-distribution of a series of data points.
TINV	The value of the inverse of the T-distribution of a series of data points.
TREND	The values that fall along a linear trend.
TRIMMEAN	A value representing the mean of the interior of a data set.
TTEST	A value representing the probability of a t-Test.
VAR	The value of a sample's variance.
VARP	The value of the variance of a complete population.
WEIBULL	A number representing the Weibull distribution of a series of data points.
ZTEST	A number representing the two-tailed P-value of a z-test.

Information Functions

These functions are for when you want to check on some characteristic of a cell's contents. This would mean such things as what is the location or contents of a cell, whether it is blank, or if contains an odd number. (That's an uneven value—not something that looks peculiar.)

Use This Function	To Get This
CELL	Data pertaining to a cell's location, formatting, or contents.
COUNT	A count of the all the cells in a range that contain a number.
COUNTA	A count of the number of values to be found in a list of arguments.
COUNTBLANK	A count of the empty cells falling in a range of cells.
COUNTIF	A count of cells that contain numbers or text, and which are in a range.
ERRORTYPE	An error number that corresponds to Excel's error messages.
INFO	Data pertaining to your computer's current operating environment.
ISBLANK	A TRUE answer if the cell is blank.
ISERR	A TRUE answer if the cell's value is an error (other than #N/A).
ISERROR	A TRUE answer if the value in the cell is an error.
ISEVEN	A TRUE answer if the value in the cell is an even number.
ISLOGICAL	A TRUE answer if the cell holds a logical value.
ISNA	A TRUE answer if the cell holds the #N/A error value.
ISNONTEXT	A TRUE answer if the cell holds a non-text value.

continues

Information Functions   Continued

Use This Function	To Get This
ISNUMBER	A TRUE answer if the cell contains a numeric value.
ISODD	A TRUE answer if the cell contains an odd number value.
ISREF	A TRUE answer if the cell contains a reference to another cell.
ISTEXT	A TRUE answer if the cell contains textual data.
N	Textual data converted to a numeric value.
NA	A cell containing the #N/A error value.
TYPE	The type of the data in the cell.

Lookup & Reference Functions

These are functions you'd use when you're using Excel to do database kinds of tasks. For example, you can choose or lookup a value from a list, or find out in which column a cell is located.

Use This Function	To Get This
ADDRESS	A cell reference formatted as text.
AREAS	The number of areas (ranges) in a formula reference.
CHOOSE	A single choice from a list of values.
COLUMN	The column number of a reference.
COLUMNS	The number of columns in a reference.
HLOOKUP	A particular value to be found in the top row of an array of cells.
INDEX	The value in a cell obtained from a row and column reference.
INDIRECT	The reference indicated by a text value.

Use This Function	To Get This
LOOKUP	A value to be found in a cell or an array of cells.
MATCH	The relative position of cell in an array, the contents of which match a specified value.
OFFSET	The value in a cell that is offset in an array.
ROW	The row number of a cell reference.
ROWS	The number of rows in an array of cells.
TRANSPOSE	The transpose of an array of cells.
VLOOKUP	The value of a cell that's found by looking in the first column of an array of cells, and moving across its row.

Logical Functions

These functions are what's known in the trade as Boolean functions—after George Boole, who invented a kind of algebra. They let you compare numbers or parts of numbers, and make decisions based on the results of those comparisons.

Use This Function	To Get This
AND	A TRUE answer if all its arguments are true.
FALSE	A logical FALSE inserted into the specified cell.
IF	A TRUE or FALSE evaluation of the contents of a cell's arguments.
NOT	A logically reversed answer in the cell you specify.
OR	A TRUE answer if any of the cell's arguments evaluate to TRUE.
TRUE	A logical value of TRUE.

Text Functions

These functions let you manipulate the content of cells that contain text rather than numbers. Things like converting a number to text, finding parts of words, or removing nonprintable characters.

Use This Function	To Get This
CHAR	A character corresponding to the argument number.
CLEAN	All the nonprintable characters removed from the text.
CODE	A numeric code corresponding to the first character in a string of text.
CONCATENATE	Two text strings combined into one text, longer, string.
DOLLAR	A number converted to text, using a currency format.
EXACT	An answer as to whether two text values are identical.
FIND	A text string that can be found within a longer text string.
FIXED	A number to be formatted as text, with a fixed number of decimals.
LEFT	The leftmost characters from a text value.
LEN	The number of characters in a string of text.
LOWER	A conversion of text in a cell to lowercase letters.
MID	The number of text characters you specify, from within a longer text string starting from the position you specify.
PROPER	Capitalize the first characters in each word in a text string.
REPLACE	Replace certain characters within a text string in a cell.

Use This Function	To Get This
REPT	Repeat the occurrence of text a specific number of times.
RIGHT	The rightmost characters in a string of text within a cell.
SEARCH	A text string obtained from within another.
SUBSTITUTE	The substitution of "new" characters for "old" characters within a text string.
T	A conversion of arguments to text.
TEXT	Text formatted as a number converted to its text equivalent.
TRIM	Space characters removed from a string of text within a cell.
UPPER	The conversion of lowercase text in a cell to uppercase text.
VALUE	The conversion of text into a number.

Appendix D
Help for Excel 4 Fans

Whether you're holding off upgrading to Excel 5, or have recently upgraded and are feeling lost, this section provides a bit of help for you.

No! I Refuse to Upgrade to Version 5!

What? You mean you haven't upgraded to Excel 5? Don't worry; you can still use most of what's in this book.

Ninety percent of what you learn in this book about worksheets, cell addresses, performing calculations, and formatting cells holds true for practically all spreadsheet programs, whether it's Excel 4, Excel 5, Lotus 1-2-3, or even Visicalc or Multiplan. You're always going to enter numbers and text into cells at the intersection of rows and columns. You're always going to perform math on those numbers. And you're always going to want to format the worksheet attractively.

Worksheets, Workbooks, Etc.

The most obvious difference between Excel 4 and Excel 5 is that Excel 5 is three-dimensional. Each file consists of a stack of worksheets "bound together" into a workbook. In Excel 4, each file consists of a single worksheet. That means that Excel 4 users won't be able to switch between worksheets without opening a separate file. Not a big deal, once you get used to it.

Excel 5 handles macros in a whole new way, using Microsoft Visual Basic, a common language Excel shares with many other Microsoft programs. In Excel 4, in contrast, your macros are collected into a single worksheet called a macro sheet. If you're an Excel 4 user, you probably won't find the information on macros in this book very helpful.

Minus a Few Extras

Excel 5 provides a series of Wizards, which are special mini-programs that help you accomplish things like creating a chart or filling in the arguments for a formula. Excel 4 doesn't provide such deluxe help; more operations are "manual-mode-only." You may have to delve into your Excel 4 documentation (gasp!) to find out how to perform some of the tasks that we perform with Wizards in this book.

Excel 5's other gismos that you won't see in Excel 4 include the TipWizard (which provides usage tips), enhanced database support, and a Visual-Basic based macro language. If you have Excel 4, some of the steps in this book might not work exactly the same. If something doesn't work, check your Excel 4 documentation to find out what you need to be doing instead.

Different Toolbar Buttons

Excel 4's toolbar offers many of the same buttons as Excel 5's. Here's a quick rundown of the ones on the Standard toolbar.

Icon	Purpose
	Opens a new worksheet
	Opens an existing worksheet
	Saves the current worksheet
	Prints the current worksheet
Normal	Applies cell style
Σ	Sums a column or row of numbers
B	Sets bold attribute
I	Sets italic attribute
A	Increases text size
A	Decreases text size

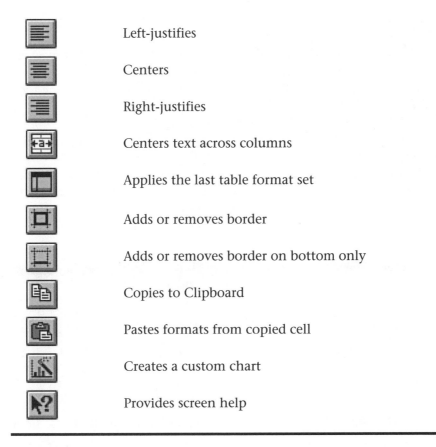

Left-justifies

Centers

Right-justifies

Centers text across columns

Applies the last table format set

Adds or removes border

Adds or removes border on bottom only

Copies to Clipboard

Pastes formats from copied cell

Creates a custom chart

Provides screen help

To display a different toolbar in Excel 4, just right-click on the currently displayed toolbar, and select one from the menu that appears.

Help! I've Upgraded to Version 5 and I'm Lost!

One of the nice things about Excel 5 is that you can still use the Excel 4 menus if you prefer them. If you'd like to keep up with the times and still do things the "old" way, start by choosing Options from the Tools menu. Then in the Menus area of the General tab, click on the Microsoft Excel 4.0 Menus check box. To return to Excel 5 menus, choose New Menus from the **O**ptions menu.

If you save your Excel 4 file under Excel 5, it becomes an "Excel 5 file." That means you, a friend, or a co-worker won't be able to use Excel 4 to call it up later.

Can I Use My Old Files?

I'm glad you asked that question. The answer is, "of course." Excel has the smarts to know the difference between its version 4 and 5 file formats. All you have to do is to open an Excel 4 file, and Excel does the conversion automatically—and at the same time reminds you that it's doing so.

When you save your work in Excel 5, by default it will store it as Excel 5 data, with its preference being to incorporate it into a workbook file. Here's a table that lists the specifics:

Excel 4 File When Loaded	That File When Saved Under Excel 5
A chart	A workbook made up of a single chart sheet.
A Macro worksheet	A workbook made up of a single Excel 4 macro worksheet. (It will not be automatically converted to Visual Basic.
A Worksheet template	A Workbook template.
A Workbook	A workbook containing any bound sheets. Single worksheets become workbooks containing a single worksheet.
A Workspace	A Workspace.

Glossary

Speak Like a Geek: The Complete Archive

$ 1. When used with a money amount, automatically formats the cell as currency. 2. When used in a cell reference, denotes an absolute cell reference.

active sheet   The worksheet of your workbook that is currently being displayed and acted upon. Only one sheet can be active at a time.

Add-ins   Commands and features that you can add to Excel to make it more powerful or easier to use.

annotation   An explanation or description that's not part of the main worksheet. It's a good way to add clarifying information or data.

ANSI   An acronym for American National Standards Institute. This Institute standardized a graphics character set (ANSI characters) for the PC back when graphics were very primitive. Some programs still rely on ANSI characters to form their graphics. (Excel doesn't.)

application   A software program that does something interactive and useful with a user. Contrast this with system software (such as DOS), which primarily interacts with your computer's hardware.

argument   Independent data-holding items that are used to pass values into and out of functions. For example, if a function is =SUM(*argument*), you would replace *argument* with the values you wanted summed, such as A3+A4. Roughly synonymous with parameters.

axis   A reference line for plotting the data. You can have up to three axes on your chart: X runs left to right, Y runs down to up, and Z runs front to back. (The latter is found on 3-D charts only).

brain-damaged   What software is when it behaves stupidly, and it's not because of something you've done.

call up   To bring into view and make active. To call up a dialog box, for example, you click on the menu command that activates it.

cell   A small rectangle where a row and column intersect. Each one is a basic building block of an Excel worksheet and can contain a label, a number, or a formula.

cell reference   The built-in name of a cell that Excel gives it automatically, like A1 or C14. It is derived from the letter of the column and number of the row in which the cell resides.

chart   A graphical representation of part of the data in your worksheet.

chart title   A name for your chart.

click   Quickly press and release a mouse button once. It's used to denote selection.

context-sensitive help   Help information that pertains directly to the part of the software which is currently being used.

copy   To duplicate the contents of a cell into another cell.

criteria   A pattern that tells Excel what to look for. The search criteria can consist of an entire record, an entire field entry, or a portion of one or more field entries.

cut   To remove the contents from a cell without removing the cell itself. When you cut a cell, Excel moves the cell's contents in the Clipboard. That way, you can paste the contents into another cell, thereby moving the contents from one cell to another.

data   Plural of datum, it is a collection of raw facts or figures. You put data together in a meaningful way so as to derive information.

database   An alternative to a regular spreadsheet for storing lists of information (for example, addresses) which require organization rather than calculation. **See *Fields* and *Records*.**

data marker   The symbol that actually represents your data. This could be a bar, a line, a piece of pie, or single dots.

data series   A series of data values in a chart. For example, if you are plotting the grades of six students over a three-month period, the grades for each student comprise a data series.

dither   A process where colors or shades are approximated by varying the intensity and spacing of single-color dots. For example, a grid of red and white alternating dots makes a dithered pink object.

DOS prompt   The words or letters that appear right next to your computer's screen cursor. They normally tell you which is your computer's currently-active disk drive, and where in its file organization you are.

double-click   Quickly press and release a mouse button two times. It's the mousy equivalent of pressing the Enter key.

drag   Moving an object on your screen by using the mouse pointer. With the object under the mouse pointer, press and hold the leftmost mouse button as you move the mouse (and on-screen mouse pointer) to a new screen location.

drag and drop   The behavior where you "grab" onto a highlighted cell with the mouse pointer, move it to another location in your worksheet, and then drop it. It's a quick and easy way to move the contents of a cell.

exit   To close down a software application, removing it from memory and closing any disk files it may have open.

fields   In a database, a field is a category about which information is recorded for each entry. For example, in an address book, ZIP code is a field because it's a category which each entry in the address book includes.

file name   The designation under which a workbook is saved on disk. An Excel file name comprises up to eight letters, a period, and an extension (usually .XLS).

find & replace   To look for an occurrence of specific characters in a cell, and to exchange them for other characters. In Excel, you can also Find (without replace), in which case you simply look for a cell containing the characters you specify.

font   A collection of letters in a single typeface. Some people consider different sizes of a typeface to be different fonts; others do not.

format   The form or layout of a worksheet or one of its elements.

formula   A statement of rules that is used to solve an arithmetic problem. Excel formulas always begin with an equal sign (=).

function   A routine that accomplishes some task. Most Excel functions take information from your worksheet in pieces called arguments (which see) which they use in their work.

gridlines   1. Lines that extend along the charts axis to make it easier for you to see the value of your data markers. 2. Lines on your worksheet that allow you to see individual cells.

hard disk   A semi-permanent storage device. When you save a spreadsheet, a copy of what you're working on (which is already in RAM) is sent out to your hard disk. Later, when you load the spreadsheet, that copy is copied to RAM so you can work on it. See *memory*.

iteration   A single attempt at doing a calculation.

keyword   A word in macro code that Excel recognizes as a command.

landscape   A page oriented so that its longest axis runs from left to right—much like a wide-screen movie. Its opposite is *portrait*.

legend   Captions for your data markers; it lets you know this line on the chart represents widgets, and that one represents thingamajigs.

macro   A collected series of keystrokes, menu selections, or commands that are stored in a macro sheet.

memory   The part of your computer that stores what you're working on, while you're working on it. Your computer has two kinds of memory: Read-only memory (ROM) that holds permanent information, and random-access memory (RAM) that holds programs and data.

monitor   The thing that looks like a TV screen that your computer uses to let you know what you're doing as you interact with it.

move   To remove the contents of one cell and place them into another cell.

MS-DOS   Short for Microsoft Disk Operating System. It is the software that actually "runs" your computer's hardware, while Excel and Windows work together with you to help you do your job.

name   A bunch of cells collected together under their own name.

number   A value or amount represented by a series of digits.

operator   Short for arithmetic operator. Operators are placed between numbers in order to perform calculations on them. Valid operators in Excel include + (add), – (subtract), * (multiply), and / (divide).

parameter   A value (or values) that is passed to a function so that it can accomplish its task. Excel parameters are the words held within function parentheses, and separated by commas.

paste   To insert data from the Clipboard into a cell.

perfory   The little hole-filled strips at the edge of computer printer paper.

pivot table   A flexible grid that lets you drag columns and rows around on-screen (pivot them) to analyze data in various ways.

plot area   The area on your chart where the data markers are drawn to illustrate your data.

portrait   A page orientation where the long axis runs up and down, much like the normal business letter. Its opposite is *landscape*.

print area   A defined group of cells that you want printed. You define the print area using the Sheet tab of the Page Setup dialog box. If you don't define a specific print area, then Excel prints your entire worksheet.

program group   A named Windows entity that holds any number of program icons. When you click on such an icon, the Program Manager loads its associated program into your computer's memory and then runs it.

query   A fancy word for question. A query might ask, "Who are my top ten sales people?" or "Which of my customers owes me money?" But of course, Microsoft Query doesn't really speak in complete sentences, so you need to learn how to phrase your questions.

RAM   Random-access memory. Your computer's scratch-pad memory that is used to hold programs and their data as you work with them. Made up of tiny, little capacitors, it does not retain its data when your computer is turned off. See *memory*.

range   A collection of cells that are acted upon as a group. The cells can be arranged in a single column or row, or as a rectangular block that's defined by the cell at the upper left corner to the one at the lower right corner.

record   An entry in a database. For example, in an address book database, all the information for John Smith, including his name, address, and phone number, comprises a single record.

relative operator   A relative operator tells Excel to look for an entry that does not exactly match the entry you type. Excel finds records that come before or after the record you specified.

result set   The data list that MS Query extracts. The result set is displayed in the data pane.

ROM   Read-only memory. Permanent memory that comes programmed by your computer manufacturer, it retains its data even when your computer is turned off. Holds basic operating information that your computer uses to run itself. See *memory*.

sans serif font   A font whose letters don't have a line or curve projecting from the ends of their ascenders and descenders. Uses the French word sans which means without.

save   To store the contents of your file on a hard or floppy disk. Excel does this automatically, if you specify for it to do so. Excel also prompts you to save your work when you exit the program.

serif font   A font whose letters have a line or curve projecting from the ends of their ascenders and descenders (the vertical strokes).

shell   A controlling program that provides a way for you to command your computer. It takes care of things like listing program file names, and then loading and running the programs when you click on their associated icon.

sort keys   Excel is pretty good about avoiding jargon, but if you want to rub elbows with database jargonauts, you have to know what a *sort key* is. A sort key is a database field that's used to sort the records in a list. For example, if you sort by last name, the Last Name field is called a sort key.

split   To break into parts. In Excel, you can split a screen in up to four parts.

syntax   The rules that govern the sequence in which commands, formulas, or functions are entered into Excel. If what you type doesn't comply with Excel's syntax, then you'll see an error message, and Excel will be unable to perform the task you're trying to get it to do.

template   A pattern for a workbook. Template workbooks don't actually contain data. Instead, you open a template, fill it with data, and save it as a regular workbook.

toggle   Some things in a computer can be on or off; one state or another. A toggle moves a thing between its two states. For instance, pressing a key can type a capital or lowercase character. The Caps Lock key is an example of a toggle.

utility   A kind of housekeeping program, it's a program that computer software makers include free with their product. The most common utilities are those for installing software, and for converting from one brand or file format to another.

wild-card character: Any character that takes the place of another character. Think of a wild-card character as a wild card in a game of poker. If the Joker is wild, you can use it in place of any card in the deck.

workbook   In Excel, it is an organized collection of spreadsheets.

worksheet   Another name for spreadsheet. A rectangular collection of rows and columns of "intelligent" cells that allow you to efficiently manipulate numbers and text.

wrap   When text in a cell moves down from line to line so that it fits into the space available, it is said to wrap.

zoom   To change the view with which you see your spreadsheet. Zooming out is like the view Wiley Coyote gets as his rocket flies up. Zooming in is like what he sees as he falls toward the valley floor.

Index

Symbols

#NAME message, 98
$ (dollar sign), 117
$ (dollar symbol), 267
% (percent sign), 117
- (hyphen), 117
/ (slashes), 117
= (equals sign), 93
1-2-3 macros, running in Excel,
   213-214
3-D charts, 197

A

About Microsoft Excel option, 67
absolute cell references, 86
accessible file types in Microsoft
   Query program, 182-183
active sheets, 267
Add Criteria command (Criteria
   menu), 188
Add Tables dialog box, 185
Add-ins, 267
Add-Ins command (Tools menu), 77,
   183, 219
adding
   numbers across columns in
      worksheets, 47-49
   records in lists with data
      forms, 148
address books, 223-224
addresses in cells, 37
Alignment option (Format Cells
   dialog box), 119
Alt key, 27
Alt+F+X keys, Exit command, 69
Alt+F4 keys
   Control-menu box, 48
   exiting Windows, 30
Analysis add-in, 219
annotations, 267
ANSI (American National Standards
   Institute) characters, 267
applications, 267
Area charts, 196
arguments in functions, 94, 267
arithmetic mean, *see* averaging
arithmetic operators, *see* operators
Arrange command (Window menu),
   55, 113
arrow, mouse pointer as, 10
arrow buttons, 53
Arrow keys, 27
ascending/descending sort order, 153
audio/video collection records, 241
auto maintenance records, 225
autoexecuting macros (1-2-3), 214

Autofill, 105-107
AutoFilter, 155-156
AutoFormat, subtotaled lists, 163
AutoFormat command (Format menu), 120-122, 164
automatic
  averaging, 98
  list sorting, 152
  naming of cells, 87
  subtotals, 159
Autosave add-in, 77-78, 219
Autosave command (Tools menu), 78
AutoSum button (Standard toolbar), 46, 93
AutoSum function, 93
averaging number lists, 97
axes of charts, 195, 268

B

Backspace key, 27
backup files, 75
Bar charts, 196
Boolean functions, *see* logical functions
Border option (Format Cells dialog box), 119
borders
  windows, 23
  worksheets, 122-123
buttons on Standard toolbar, 264-265

C

C>, C:\> (DOS prompt), 18, 222
Calculation option (Options dialog box), 216-218
calculation types in pivot tables, 175
calculations and iterations, 270
calendars, 232
calling up, 268
Caps Lock key, 27
cell pointer, 4, 9
cells, 36-37, 268
  absolute references, 86
  addresses, 37
  copying/moving in worksheets, 104-105
  deleting, 108-109
  formatting options, 118-120
  in worksheets, 4, 14
  inserting single, 108
  labels, 4
  moving, 89, 271
  names, 10, 83-89
    automatic naming, 87
    deleting, 88-89
  ranges, 82-83
  references, 83, 268
  relative references, 86
  shading, 123
  styles, 112
Cells command (Format menu), 60, 118
Cells command (Insert menu), 108
centering worksheet titles, 122
Chart command (Insert menu), 198
Chart option (Options dialog box), 217-218
Chart toolbar, 201
charts, 5, 14, 193-203, 268
  changing data series, 202
  formatting, 199
  legends, 270
  plot area, 271
  titles, 268
ChartWizard button (Standard toolbar), 194
ChartWizard dialog boxes, 198
check boxes in dialog boxes, 29
checkbooks, 235-236
chores lists, 236
class schedules, 237
clicking, 21
closing
  Help window, 69
  workbooks, 78
collapsed lists, formatting, 164
colons in cell references, 86
Color option (Options dialog box), 217-218
colors in worksheets, 124-125
Column charts, 196
Column command (Format menu), 59
Column command (Insert menu), 108

column labels, 169
column letters, 9
columns
    cross-adding in worksheets, 47-49
    hiding, 59
    in worksheets, 4
    inserting, 107-108
Combination charts, 196
combining data for new lists, 182
command buttons in dialog
  boxes, 30
Complete installation, Excel
  option, 222
components of functions, 243-244
configuring Excel workspace,
  215-218
Contents command (Help menu),
  63-64, 68
context-sensitive help, 68, 268
Control-menu box, 30, 48
Copy button (Standard toolbar), 105
copying, 268
    cells, 104
    filtered lists, 157
    workbook styles, 113
    worksheets, 58
Create Names dialog box, 87
criteria in queries, 187-189, 268
    AutoFilter, 157
    removing, 189
Criteria button, 147
Criteria menu commands
    Add Criteria, 188
    Remove All Criteria, 189
cross, mouse pointer as, 10
Crosstab ReportWizard, 168
Ctrl key, 27
Ctrl+1 keys, Format menu, 124
Ctrl+Home keys, accessing cell A1, 28
Ctrl+macro letter keys, 1-2-3
  macros, 66
Ctrl+V keys, Paste command, 89
Ctrl+X keys, Cut command, 89
Cue Card window, 184
currency, 117
custom filters, 157
Custom installation, Excel
  option, 222

Custom Lists option (Options dialog
  box), 217-218
custom sort orders, 154-155
CUSTOM.DIC dictionary, 110
customizing
    charts, 202
    Excel workspace, 215-218
    pivot tables, 172
Cut button (Standard toolbar), 105
cutting, 268

D

data, 268
data area in pivot tables, 169
Data Form dialog box, 146-148
data forms in lists, 146-148
Data Markers, charts, 196, 269
Data menu commands
    Filter, 155
    Form, 146-148
    Get External Data, 183
    PivotTable, 170
    Refresh Data, 174
    Sort, 153
    Subtotals, 161
data series in charts, 196, 202, 269
database functions, 96, 250-251
database programs, 143, 269
date & time functions, 95, 251-252
dates, 117
day planners, 231
decimals, changing fractions
  into, 120
defaults of workbook names, 75
Define Name dialog box, 85, 88
Del(ete) key, 28
Delete command (Edit menu), 109
deleting
    cell names, 88-89
    cells, 108-109
    macros, 213
    records from lists, 148
    styles, 113
dictionary, 110
directories, installing Excel, 222
displaying Program Manager Control
    menu, 30

dithering, 269
documents as workbooks, 3, 34
dollar sign in cell references ($),
  86, 117
Donut charts, 197
DOS prompt (C>, C:\>), 18, 222, 269
double-clicking, 21, 269
Drag & Drop, 104, 269
dragging, 21, 269
drop-down lists in dialog boxes, 29

E

Edit menu commands
  Delete, 109
  Fill, 106
  Find, 110-111
  Move or Copy Sheet, 58
  Redo, 111
  Replace, 111
  Undo, 111
  Undo Sort, 154
Edit option (Options dialog box),
  216-218
editing
  lists, 145-149
  pivot tables, 174
elements
  of charts, 195-196
  of functions, 94-96
ellipsis (...) in menu commands, 25
emergency number phone listings,
  224
End key, 28
Enter key, 26
equals sign (=), 93
Esc key, 26
Examples and Demos command
  (Help menu), 66
Excel
  icon, 34, 44
  exiting, 48
  installing, 221-222
  starting, 34
  upgrading, 263
  version 4, retaining files/menus,
    265-266

executable instructions, macros,
  211-212
exercise logs, 228-229
Exit command (File menu), 69, 189
Exit Windows command (File Manager File menu), 31
exiting, 269
  Excel, 48
  Microsoft Query, 189
  Windows, 30
  workbooks, 78
expanding cell names, 88
extensions in file names, 72
extracting data for new lists, 184-186

F

F1 key (Help), 4, 62, 68
fields, 146, 269
File Manager
  Exit Windows command (File
    menu), 31
  File Manager icon, 20
File menu commands
  Exit, 69, 189
  Open, 55
  Open Query, 187
  Print, 5, 130
  Print Preview, 134
  Return Data to Microsoft
    Excel, 186
  Run, 222
  Save, 73
  Save As, 45, 74
  Save Query, 186
  Summary Info, 76
file names, 72-73, 269
File Open button (Standard
  toolbar), 55
files
  backup, 75
  retaining version 4 in
    version 5, 266
  types accessible in Microsoft Query
    program, 182-183
  XLQUERY.XLA, 183
Fill command (Edit menu), 106

Filter command (Data menu), 155
filtering lists, 151, 155-157
financial functions, 95, 244-247
Find & Replace, 270
Find command (Edit menu), 110-111
finding specific records in lists, 147
Font option (Format Cells dialog box), 119
fonts, 124, 270, 273
Form command (Data menu), 146-148
Format Cells dialog box, 60, 112, 117-118
Format menu commands
   AutoFormat, 120-122, 164
   Cells, 60, 118
   Column, 59
   Row, 59
   Style, 112-113
Format Painter button (Standard toolbar), 107
Format Plot Area dialog box, 202
Format Toolbar, 125
formatting, 270
   cells, 118-120
   charts, 199
   collapsed lists, 164
   guidelines, 126
   numbers automatically, 116-117
   pivot tables, 178
   Standard toolbar, 125
   subtotaled lists, 163
Formatting toolbar, 10, 42-43, 124
formula bar, 10
formulas, 92-93, 270
   hiding, 60
   in cells, 36
   in worksheets, 46-47
fractions, 117, 120
Freeze Panes command (Window menu), 57
function keys, 26
Function Wizard, 98-99
functions, 12, 94-96, 243-244, 270
   AutoSum, 93
   calculating results of other functions, 100
   components, 243-244

   database, 96, 250-251
   date/time, 95, 251-252
   financial, 95, 244-247
   information, 96, 257-258
   logical, 96, 259
   lookup/reference, 95, 258-259
   mathematical/trigonometric, 95, 247-250
   names, 94
   statistical, 95, 253-256
   text, 96, 260-261

G

general approach to using worksheets, 12-14
General option (Options dialog box), 216-218
Get External Data command (Data menu), 183
Get External Data dialog box, 186
Go To dialog box, 90
graphics in presentations, 233-234
greeking text, 135
gridlines in charts, 11, 196, 270
grouping data in pivot tables, 176-177
Grouping dialog box, 176
guidelines
   for mouse operation, 20-21
   formatting, 126
   lists, 144

H

hard disks, 270
headers/footers, 133
headings for macros, 211
Help
   context-sensitive, 68
   F1 key, 4, 68
   Multiplan, 66
   Worksheet Functions topic, 96
Help button (Standard toolbar), 68-69
Help menu commands, 62-67
   Contents, 63-64, 68

Examples and Demos, 66
Index, 65
Search for Help on, 64-65
Technical Support, 67
Help window, 69
hiding
  formulas, 60
  pivot table data, 177
  rows/columns, 59
highlighting data for charts, 198
home inventories, 240
Home key, 28
horizontal scroll button, 53
household budgets, 234-235
hyphen (-), 117

I

I-beam, mouse pointer as, 10
icons, 20, 21-22
  Excel, 34, 44
  File Manager, 20
  MS DOS, 218
  program, 21
Index command (Help menu), 65
information functions, 96, 257-258
input flow of worksheets, 13-14
Ins(ert) key, 28
Insert dialog box, 108
Insert menu commands
  Cells, 108
  Chart, 198
  Column, 108
  Name, 85
  Page Break/Remove Page
    Break, 136
  Rows, 108
inserting columns/rows/single
  cells, 108
installing Excel, 221-222
insurance inventories, 240
invoice records, 242
iterations of calculations, 270

J-K

key combinations
  Ctrl+Home keys (accessing cell
    A1), 28
  Alt+F+X keys (Exit command), 69
  Alt+F4 keys (Control-menu
    box), 48
  Alt+F4 keys (exiting Windows), 30
  Ctrl+1 keys (Format menu), 124
  Ctrl+macro letter keys (1-2-3
    macros), 66
  Ctrl+V keys (Paste command), 89
  Ctrl+X keys (Cut command), 89
  End+Down Arrow keys (last cell in
    column), 28
  End+Right Arrow keys (last cell to
    right), 28
  F1 key (Help), 62
  moving through worksheets with
    keyboard, 52
keyboard keys for Excel use, 26-28
keywords, 270

L

labels, 12
  columns, 169
  cells, 4, 36
  rows, 169
  worksheets, 44-45
landscape orientation, 270
Laptop installation (Excel
  option), 222
launching Excel, 34
legends in charts, 196, 270
Line charts, 196
lists
  adding records with data
    forms, 148
  averaging number, 97
  combining data for new lists, 182
  deleting records, 148

editing, 145-149
extracting data for new lists, 184-186
filtering, 151, 155-157
finding specific records, 147
guidelines, 144
searching with relative operators/ wild-card characters, 147-149
sorting, 151-152
subtotaling, 160-162
locating records with data forms, 146-148
logical functions, 96, 259
lookup & reference functions, 95, 258-259
Lotus 1-2-3 command compatibility with Excel, 66

M

Macro command (Tools menu), 212
macros, 14, 206, 270
deleting, 213
executable instructions, 211-212
headings, 211
language, 264
Lotus 1-2-3
autoexecuting, 214
running in Excel, 213-214
operating, 212-213
recording, 208-210
Zoom_In/Zoom_Out code listings, 210-211
mailing lists, 5
Main program group, 218
margins in worksheets, 133-135
mathematical/trigonometric functions, 95, 247-250
mathematic operators, 93
memory, 271
menu bar, 10
menus, 24, 38-39, 265
merging styles, 113
messages, #NAME, 98
Microsoft Office program group, 34

Microsoft Query program, 182
accessible file types, 182-183
exiting, 189
window, 184
Microsoft Windows, *see* Windows
Minimize button, 23
Module options (Options dialog box), 217-218
monitors, 271
mortgage amortization records, 238-239
mouse
guidelines for operation, 20-21
moving through worksheets, 52
mouse pointer, 10
Move or Copy Sheet command (Edit menu), 58
moving
cell contents, 271
cells, 89
cells in worksheets, 104
through worksheets with mouse, 52-53
windows, 24
worksheets, 58
MS DOS icon, 218
MS-DOS (Microsoft Disk Operating System), 271
multi-word names for ranges, 84
Multiplan help, 66
multiple ranges in pivot tables, 171-172
multiple workbooks/worksheets, 54-55

N

Name command (Insert menu), 85
#NAME message, 98
names of cells, 271
naming
cells, 83-89
files, 72-73
ranges, 83-89
scattered cells, 88
workbooks, 75
worksheets, 59

New Menus command (Options menu), 265
New Workbook button, 44
Normal style, 112
number lists, averaging, 97
Number option (Format Cells dialog box), 118
numbers, 271
    as text in sorting, 152
    automatic formatting, 116-117
    in cells, 36
    in worksheets, 45-46
        adding across columns, 47-49
    standard, 116

O

on-line printers, 137
Open command (File menu), 55
Open dialog box, 113
Open Query command (File menu), 187
operating macros, 212-213
operators, 271
    mathematic, 93
    relative, 272
option buttons in dialog boxes, 29
Options command (Tools menu), 154, 215
Options menu commands, New Menus, 265
orientation
    landscape, 270
    portrait, 271
outline symbols, subtotaling, 162
Overtype mode, 28
overviews
    Excel program, 3-5
    Windows history, 17-18
    worksheets, 8

P

Page Break command (Insert menu), 136
page breaks
    in worksheets, 136

Page Dn/Page Up keys, 28
Page Setup dialog box, 132-134
paper jams, 138
parameters, 95, 271
parentheses in functions, 94
passwords, 76
Paste button (Standard toolbar), 105
pasting, 271
Patterns option (Format Cells dialog box), 119
percent sign (%), percentages, 117
perfory, 271
phone listings of emergency phone numbers, 224
Pie charts, 197
pivot tables, 168-169, 271
    adding/removing data, 173
    customizing, 172
    editing, 174
    formatting, 178
    grouping/ungrouping/hiding/ showing data, 177
    multiple ranges/worksheets, 171-172
    rearranging, 172
    summary functions and calculation types, 174-175
PivotTable command (Data menu), 170
PivotTable Field dialog box, 175
PivotTable Wizard, 169-171
PivotTable Wizard dialog boxes, 170-171
planning charts, 197-200
plot areas of charts, 196, 271
portrait orientation, 271
preplanning, subtotaling, 160
presentation graphics, 233-234
print area of worksheets, 272
Print button (Standard toolbar), 130
Print command (File menu), 5, 130
print preview, 14
Print Preview command (File menu), 134
Printer dialog box, 138
printers, 137
printing worksheets, 5, 130
problems with printing, 137

program groups, 272
   icons, 21
   Main, 218
   Microsoft Office, 34
   windows, 20
Program Manager Control menu, 30
Program Manager window, 20
programs
   database, 143
   Microsoft Query, 182
project managers, 230
protection, Password/Write Reservation, 76
Protection option (Format Cells dialog box), 119

Q

queries, 272
   changing, 186
   criteria, 187-189
   saving, 186-187
Query add-in, 219
Query and Pivot toolbar, Refresh Data button, 174
quitting
   Excel, 48
   Microsoft Query, 189
   Windows, 30
   workbooks, 78

R

Radar charts, 197
RAM (Random-access memory), 272
ranges, 272
   cells, 82-83
   multiple, with pivot tables, 171-172
   naming, 83-89
Record Macro command (Tools menu), 207
recording macros, 208-210

records, 272
   auto maintenance, 225
   exercise logs, 228-229
   in lists
      deleting, 148
      editing with data forms, 148
   locating with data forms, 146-148
   mortgage amortization, 238-239
   sports stats, 227
   student grades, 226-227
Redo command (Edit menu), 111
reference functions, 258-259
references to cells, relative/absolute, 83, 86
Refresh Data button (Query and Pivot toolbar), 174
Refresh Data command (Data menu), 174
registers for checking accounts, 235
relative operators, 147-148, 272
Remove All Criteria command (Criteria menu), 189
Remove Page Break command (Insert menu), 136
removing criteria in queries, 189
Rename Sheet dialog box, 59
renaming worksheets, 59
Replace command (Edit menu), 111
Report Manager add-in, 220
resizing windows, 23
Result sets, 272
retaining
   Excel 4 files in version 5, 266
   Excel 4 menus, 265
Return Data to Microsoft Excel command (File menu), 186
ROM (Read-only memory), 272
Row command (Format menu), 59
rows
   hiding, 59
   in worksheets, 4
   inserting, 107-108
   labels, 169
   numbers, 9
Rows command (Insert menu), 108
Run command (File menu), 222
running macros, 212-214

S

sales contacts lists, 237
sans serif
  fonts, 273
  typefaces, 126
Save As command (File menu), 45, 74
Save command (File menu), 73
Save Options dialog box, 75-76
Save Query command (File
  menu), 186
saving, 273
  queries, 186-187
  workbooks, 73-74
  worksheets, 13
scatter charts, *see* XY charts
screens, splitting, 273
scroll bars/boxes/buttons, 53
Search button (Help window), 64
Search for Help on command (Help
  menu), 64-65
searching lists with relative opera-
  tors/wild-card characters, 147-149
Select Data Source dialog box, 184
selecting menu commands, 25
Series dialog box, 106
serif
  fonts, 273
  typefaces, 126
shading cells, 123
shell, 273
Shift key, 26
shortcut keys
  Alt+F+X keys (Exit command), 69
  Alt+F4 keys (exiting Windows),
    30, 48
  Ctrl+1 keys (Format menu), 124
  Ctrl+Home keys (accessing cell
    A1), 28
  Ctrl+macro letter keys (1-2-3
    macros), 66
  Ctrl+V keys (Paste command), 89
  Ctrl+X keys (Cut command), 89
  End+Down Arrow keys (last cell in
    column), 28
  End+Right Arrow keys (last cell to
    right), 28
  F1 key (Help), 62

showing pivot table data, 177
single cells, inserting, 108
single-word names for ranges, 84
slashes (/), 117
Slide Show add-in, 220
Solver add-in, 220
Sort command (Data menu), 153
sort keys, 273
sorting
  ascending/descending order, 153
  custom order, 154-155
  lists, 151-152
  numbers as text, 152
Spacebar, 27
specific criteria in queries, 187-189
Spelling command (Tools menu),
  109-110
Split command (Window menu), 56
splitting
  screens, 273
  windows, 56-57
sports stat sheets, 227
standard deviation, 97
standard numbers, 116
Standard toolbar, 10, 40-42
  buttons, 264-265
    AutoSum button, 46, 93
    ChartWizard button, 194
    Copy/Cut buttons, 105
    File Open button, 55
    Format Painter button, 107
    Help button, 68-69
    Paste button, 105
    Print button, 130
    TipWizard button, 69
    Undo button, 154
  formatting, 125
starting
  Excel, 34
  Windows, 18-20
statistical functions, 95, 253-256
student grade records, 226-227
Style command (Format menu),
  112-113
styles
  cells, 112
  copying/deleting/merging, 113
  Normal, 112
subdirectories, XLSTART, 218

Subtotal dialog box, 161
subtotaling
    automatic, 159
    lists, 160-162
    outline symbols, 162
    preplanning, 160
Subtotals command (Data menu), 161
summary functions in pivot tables, 174-175
Summary Info command (File menu), 76
syntax, 273
System Info button, 67

T

tabbing worksheets, 53
tables, pivot, 168-169, 271
tabs in dialog boxes, 30
Technical Support command (Help menu), 67
templates, 218, 273
text boxes in dialog boxes, 29
text color, 125
Text format, 118
text functions, 96, 260-261
three-dimensional
    charts, 197
    worksheets, 263
time functions, 251-252
Tip Wizards, 69, 264
titles
    charts, 196, 200, 268
    worksheets, 122
toggling, 273
toolbars, 10, 39-43
Toolbars command (View menu), 40, 201
Tools menu commands
    Add-Ins, 77, 183, 219
    Autosave, 78
    Macro, 212
    Menu Item, 207
    Options, 154, 215
    Record Macro, 207
    Spelling, 109-110
    Zoom In, 209

Transition option (Options dialog box), 217-218
trigonometric functions, 247-250
troubleshooting printing problems, 137
typefaces, sans serif/serif, 126
Typical installation (Excel option), 222

U

Undo button (Standard toolbar), 154
Undo command (Edit menu), 111
Undo Sort command (Edit menu), 154
Unfreeze Panes command (Window menu), 57
ungrouping data in pivot tables, 176-177
unhiding worksheet elements, 59
updating pivot tables, 174
upgrading to Excel 5, 263
utilities, 273

V

values as parameters, 271
vertical scroll button, 53
video collection records, 241
View Manager add-in, 220
View menu commands
    Toolbars, 40, 201
    Zoom, 54, 208
View option (Options dialog box), 216-218
viewing multiple workbooks/ worksheets, 54-56
Visual Basic, recording macros, 210

W

wedding planners, 229-230
wild-card characters, 147-149, 274
WIN command, 18, 222
Window menu commands
    Arrange, 55, 113
    Freeze/Unfreeze Panes, 57

Split, 56
Windows
    exiting, 30
    overview of history, 17-18
    starting, 18-20
windows
    borders, 23
    Cue Card, 184
    Help, 69
    Microsoft Query, 184
    moving, 24
    Program Manager, 20
    resizing, 23
    splitting, 56-57
Windows Program Manager, installing Excel, 222
Wizards, 263-264
workbooks, 14, 34, 274
    as templates, 219
    closing, 78
    copying styles, 113
    default names, 75
    Excel documents, 3
    file names, 72
    saving, 73-74
    viewing multiple, 54-55
    worksheets as, 8-12
Worksheet Functions help topic, 96
worksheets, 35-36, 43-48, 274
    accessing, 51-60
    borders, 122-123
    cells, 4, 14
    colors, 124-125
    columns, 4
    copying/moving, 58, 104-105
    general approach to using, 12-14
    margins, 135
    multiple, with pivot tables, 171-172
    names, 86
    naming/renaming, 59
    overview, 8
    page breaks, 136

print area, 272
printing, 5, 130
ranges, 82
rows, 4
saving, 13
tabs, 11, 35, 53
three-dimensional, 263
titles, 122
unhiding elements, 59
viewing multiple, 54-56
zooming, 54, 135
workspace
    configuring in Excel, 215-218
    saving, 74
wrapping, 274
Write Reservation protection, 76

X-Z

XLQUERY.XLA file, 183
XLSTART subdirectory, 218
XY charts, 197

Zoom button, 136
Zoom command (View menu), 54, 208
Zoom In command (Tools menu), 209
Zoom_In macro, 206-211
Zoom_Out macro, 209-211
zooming worksheets, 54, 135, 274